TEACHING
DIVERSE
POPULATIONS

SUNY SERIES,
THE SOCIAL CONTEXT OF EDUCATION

CHRISTINE E. SLEETER, EDITOR

TEACHING DIVERSE POPULATIONS

FORMULATING A KNOWLEDGE BASE

EDITED BY

ETTA R. HOLLINS,
JOYCE E. KING,
AND
WARREN C. HAYMAN

STATE UNIVERSITY OF NEW YORK PRESS

Published by
State University of New York Press, Albany

© 1994 State University of New York

For information, address State University of New York
Press, State University Plaza, Albany, N.Y., 12246

Production by Diane Ganeles
Marketing by Lynne Lekakis

Library of Congress Cataloging-in-Publication Data

Teaching diverse populations: formulating a knowledge base / edited
    by Etta R. Hollins, Joyce E. King, Warren C. Hayman.
        p.   cm. — (SUNY series, the social context of education)
    Includes bibliographical references (p.   ) and index.
    ISBN 0-7914-1721-2. —ISBN 0-7914-1722-0 (pbk.)
        1. Intercultural education—United States.   2. Education—Social
    aspects—United States.   3. African-American students—Education—
    United States—Case studies.   4. Teachers—Training of—United
    States.   I. Hollins, Etta R., 1942–   .   II. King, Joyce Elaine,
    1947–   .   III. Hayman, Warren C., 1932–   .   IV. Series.
    LC1099.3.T43 1994
    370.19'6'0973—dc20   93-18084
                                                            CIP

10   9   8   7   6   5   4   3   2

Contents

Foreword

Since 1980 there have been several publications presenting a knowledge base for beginning teachers. These publications address teaching culturally diverse populations through a very generalized view of multicultural education or not at all. A recent publication entitled *What Teachers Need to Know: The knowledge, skills, and values essential to good teaching* does not address issues of cultural diversity, although the title appears all inclusive. The approach taken in these publications either implicitly or explicitly supports the continued use of a generic teaching model in the nation's schools. Many separate publications have appeared that address teaching "at-risk," "underserved," or "disadvantaged" populations. These publications tend to treat cultural diversity as a problem and implicitly or explicitly advocate remediation, re-socialization, or compensatory education for the children. Such approaches have proven less than satisfactory in the past.

The knowledge base for teacher preparation should be solidly founded on what is known about teaching diverse populations. That is, cultural diversity is not a problem and should not be an appendage to teacher preparation programs, but rather, should be the yarn from which such programs are woven. Formulating such a knowledge base for teacher preparation requires a synthesis of existing knowledge about teaching culturally diverse populations and a determination of what more needs to be known. This publication addresses this issue.

The significance of the present volume can also be found in the authors' attempt not to rehash old ideas but to chart bold new territory in theory formulation and to show the relationships of these ideas to practice. Sleeter and Grant (1987) have pointed to the fail-

ure of much of the contemporary literature on multicultural education to provide a thorough discussion of the theoretical frameworks
supporting their goals.

This volume presents a review of the literature on schooling for
culturally diverse populations in a way that provides (1) a vision of
the purpose, form and context of schooling for culturally diverse
populations; (2) a view of teacher preparation programs and
teacher effectiveness with culturally diverse populations; (3) a holistic view of salient issues involved in the context and process of
schooling for culturally diverse populations; (4) an indepth examination of the schooling process for one cultural group; and (5) approaches for extending the view of education beyond the walls of
the classroom.

The focus of this monograph is on indigenous populations who
have been traditionally underserved by the nation's public schools.
Indigenous ethnic minority populations include African American,
Appalachian, Native Alaskan, Native American, and Latino-
American.

The ethnic minority populations represented in this volume are
original and longterm inhabitants of this land and tend to be fluent
speakers of a dialect of the English language. These students are
not usually found in bilingual or English as a Second Language
classes. They are not recent immigrants fleeing from war torn countries where they were victimized and traumatized. They are children who have been victimized and traumatized by the society and
educational system in the United States. There is no mecca in the
world for these children, except that to be created by changing the
purpose, form, and context of public schooling and classroom instruction. Changing the schooling process for these children requires changing the content of teacher preparation programs, that
is, developing a new knowledge base for teacher education.

Initially this volume was developed as a vehicle for a national
teleconference entitled, "The Challenge of Cultural Diversity in
Teacher Preparation and Assessment." The first teleconference was
held in March 1991 and the second in November 1991. A total of
three hundred and fifty colleges and universities participated. The
panel at the first teleconference included Joan Baratz-Snowden, the
National Board for Professional Teaching Standards; Lovely Bil-
lups, The American Federation of Teachers; Ed Foglia, the National
Education Association; Donna Gollnick, National Council for the
Accreditation of Teacher Education; Shirley Robards, Association of
Teacher Educators; and Henry Trueba, The Holmes Group.

A video tape of the teleconference was available to those requesting it and contributors to the knowledge base formulated for the teleconference agreed to have their papers compiled into a book for broader distribution.

Those requesting the video tape and the printed material wanted to use it for a variety of purposes. Teacher educators wanted to use it to improve their teacher preparation programs' structure as well as content. They also indicated its usefulness as text material for specific courses. The material was, of course, of special interest to scholars and researchers for its thorough review of the literature. Public school educators have indicated that the material is useful in formulating better theories about the process and content of instruction for culturally diverse populations that will inform their everyday practice. Thus, the format of this book is intended to serve the needs of this diverse audience.

The book is organized into three parts. Each part begins with an introduction that helps the reader understand the intent of the section and the relationship among the chapters within the section. Each part is concluded with a composite list of references. The references have been compiled in this way for the convenience of scholars and researchers. Each chapter begins with "Questions to think about" which help focus the reader's attention on primary issues concerning the particular topic and, where appropriate, to make links between issues that extend across chapters.

In Part I of the book, "Shaping a Vision for the Schooling of Diverse Populations," the contributors implore the research literature to challenge many contemporary practices in the schooling process. The first chapter in this volume examines the relationship between culture and learning in school, raising questions about the process of classroom instruction. The second chapter extends the question raised in the first chapter to challenge the appropriateness of the present purpose of schooling for culturally diverse populations, particularly African American students.

In Part II of the book, "Developing a Holistic View of Schooling for Diverse Populations," the contributors present a review of the literature related to issues in the education of five different ethnic minority groups. The first chapter in this section presents the case for including Appalachian students as an ethnic minority group and examines their unique educational needs. The second chapter describes the beginning of an American Indian magnet school and identifies the issues that are still under consideration. The third chapter reviews the research on effective schools for Mexican American students. The fourth chapter describes research in a Latino/ Puerto Rican collaborative that includes professors and students as researchers. The final chapter in this section examines the preparation of teachers for culturally diverse populations, particularly African American students.

Part III, "Taking a Closer Look at Schooling for One Sociocultural Group: African Americans," provides a more detailed examination of the literature for this particular group. The first chapter provides a broad overview of the benchmarks in research on effective instruction for African American students. The second chapter reviews the research literature on cognitive styles for African American students. The third chapter examines the relationship between African American English and mathematical logic. The fourth chapter raises questions about the relationship between ethnic identity and learning in school. The fifth chapter reviews the research on attributes of African American teachers who are effective with African American students. The final chapter provides a fitting epilogue for the entire book by raising questions about relating schooling practices to the "deep structure" of culture.

This review of the literature goes beyond what is usually included in multicultural education. This volume focuses more on the process and purpose of schooling rather than curriculum content and social transformation, although our contributors do not ignore these other factors. We have provided a thorough review of the literature on African American students for two reasons: (1) to provide the reader with greater depth in understanding the complexity of the issues involved in the research and practice of schooling for diverse populations, and (2) African American students have been studied more and over a longer period of time than most other ethnic groups.

In our review of the literature our goal was for accurate representation of what exists; however, we do not make a claim of absolute objectivity. It is obvious that most of the contributors are advocates of a particular way of thinking about teaching and learning. For example, most of us believe that culture is an essential part of the schooling process. We do not believe that equity in educational outcomes can be attained by employing a decontextualized approach. We believe that if it were possible to totally decontextualize classroom instruction or to develop a generic approach, the academic performance of underserved populations would not improve dramatically. Most of us contend that what presently happens in schools is derived from mainstream middle-class culture and incorporates precious little from the other cultures within this society. We are not advocating that all of what happens in schools must exactly replicate what happens in every culture represented in schools. We do believe that there are aspects of culture that must be attended to if we are to provide equitable education for all students. We also believe that, for the most part, this can happen in multicultural/multiethnic classrooms.

IRVING P. MCPHAIL

Acknowledgments

The editors are greatly indebted to the contributors for the high quality of their work, their sincerity and strong commitment to resolving the issues and challenges of providing appropriate schooling for culturally diverse populations, and their promptness in meeting deadlines and responding to our requests. We are very pleased that we have collaborated in producing this high quality and presently unique volume.

We are grateful to the Ford Foundation for providing a grant award to support the teleconference on "The Challenge of Cultural Diversity in Teacher Preparation and Assessment," for which the papers that now appear as chapters in this volume were initially developed. We are especially grateful to Barbara Hatton at the Ford Foundation who worked with us throughout our planning and completion of this project.

We are grateful to Irving McPhail for his assistance in reviewing the manuscript in its early stages. His comments and suggestions were invaluable.

We are thankful to California State University at Hayward for providing a Research, Scholarship, and Creative Activity award that supported release time for the senior editor, Etta R. Hollins, and for the support provided through Santa Clara University for Joyce E. King as well as Johns Hopkins University for Warren C. Hayman.

PART I

Shaping a Vision for the Schooling of Diverse Populations

Introduction

Part I begins with a review of the literature on cultural congruence in instruction by Kathryn Au and Alice Kawakami. The authors are careful to point out that "culturally congruent educational practices incorporate features of the students' home culture but do not result in activities and environments identical to those of the home." The research literature has been divided into five categories that represent those aspects of the home culture identified as having a significant influence on academic performance when addressed in positive ways by classroom teachers. These aspects include variations in (1) dialects of the English language, (2) participation structures (rules for social interaction), (3) narrative and questioning styles, (4) native language spoken (ESL), and (5) peer group relationships. These variations exist between and within ethnic and cultural groups, but are group based rather than individualistic.

Traditional classroom instruction is based on mainstream cultural practices that either disregard important variations among groups of students or attempt to assimilate all students into mainstream ways of thinking and behaving. Au and Kawakami point out that changes in classroom instruction that address these variations found among groups of students can improve academic performance without altering the purpose of education or the goals of schooling. These authors support the development of a "composite culture that can meet the learning requirements of all students." They further

1

point out that "typical practices that appear ineffective for students of diverse backgrounds are those that devalue the home language or dialect, rely too heavily on classroom recitation, fail to recognize community variations in styles of narration and questioning, and ignore peer group dynamics."

The second chapter in this volume points to cultural knowledge as a missing link in the education of African American children. The author, Joyce E. King, defines cultural knowledge as "those learned behaviors, beliefs and ways of relating to people and the environment that members of a cultural group acquire through normal processes of enculturation. . ." The author presents a review of the literature organized around four research perspectives that include culture centered, culturally congruent, cultural difference and cultural deficit. She describes the need for culture centered research in the human sciences and presents an overview of research on the relationship between African American cultural knowledge and the context of mainstream schooling.

The central question in the second chapter is: What should be the purpose of schooling for African American students as well as other ethnic minorities? King argues that the purpose should be the liberation of oppressed groups and "humanistic social transformation." She contends that those who advocate cultural difference and cultural deficit perspectives support re-socialization of ethnic minority youngsters to mainstream ways. This re-socialization process is believed to serve the interest of the culture in power and does not serve the purpose of liberating oppressed groups. It can be inferred from King's discussion that culturally congruent instruction does not go far enough. That is, developing or identifying effective approaches to acquiring predetermined bodies of knowledge does not include the skill of social criticism and thus, falls short of the goal of transforming the society. Besides, in keeping with this argument, the knowledge presently included in the schooling process is derived from the dominant culture and would need serious revamping to meet the needs of the oppressed.

In chapter one the classroom is presented as a microcosm of the larger society. Thus, it can be inferred that by creating a "composite culture" and a "democratic classroom community," we are moving towards transforming the society at large; or at least providing opportunities for youngsters to acquire those attitudes, values, and behaviors that we believe are fundamental to a democratic society. In this sense, both chapters describe ways of thinking about transforming the schooling process and the society at large: Au and

Kawakami focus on culture, pedagogical practices, academic performance, and the social context of instruction. King focuses on the relationship between culture and social perspectives in conceptualizing the schooling process and transforming the society. King's vision of schooling for African American and other ethnic minority children requires an explicit approach to aligning the purposes, goals, and practices of schooling with that of creating a more just and humane society. While claiming that the purpose and goals of schooling need not change, Au and Kawakami present a vision that includes an implicit, yet strategic, approach to social transformation through the schooling process intended to accomplish goals similar to those advocated by King.

CHAPTER 1

Cultural Congruence in Instruction

KATHRYN H. AU and ALICE J. KAWAKAMI

Questions to Think About

1. What should teachers understand about the home, community, and peer group values of students of diverse backgrounds?
2. How can teachers be helped to use knowledge of cultural differences to improve the quality of classroom instruction?
3. What can teachers do to create composite cultures in classrooms with students of different ethnic backgrounds?
4. How can preservice and inservice programs be broadened to provide teachers with information about culturally congruent instruction?

Research on cultural congruence in instruction offers a basis for understanding how schooling might be made more beneficial for students from diverse backgrounds. Studies of cultural congruence are based on the premise that school learning takes place in particular social contexts, often through teacher-student interactions. From the perspective of Vygotsky (1978) and other social constructivists, learning occurs when the student's performance is assisted by that of a more capable other, who may be a teacher or a peer. Learning takes place in the context of social relationships, and both learning and failure to learn are considered socially organized activities (McDermott 1987).

The overall hypothesis in research on cultural congruence is that students of diverse backgrounds often do poorly in school because of a mismatch between the culture of the school and the culture of the home. Students have less opportunity to learn when school lessons and other activities are conducted, or socially organized, in a manner inconsistent with the values and norms of their home culture. A related hypothesis is that students of diverse backgrounds will have better learning opportunities if classroom instruction is conducted in a manner congruent with the culture of the home. This type of instruction has also been termed *culturally compatible* instruction (Jordan 1985) and *culturally responsive* instruction (Erickson 1987).

Cultural congruence in instruction does not mean an attempt to replicate a home or community environment in the classroom. Research on cultural congruence recognizes that the home and school are different settings with different functions in students' lives. Culturally congruent educational practices incorporate features of the students' home culture but do not result in activities and environments identical to those of the home. For example, reading lessons with participation structures congruent with the culture of Native Hawaiian children are still clearly recognizable as school reading lessons (Au 1980).

Nor does cultural congruence in instruction necessarily entail changes in the purposes of education or the goals of schooling. As Singer (1988) notes, research exploring cultural congruence has to date adopted an "inherently moderate" position by accepting that the goals of schooling for students of diverse backgrounds are essentially the same as the goals for students of mainstream backgrounds, that is, to help them acquire the skills and knowledge needed for success in the larger society. However, cultural congruence in instruction need not be associated only with conventional school goals (for an example, see Lipka 1990).

It should be understood at the outset that the intent of this review is not to stereotype but to report the results of research that seem to have implications for improving the schooling of students of diverse backgrounds. The assumption has been made that the members of certain ethnic communities may have a preference for values and communication processes different from those of the mainstream. It should be understood that, in particular situations, individuals in these communities may refer to mainstream values and use mainstream communication processes. It should also be understood that members of these communities may vary greatly in occupation, educational background, and other indicators of social and economic status.

For the purposes of this review, studies of cultural congruence are organized into five categories:

(1) research on dialect speakers,
(2) research on participation structures,
(3) research on narrative and questioning styles,
(4) research with students who speak English as a second language (ESL students), and
(5) research on peer groups.

This organizational scheme was developed for the purposes of highlighting certain themes in the literature and is by no means definitive. In fact, many of the studies could easily be placed in several different categories.

Research on Dialect Speakers

Many students of diverse backgrounds are speakers of a nonmainstream variety of English, including dialects or creoles. For example, many African American children grow up speaking Black English or African American language, while many Native Hawaiian children grow up speaking Hawaiian Creole English. Thus, issues of language and dialect are often inseparable from issues of culture.

Labov (1966, 1970) conducted some of the first research on communication processes with African American students. He discovered that children's willingness to speak at length was a function of their social relationship with the person they were addressing, as well as of the topic and setting. Children said little in formal, testlike situations but used extensive, complex language in informal settings. Labov argued that schools tended to underestimate the language ability of many African American children, simply because they were speakers of a nonmainstream variety of English.

Piestrup (1973) identified six different styles being used by teachers in first grade classrooms. Students of teachers who used the Black Artful style participated enthusiastically in reading lessons and had the highest reading scores among the classes studied. The term Black Artful was used to describe a manner of teaching that incorporated use of Black English and a rhythmic form of verbal play. Black Artful teachers focused closely on children's learning to read, pressed hard for children to try their best, and held high expectations for their achievement. They encouraged children to speak and listened to their responses. They were aware of differences between the children's vocabulary and the vocabulary in reading materials, and addressed these differences to improve children's comprehension of the text.

According to Piestrup, teachers with some of the other styles had difficulty keeping their lessons focused on learning to read. They ran the risk of alienating children by subtly rejecting their speaking of Black English. Piestrup recommended that teachers involve children in learning to read in a way which builds on their lively patterns of speaking. This conclusion was reinforced by Boykin (1984), who argued that African American students should be taught to read with approaches sensitive to their linguistic and cultural backgrounds.

Collins (1988) suggested that teachers' differential treatment of students was associated with reading group placement, as well as with students' use of Black English. Collins found that the low reading group received more phonics drill than the other groups. The teacher frequently corrected the pronunciation of low group students, thus placing the emphasis in lessons on word identification rather than reading comprehension. Boykin's (1984) analysis of typical reading programs also pointed to the need for a more holistic, meaning-oriented approach to reading instruction for African American children.

Collins, like Labov and Robbins (1969), reached the conclusion that linguistic differences or interference at the level of phonology and syntax plays a relatively minor role in reading comprehension problems.

> Instead, the more important causes of reading difficulties are the social conflicts in the classroom that are triggered by the symbolic meaning of BEV [Black English Vernacular] as an emblem of ethnic identity. (Collins 1988, p. 306)

In summary, research on speakers of nonmainstream varieties of English suggests that their performance may be enhanced in situations where teachers have the ability to recognize and build upon their strengths in language. The academic achievement of these students may be threatened in situations in which teachers have the mistaken assumption that student's language is somehow inferior.

Research on Participation Structures

In classrooms where teacher-guided lessons occupy much of the instructional time, the teacher's role and relationship to the class is critical in supporting students' learning. The studies to be reviewed in this section focus on ways that the teacher's ability to foster learning is affected by the structuring of interactions with students, and whether interactions are structured in a culturally congruent or incongruent manner.

Philips (1972) laid the groundwork for much research on cultural congruence in her study conducted on the Warm Springs Indian reservation. Philips attempted to account for teachers' observations that children were reluctant to speak in class, and that this reluctance increased as students got older. Philips explained the significance of this problem:

> . . . if talk fails to occur, then the channel through which learning sessions are conducted is cut off, and the structure of classroom interaction that depends on dialogue between teacher and student breaks down and no longer functions as it is supposed to. Thus, while the question "Why don't Indian kids talk more in class?" is in a sense a very simple one, it is also a very basic one, and the lack of talk a problem that needs to be dealt with if Indian children are to learn what is taught in American schools. (p. 372)

In other words, school instruction, which occurs largely through verbal interactions, is hampered in the absence of an on-going dialogue between students and teacher.

Philips developed the concept of the *participant structure* (also referred to as *participation structure*), or structural arrangements for interaction. She identified participant structures in which students were reluctant to speak, and those in which they were much more verbal. Students experienced difficulty when the teacher closely controlled who would speak and when while she was interacting either with the whole class or with a small group, such as a reading group. They did not volunteer to answer and frequently refused to speak in front of the class or group.

Students were more comfortable in a participant structure in which they were working independently and could initiate interactions with the teacher, either by raising their hands or by going over to speak to the teacher at her desk. They also showed greater verbal participation in a structure that allowed them to work in small, student-run groups, indirectly supervised by the teacher.

Philips discovered that the reluctance of students to speak in certain classroom conditions could be traced to differences between the social conditions for verbal participation in the school versus the community. She identified differences in three areas.

First, in the classroom the teacher sets herself apart from the rest of the participants, the students, when she directs and plans activities. In community events students are accustomed to seeing the group work together as a whole. Thus, students tend to see themselves as within the same group, and the teacher as an outsider.

Second, the teacher sees herself as a leader with the role of issuing instructions. Similarly, she feels that the students' role is to comply with her instructions. In the community, however, students have learned that leadership is not based simply on holding a particular position and that individuals have the right to choose whom they will follow.

Third, classroom activities seldom include all students, while community activities are open to all who wish to participate. Also, the teacher determines the degree of students' participation, for example, in reciting in front of the class. In the community, individuals decide on the degree to which they will participate, having determined in private that they are capable of performing successfully.

In short, Philips demonstrated that students were more willing to speak in classroom situations that involved conditions similar to those in community social situations. In particular, Philips' highlighted the importance of the teacher considering students' rights to take the initiative to speak, when they had decided they could perform capably, and to organize themselves to accomplish tasks within a small group.

Mohatt and Erickson (1981; see also Erickson & Mohatt 1982) reported the results of research comparing the teaching approaches used by two first grade teachers working on the Odawa Indian Reserve. Teacher I was Indian and a member of the local community. Teacher II was a non-Indian who was teaching Indian children for the first time. The two teachers were found to have different styles, with that of Teacher I being much like that used in Odawa homes.

Teacher I's style was quite slow and deliberate. She exercised control over the class as a whole and did not single individual children out in front of the group. Rather, she dealt with individuals in intimate, private situations. She also invited children to respond by pausing for an average of 4.6 seconds before beginning to speak again herself.

Teacher II's style showed a more rapid pace. He attempted to keep control over all arenas of activity at the same time by issuing directives to the whole class, to the small reading group, and to individuals. In other words, he did not meet in private conferences but called out directions to individual children from across the room. In comparison to Teacher I, his directives were more explicit and given more frequently. He waited for an average of only two seconds for children to answer before he filled in the silence.

Teacher II was gradually able to change his style, so that he began to spend more time working with small groups and individual children. However, he continued to turn the "teacher spotlight" on individual children by singling them out to answer and by calling out directives to them.

A substantial body of research provides evidence of differences in the communication processes favored by teachers and students from different Native American communities in North America. Findings similar to those discussed above are reported by Dumont (1972) in research in Cherokee and Sioux classrooms, by Lipka (1990) in a study of Yup'ik Eskimo classroom, and by Scollon and Scollon (1981), Van Ness (1981) and Barnhardt (1982) in research with Alaskan Athabaskans. The research suggests that students and teachers from these communities attach a greater importance to individual autonomy, self-determination, and a non-hierarchical style of leadership, than do their mainstream counterparts. The role of the teacher must be shaped by these values if students are to benefit fully during teacher-guided lessons.

Studies examining the role of the teacher have also been conducted in classrooms with Native Hawaiian students. Boggs (1980) identified a number of home speech events involving Hawaiian children five years and younger. He differentiated between two types of events: (1) those where parents or other adults engaged in entertaining infants or in verbal play with slightly older children, and (2) those used when the parent was upset, trying to deal with a problem situation, or punishing the child. According to Boggs, the children come to appreciate spontaneity and fun in speech events through the first kind of experience, labelled by one parent as "laughing it up with the kids." However, through the second kind, which can be called scolding events, they become extremely sensitive to cues that the adult wants only to hear a certain response. Boggs' work implies that Hawaiian children's home experience makes salient two basic categories for interactions with adults: very light hearted or very serious.

Discontinuity between home and school speech events were evident in classroom observations made by Boggs (1972).

> When the teacher asked a question at least a dozen hands would
> generally shoot up and then, before anyone could be recognized to
> reply, several would blurt out the answer. When an individual did
> not have the floor he sometimes spoke confidently and sometimes
> shyly, but did not volunteer any information not called for. Often a
> child would gain recognition and then have nothing to say. Reports
> to the teacher on the behavior of other children meanwhile would
> interrupt any other communication. (p. 301)

Teachers found this situation upsetting because the children were
violating mainstream rules for classroom recitation. Those who
were supposed to be speaking were unresponsive, while those who
should have been silent were brimming over with things to say.
Boggs suggests that children nominated do not speak because they
are reacting to adult authority in a dyadic relationship. Children
who are not called upon persist in answering or tattling because of
a presumed lessening of adult authority in a collective relationship.
In effect, Hawaiian children's performance in classroom recitation
may suffer because they inappropriately equate their roles in this
event with their roles in scolding events and verbal play events,
home speech events perceived in some ways to be analogous.

Other studies conducted with Hawaiian students point to the
collaborative nature of home and community speech events, which
contrast with the individual performance orientation of school
speech events. Watson (1975) and Watson-Gegeo and Boggs (1977)
examined closely Hawaiian children's behavior in a speech event
called *talk story*. Watson (1975) briefly defines talk story as "a rambling personal experience narrative mixed with folk materials" (p.
54). Talk story is characterized by a high proportion of turns involving joint performance, or the cooperative production of responses by
two or more children. Performance in collaboration with others is
more highly valued than individual performance, and an audience
of other children is likely to be more impressed by a speaker successful in drawing others into the conversation, than by one who
keeps the floor to himself.

Within the framework provided by the work of Boggs, Watson-
Gegeo, and others, researchers at the Kamehameha Elementary
Education Program (KEEP) investigated ways that school reading
instruction could be made more beneficial for Hawaiian children
(Au et al. 1986). The emphasis in beginning reading instruction was
changed from word identification to comprehension, and students
were taught in small group lessons in which teachers engaged students in a highly interactive form of discussion.

In a study of cultural congruence in instruction, Au (1980) identified similarities to talk story in one of these reading discussion lessons, taught by a Hawaiian teacher to a group of young Hawaiian students. In most of the participation structures identified, the children were allowed to produce responses cooperatively. Slightly more than half the time in story discussion was spent in these talk story-like structures.

The teacher's exercise of authority seemed to be guided by two principles: breathing room and equal time. She gave the children breathing room by withholding criticism of their responses, except when they wandered from the topic of discussion. Answers given in Hawaiian Creole English, if appropriate in content, were always accepted. Most importantly, the teacher created breathing room by permitting and even encouraging the occurrence of talk story-like participation structures that allowed the children to produce responses cooperatively.

The second principle, equal time, was seen in the teacher's concern for the fair allocation of turns and speaking time within the group of children. Teacher nomination was used to ensure that children less successful in obtaining turns on their own were given a chance to speak. Equal time even seemed to apply to the distribution of speaking rights between teacher and children; the longest single utterance in the lesson was a student narrative, not a teacher lecture.

Au and Mason (1981, 1983) analyzed lessons given by two teachers to the same group of six Hawaiian students. The teachers were similar in degree of education and experience, but Teacher LC (low contact) previously had little contact with Hawaiian children, while Teacher HC (high contact) had worked successfully with Hawaiian children for five years. Consistent with their backgrounds, it was found that the two teachers managed interaction in their lessons very differently.

Teacher LC structured her lessons following the rules for conventional classroom recitation. The highest percentage of time in her lessons was spent in the exclusive rights structure, in which the teacher nominated a particular child as the sole speaker. Teacher LC never wished to permit more than one child to speak at a time.

The key characteristics of Teacher HC's lessons were quite different and consistent with the findings in the previous analysis of a talk story-like reading lesson. The largest proportion of time was spent in the open turn structure. During this structure the teacher did not assign speaking rights to any of the children. She posed a question and the children then negotiated for speaking turns among themselves.

The exclusive rights structure was not a part of Teacher HC's lessons, just as the open turn structure was not a part of Teacher LC's lessons. Although Teacher HC called on different children, she never assigned a child exclusive speaking rights in a manner entirely preventing other children from engaging in joint performance with the main child speaker. However, while Teacher HC did not control the role and number of child speakers, she always controlled the topic of discussion.

Au and Mason examined the two teachers' lessons for differences in achievement-related student behavior. Students spoke an equal number of times in both teachers' lessons, but they gave a much higher number of reading-related responses in Teacher HC's lessons, showing that they were more focused on academic work. Idea units in the text were discussed at a much higher rate and children produced more logical inferences, indicating that talk story-like reading lessons stimulated a higher quality of involvement with and interest in text. Au and Mason concluded that, over time, participation in talk story-like reading lessons could result in improvements in Hawaiian children's learning to read.

In talk story-like reading lessons, cultural congruence is achieved when the teacher allows the children to collaborate in producing answers. The teacher's role centers on monitoring the flow of ideas and guiding the discussion, not on lecturing or dictating who will speak when.

In summary, research on participation structures points to the importance of conducting classroom lessons in a manner consistent with the values of students' home cultures. Depending on the particular group of students, teachers may need to consider departing from conventional classroom recitation in various ways. These departures include showing a greater respect for individual autonomy by not "spotlighting" individual children, and addressing questions to the group and permitting the students to collaborate in their responses. The general idea is for teachers to seek a balance of rights in participation structures, so that classroom lessons can be focused on academic content and not on issues of management.

Research on ESL Students

Studies of students who speak a first language other than English suggest that cultural congruence may be achieved when the teacher defines her social relationship to students in other than mainstream ways. Cazden, Carrasco, Maldonado-Guzman, and Erickson (1980) conducted research in primary classrooms in Chicago to investigate two issues. The first was whether the teachers, who were bilingual Chicanas, organized instruction and classroom management in culturally congruent ways. The second was whether Spanish and English were used by the children and teachers for different social interaction purposes.

The results suggested that the teachers interacted with the children in a manner consistent with Hispanic community definitions for social relations between adults and children. When speaking with the children, the teachers communicated *carino* (love or tenderness) by showing concern for the children's well-being and a knowledge of their families. The teachers also encouraged children to help one another. Children showed a great deal of skill in their teaching interactions with peers (Carrasco, Vera, & Cazden 1981).

The teachers and children did not appear to use Spanish and English for different social interaction purposes. Teachers showed features of *cariño* in their interactions with children regardless of the language used, and both languages were used in situations of peer helping.

McCollum (1989) compared whole class lessons taught by Mrs. Ortiz, a Spanish-speaking Puerto Rican teacher, to those taught by Mrs. Thomas, an English speaking Anglo American teacher, in their third grade classrooms. In general, Mrs. Thomas used the conventional classroom recitation pattern identified by Mehan (1979). She often called on individual students to respond and ignored student initiations.

The lessons taught by Mrs. Ortiz involved a give and take much more like that of everyday conversation. Mrs. Ortiz seemed to act to facilitate interaction rather than to control it closely. Instead of calling on individuals, Mrs. Ortiz frequently invited students to answer. She often acknowledged student initiations and seldom indicated that their topics were inappropriate, although in many instances students discussed information about their personal lives. Mrs. Ortiz allowed these digressions to go on for a while before steering students back to the lesson.

McCollum described learning as being accomplished in a reciprocal or dialogic manner in Mrs. Ortiz' classroom, as opposed to being transmitted in a unidirectional manner in Mrs. Thomas' classroom. She suggested that the pattern of conducting lessons in the Spanish speaking classroom reflected a different social relationship between the teacher and students. In Mrs. Ortiz' classroom the teacher-student relationship included the sharing of personal information during lessons. There was less of a boundary between personal conversation and curriculum oriented conversation.

In summary, in mainstream classrooms the teacher's role is often assumed to require that he or she issue directives, emphasize individual performance, and maintain a strict boundary between personal conversation and lesson discussion. However, these assumptions may be in conflict with the values of certain communities. Research conducted in classrooms with Spanish speaking students suggests that the role of the teacher can be adjusted in ways that lead to cultural congruence in instruction, in terms of students' willingness to participate in lessons and in terms of improvements in students' learning.

Ramirez (1981) pointed to the importance of examining teachers' attitudes toward the speech of bilingual students. He describes a study of two teachers engaged in Spanish reading instruction. The first teacher focuses students' attention on understanding the text. This teacher allowed students to interpret the text and to give explanations in their dialect of Spanish. In contrast, the second teacher emphasized standard pronunciation rather than students' answers to comprehension questions. Ramirez suggested that an overemphasis on standard Spanish pronunciation rather than text comprehension could eventually result in lower rates of student participation and achievement.

The results of this study by Ramirez imply that negative attitudes toward students' language comes into play with both ESL students and dialect speakers. Students' language ability is downplayed and they are given inferior, low-level forms of instruction, due to their first languages (whether Spanish or a nonmainstream variety of English) being of a lower status than Standard American English.

Moll and Diaz (1987) looked at possibilities for reorganizing instruction to capitalize on the linguistic and intellectual strengths of Spanish speaking students. Their research was conducted in Latino working-class communities. The first study, which centered on reading lessons, took place with third and fourth grade students all labeled as limited-English speakers. The children spent part of the day with one teacher receiving instruction in Spanish, and the other part of the day with a second teacher, receiving instruction in English.

In the Spanish reading class, Moll and Diaz observed the pattern of differential treatment of reading groups reported by Collins

(1988), Allington (1983), and others. The instructional emphasis in the low group was on decoding, and in the high group on comprehension. The English reading teacher did not ask the children any comprehension questions, as the Spanish reading teacher did. In the English class the instructional emphasis for *all* reading groups was on decoding, indicating that the teacher was treating all the students as if they were poor readers. Moll and Diaz suggested that the problem stemmed from the children's reading aloud in English with an obvious Spanish accent. This apparently led the teacher to assume that the children lacked decoding skills and were in need of additional practice.

Moll and Diaz pointed to difficulties with the model of reading followed by both teachers. This model assumed a hierarchy of reading skills in which decoding precedes comprehension. The students who were good readers in Spanish had the best chance of becoming good readers in English. However, they were not encouraged to transfer their reading comprehension to the English class, because instruction was organized to emphasize only word identification.

To see whether transfer could be promoted, the researchers asked the English reading teacher to teach a lesson to the low group. Immediately following the lesson, one of the authors met with the children to ask them comprehension questions in Spanish. The children's responses indicated they understood the story. However, they had not been able to display this understanding in English. The authors devised a strategy of giving students "bilingual communicative support" for learning to read in English. This strategy involved teaching the children with texts appropriate for their grade level, asking the children to concentrate mainly on understanding what they were reading, and allowing the children and the adult to switch into Spanish as needed.

In summary, when students speak a nonmainstream variety of English or a first language other than English, teachers may lower their expectations for academic achievement and provide less effective forms of instruction. For example, in reading lessons teachers focus on decoding, pronunciation, or other low level skills, at the expense of reading comprehension. Successful teachers appear to be those who have respect for the language students bring from the home and community. They provide culturally congruent instruction by capitalizing upon students' existing language ability to meet school goals. For example, they enable students to use their knowledge of Spanish to learn to read English texts.

Research on Narrative and Questioning Styles

Two lines of research have investigated how students and teachers may fail to interact successfully due to differences in styles of story telling or question asking at home and at school. Michaels (1980; Michaels & Collins 1984) studied narratives told by African American children during classroom sharing time. These children used a style of narrative linking different events together with a certain pattern of intonation. This style of narrative was not familiar to teachers from mainstream backgrounds and did not conform to their expectations for an acceptable recitation during sharing time. Because teachers perceived the children to be rambling, they used questions to clarify and focus their stories and even cut them off. Children who used this narrative style were allowed less time to participate in sharing time than those whose narratives conformed to the teachers' discourse framework. From the children's point of view, teachers were interrupting them and preventing them from finishing what they had to say. Needless to say, this was a frustrating situation for both students and teachers.

Heath (1983) compared the storytelling style used in Trackton, a working-class African American community, with the style favored in school. Trackton children entered school valuing a style of storytelling that relied on the context provided by a close network of family and friends. Storytellers evaluated the stories they told, and often two or more people collaborated in telling a story. In contrast, the form of storytelling favored in classrooms involved features such as audience evaluation of a story, adult shaping of a story through questioning, and individual performance.

Heath (1983, 1982) also looked at questioning styles at home and at school. Teachers reported that children seemed unable to answer even the simplest questions. Adults reported that children were reluctant to speak in school, sometimes because the teacher asked "dumb questions" for which she already knew the answers. Heath found that Trackton adults did not question children about the attributes of objects (e.g., "What color's this?"), a form of questioning commonly used by classroom teachers. In the view of Trackton residents, it did not make sense to "talk about things being about themselves." Instead, adults might solicit an analogy from the children by asking them: "What's that like?" Trackton children learned early on to identify similarities between objects, situations, scenes, and personalities. However, they were not required to account for similarities in terms of specific attributes.

Heath reports that teachers who learned of these differences were able to devise ways of addressing them. For example, they used actual photographs of community sites in social studies units and asked questions more like those that might be asked by a member of the community. Children listened to audiotapes of one another answering questions, and gradually became familiar with school questions and forms of responding. Teachers "talked about talk" in class, labeled the types of questions they asked, and encouraged the children to listen to the way their classmates asked questions.

In summary, teachers with mainstream backgrounds often expect students to be familiar with classroom styles of telling stories or answering questions in class. They are unaware that these styles may differ from those in the children's homes and communities. Having knowledge of these differences may enable teachers to make adjustments that allow students to participate successfully in lessons and to learn typical classroom norms for telling stories and answering questions.

Research on Peer Groups

The final group of studies included in this review are investigations of the influence of peer groups. As Cazden (1988) points out, a classroom actually consists of two worlds: one created by the teacher's activities and formal lessons, and the other created by the activities and relationships within the peer group. The potential for students to support one another's learning often goes unrecognized in classrooms run according to mainstream norms that emphasize individual achievement as opposed to collaborative efforts.

Research with Hawaiian families revealed that children were often raised by multiple caretakers, particularly their siblings (Gallimore, Boggs, & Jordan 1974). As a result, children became more accustomed to being helped by siblings and peers than by adults. Jordan (1985) discovered that children carried this pattern over to the classroom. They showed high rates of peer interaction, frequently offering help to peers or requesting assistance from them. Although the children were raised in a manner that favored working together, school norms were oriented toward individual performance. Not surprisingly, teachers tended to view instances of peer helping as a form of cheating and spent much time and energy trying to stop it.

Vogt, Jordan, and Tharp (1987) described a form of classroom organization that took advantage of the children's preference for peer helping. Rather than being seated in rows, children worked in small groups at learning centers. Children at a center were encouraged to help one another. While most of the class worked at centers, the teacher taught a reading lesson to a group of about six children. Children at centers, then, were only indirectly supervised by the teacher. This system had the dual advantage of permitting peer teaching and learning interactions and making it easier for teachers to stand back and let students learn in the manner most comfortable for them. It was similar to home settings in allowing children to have flexible access to other children and to influence the types of interactions that occurred (Weisner, Gallimore, & Jordan 1988).

In a follow-up study, Vogt et al. discovered that the practices found to be effective with Hawaiian children could not be transferred directly to classrooms with Navajo children in the Rough Rock community. For example, in classrooms with Hawaiian children, the learning center arrangement functioned best when boys and girls worked together in groups of four or five. At Rough Rock there was virtually no interaction among children in groups of this type. This lack of interaction was apparently due to the separation of the sexes in Navajo culture. Preliminary analyses indicated that children would engage in peer helping when they were organized in groups of two or three with children all of the same sex.

D'Amato (1988) described "acting," a process of resistance to teachers shown by Hawaiian children. "Acting" occurs when competitive classroom processes result in violations of peer group norms. According to D'Amato, contention in peer groups of Hawaiian children takes the form of rivalry. In rivalry, players try to show that they are as good as their peers in order to win their respect and affection. Peers work to maintain a delicate balance so that individuals can see themselves as roughly equal in status. Classroom contention, on the other hand, usually takes the form of competition. In competition players try to show that they are better than their peers. Also, because the situation is under the teacher's control, children cannot work to maintain a sense of equality among peers. When teachers create situations in which children can no longer maintain relationships of equality, children are likely to unite in resistance.

D'Amato found that both the KEEP system of learning centers and talk story-like reading lessons supported rivalry and reduced the damaging effects of competition. With learning centers, children had a chance to prove themselves to their peers and to maintain relationships of equality. Since teachers supervised the centers only indirectly, they were not perceived to be violating peer group norms and so were less likely to be the targets of "acting."

D'Amato suggested that Hawaiian children's "acting" was their way of inviting the teacher to give them good reasons for cooperating in class. Because the children do not generally understand the long-term benefits of staying in school, reasons must reside in day-to-day classroom experiences. For example, in the KEEP program, activities are made interesting and meaningful to children's lives and conducted in culturally congruent ways, which children find agreeable.

According to Ogbu (1978), students from certain ethnic groups, termed castelike or involuntary minorities, resist school as a way of protesting their lack of social and economic opportunity and of maintaining their own cultural identity. In Ogbu's framework, "acting" by Hawaiian children would appear to be an example of this type of resistance.

Fordham and Ogbu (1986) highlighted the conflict experienced by African American high school students who found they had to choose between being successful in school sanctioned ways and maintaining their cultural identity. Fordham and Ogbu proposed having students rely on one another to achieve academic success by creating peer networks based on the concept of *fictive kinship*. *Fictive kinship* refers to the close, family-like relationships among African Americans and their shared identity or collective sense of peoplehood as African Americans.

Case studies conducted by Fordham (1991) documented the personal price paid by successful high school students who experienced the burden of "acting white." Fordham also described two programs effective in promoting academic success through having African American students cooperate with, rather than compete against, one another. The important feature of these programs was that they embodied an approach Fordham labeled *group sanctioned learning*. The first program, for high school students, utilized class/team competitions.

In the second program, at the University of California at Berkeley, students were initially so focused on individual competition that they did not seek help when they needed it. Once involved in support groups, students were able to achieve at much higher levels in math and science courses. According to Fordham, the experiences of students in this second program highlight the importance of school administrators promoting more collaborative forms of learning for African American adolescents, which involve them in peer support groups.

In summary, peer relationships and peer group norms may play an important part in classrooms with students of diverse backgrounds of all ages. For example, students may enter school with an orientation toward learning from peers rather than adults. Teachers may inadvertently work counter to peer group norms in ways that cause students to resist or oppose school activities. To improve students' chances for academic success, teachers must alter the organization of the classroom to build upon the positive aspects of peer relationships, such as students' willingness to help one another.

Conclusion

D'Amato (1987) and Au and Kawakami (1991) argue for a view of culture that can deal with both regular, rule-governed activity and with inventive activity. This more dynamic view of culture helps to account for effective classrooms and programs in which students of diverse backgrounds and their teachers collaborate to create and maintain a community of learners. The composite culture that promotes academic learning is in some ways congruent with the values and communication processes of students' home cultures. However, studies of effective classrooms and programs show that achieving cultural congruence in instruction is not simply a matter of matching classroom participation structures or activity settings with those of the home, although home values and communication processes must be taken into consideration.

Many classrooms in the United States are multicultural settings, with students from a number of different ethnic groups. In these cases it is particularly important for educators to be aware of how a composite classroom culture can evolve, even given the variety in students' backgrounds. Au and Kawakami (1991) emphasize the importance of having flexible classroom arrangements that give teachers and students the time to experiment and collaborate on the development of a composite culture that can meet the learning requirements of all students.

In our judgment, these composite cultures cannot evolve in situations in which schools follow conventional, mainstream practices.

Typical practices that appear ineffective for students of diverse backgrounds are those that devalue the home language or dialect, rely too heavily on classroom recitation, fail to recognize community variations in styles of narration and questioning, and ignore peer group dynamics. Typical practices often result because teachers have underestimated students' abilities, which leads to a lowering of expectations and an emphasis on low-level skills rather than higher-level thinking.

Because teachers have a key role in the shaping of the classroom community, it is important for them to be informed about research on cultural congruence in instruction in general, and about research that might provide insight into the students in their classes in particular. Having this information can help teachers recognize and deal constructively with oppositional behaviors, such as students' refusal to answer or "acting," in a manner that results in positive outcomes for teachers and students alike.

Research suggests that culturally congruent styles of teaching can be learned. For example, teachers who are not Hawaiian can learn to conduct lessons using talk story-like participation structures (Au & Kawakami 1985). Teachers can and do benefit from having information about, and guidance in adapting to, students from diverse cultural backgrounds. As an ever-growing number of students of diverse backgrounds enter America's schools, it becomes clear that research on cultural congruence in instruction should have a central place in teacher education programs.

CHAPTER 2

The Purpose of Schooling for African American Children: Including Cultural Knowledge

JOYCE E. KING

Questions to Think About

1. What should be the purpose of schooling in a culturally diverse society? Specifically, what should be the central purpose of schooling for African American and other ethnic minority students?
2. What is the relationship between *Culture Centered* schooling as described by King and "culturally congruent" instruction described by Au and Kawakami?
3. How are the purposes of schooling for African American children presented by King related to the purposes of the "composite culture" and the "democratic classroom community" described by Au and Kawakami?
4. What is the probable outcome if mainstream practices of schooling are not changed?

A log which lies in the river a long time does not become a crocodile.

—A West African proverb

For the most part researchers in various disciplines who fail to recognize the meaning and necessity of African American cultural knowledge have concentrated instead on identifying negative home and community influences on the learning and academic performance of African American students.[1] What much of this research says about the negative impact of their sociocultural background on the academic achievement of African American students reflects a narrow conception of culture and educational purposes related to re-socialization for mainstream "success." For too many students this is an unfulfilled promise of our educational and social systems.

The aim of this chapter is to broaden the professional knowledge base for teacher preparation beyond education that conforms only to the interests and "imperatives of the marketplace" (Giroux 1992). The knowledge base should address liberating educational purposes that are in the interest of African American survival and in the interest of a more democratic, just and culturally diverse society. This chapter is divided into six parts: (1) the conceptualization of cultural knowledge from four research perspectives—culture *Centered, Congruent, Difference* and *Deficit* research; (2) the necessity for culture *Centered* research in the human sciences; (3) African American cultural knowledge; (4) cultural perspectives and the knowledge base for teaching; (5) variability in Black student academic performance; and (6) the specific purposes of education for African American children derived from this synthesis of the research literature.

I. Cultural Knowledge and Educational Purpose: Four Research Perspectives

Culture is the total product of a people's being and consciousness that "emerges from their grappling with nature and living with other humans in a collective group" (Ogundipe-Leslie 1984, p. 81). *Cultural knowledge* refers to those learned behaviors, beliefs and ways of relating to people and the environment that members of a cultural group acquire through normal processes of enculturation (Spradley 1972). African American cultural knowledge includes the skills, awareness and competence that permits Black people to participate meaningfully in their culture—in all of its changing regional and socioeconomic variations. This cultural competence involves more than learning "a conglomeration of superficial aspects of life such as dance, dress, hairstyles" or other artifacts. When the transformative potential of African American cultural knowledge is adequately understood in terms of its integrity and uniqueness, this missing link in the education of African American (and other) students becomes more obvious. This analysis of the distinctiveness of African American culture will suggest that the changing needs of the American workplace and the democratic and multicultural future of our society require educational approaches that value, respect and *use* the cultural knowledge and competence of African American people.

Research regarding home and community sociocultural influences on the education of African American children and the learning process constitutes an emergent knowledge base for teaching. Four different perspectives of cultural knowledge and educational purpose in this knowledge base can be identified: a culture *Centered, Congruent, Difference* and *Deficit* research perspective. Research and scholarship from a culture *Centered* or *Congruent* perspective suggests educational approaches to transform the society and/or, the education process in certain ways. By contrast, research within the *Difference* and *Deficit* perspectives concludes that the education process needs to re-socialize African American children and/or, their parents. Educational approaches identified with each of these perspectives can be shown to have a positive effect on student learning. However, two questions need to be asked to distinguish between them and to judge their appropriateness for the education of African American students and society. What is education for? And what is the conception of African American cultural knowledge in the education process? Of course, one's personal values and commitment to justice, equity and democratic human possibility are relevant to any such judgment.

Within the culture *Centered* research perspective transformative educational outcomes—for society and education—can be linked to education processes that incorporate an autochthonous conception of cultural knowledge that reflects, values and respects the integrity of indigenous African American culture. A fundamental characteristic of this cultural heritage is that African American people have persistently challenged and transformed mainstream cultural norms and practices that devalue and dehumanize people. So education processes grounded in the integrity of the African American heritage must necessarily include social criticism as an important academic skill (King 1991b). Research within the culturally *Congruent* perspective focuses on transforming the educational process to align it more closely with students' cultural knowledge and their indigenous ways of knowing, learning and being. The skills of social criticism are not necessarily addressed but it is presumed that transformed, culturally responsive and inclusive instructional approaches that drastically improve the education of African American students will generally benefit the whole society.

From the cultural *Difference* perspective actual discontinuities between the home and mainstream school culture may be recognized and instructional content may be made more representative of diverse cultures, but re-socialization remains the primary outcome. In other words, certain strengths of autochthonous African American cultural patterns may be recognized, such as the mediating role Black parents often play in the educational success of their children, but the emphasis remains on re-socialization to accommodate dominant Euro-American mainstream cultural norms. In *Deficit*-oriented research, the focus is on re-socializing students to compensate for presumed sociocultural deficiencies in their knowledge, skills and upbringing that are thought to be misaligned with mainstream schooling and instructional practices. From this perspective traditional Black family life, parenting and cultural patterns are considered deficient, deviant, maladaptive, or pathological.

There are good reviews of *Congruent, Difference,* and *Deficit* research already available (Au & Mason 1981; Carew & Lightfoot 1979; A. Weiler 1981) in addition to Au and Kawakami in this volume. In this chapter greater emphasis is placed on culture *Centered* and *Congruent* research because of the need to rethink prevailing conceptions of African American culture, perceptions of Black students, and the learning process as well as the social purposes of education. From the culture *Centered* perspective, for example, the purpose, methods, and content of education are all involved in preparing African American students to understand, preserve and *use* their cultural knowledge and competence to achieve academic and cultural excellence (NABSE 1984). From this perspective, education should help students develop a "relevant personality" (Ladson-Billings & King 1990) that includes a collective identity, the skills, knowledge, vision and motivation to challenge societal injustice and join with others to reinvent the society (Boggs 1974; Wynter 1992).

A Transformative Definition of Education. This transformative definition of education is linked to an autochthonous conception of African American culture that pre-dates but has much in common with Paul Freire's (1971) pedagogy of the oppressed, certain multicultural education approaches (Banks 1991) and feminist pedagogy (K. Weiler 1991). Within this African American tradition the purpose of education, whether in the home, community or school, is for "black humanism" and social transformation. That this historical African American commitment to fundamental humanistic social transformation rebounds ultimately to benefit the society as a whole is a matter of record, as is the significance of education in this continuing struggle (Harding 1990). That is, for Black people education is necessarily "a retooling process: [for] rehumanization, re-Africanization, and decolonization . . ." (Wilcox 1970). In other words, as Preston Wilcox declared: "Education must become a process that educates for liberation and survival—nothing less" (p. 11).

Undoubtedly, liberation for Black people will necessarily mean the transformation of society as well. This is suggested in Derrick Bell's (1987) analysis of the "quest for racial justice." Notice that his query rejects social reform goals for Black people that achieve less than social transformation:

> . . . why do you state a goal for blacks today that would, if achieved, simply make them the exploiting rich rather than the exploited poor, the politically powerful rather than the pitifully powerless, the influential and prestigious rather than the ignored and the forgotten? (p. 250)

In order for education—including the methods, content and connections between communities and schools—to become a re-Africanizing and rehumanizing process, not for Black students alone but also to enable other students to overcome the effects of the particular ways "blackness" is stigmatized in our society, education processes must use African American cultural knowledge to link learning with liberation and human survival. Yet, the necessity for such transformative education processes, in contrast to education for re-socialization, seems to elude even the most astute researchers. Black psychologist Claude M. Steele's (1992) recommendations for "wise schooling" to help African American students who fail "to thrive in school" offers one example.

The Limitations of Education for Re-socialization. Steele (1992) identifies the "culprit that undermines black achievement": the "specter" of endemic racial devaluation (i.e., teacher expectations and racist stereotypes) that "haunts" Black students, causing them eventually to "disidentify" with school and locate other extra-academic sources of self-esteem and self-identity. He argues convincingly and correctly that "the particulars of black life and culture" must be presented in the "mainstream school curriculum" in order to "alter our images of the American mainstream." What is missing from his otherwise incisive analysis, however, is an adequate conception of these "particulars," of African American cultural knowledge, that is. In order for Black students to "thrive" in school on their own (culture centered) terms more is needed than self-esteem building and identifying with schooling and mainstream society, such as it is (Asante 1990, 1991). Students (and teachers) also need to understand the particular historical significance of the transformative *presence* of African American people in America. This is not a call for a "culture-specific learning orientation" or an ethnocentric curriculum. Including African American contributions in the curriculum as Steele recommends is important but hardly constitutes incorporating a critically transformative, indigenous conception of African American cultural knowledge that is a necessary element of a rehumanizing, re-Africanizing education process. Such a conception is needed if education is to help students "re-tool" in order to challenge and *change* the mainstream (not just its images or our images of it). Moreover, African American students need forms of education that permit them to *choose* collective liberation and survival as a goal and to see this as part of a larger struggle for social change. To do this they need the skills and knowledge to help reinvent America as a more just, democratic and culturally diverse society.

Like other analyses of education from a cultural *Difference* perspective, Steele's does not go so far as to focus on preparing students to use African American cultural knowledge for socially transformative purposes. Reforms must be carefully examined to discern their transformative potential or whether they primarily facilitate students' adaptation and accommodation to society's existing hierarchies (Grant 1989; King 1992). There are serious reasons to question the wisdom of social adaptation to mainstream definitions of success (for a few) and to examine the limitations of education for re-socialization. Consider the immense human and social costs including poverty, hunger, unemployment, homelessness and destruction of the planetary environment. Also, it is significant that while urban youth are increasingly disinterested in "success" on mainstream terms—a virtual impossibility for the majority of them given our present economic structure. Yet *Difference* and *Deficit* research continues to focus on ways to enable individual students to achieve middle-class standards of "success."[2]

II. Culture Centered Research in the Human Sciences

The need for research perspectives that place African and African American interests, consciousness and ideals at the center of any cultural analysis or study of education arises in recognition of the "connection between ideology and science," as Molefi Asante (1987, p. 6), Wade Nobles (1985, p. 14) and others have noted. Indeed, the anthropologist John Gwaltney points out that "we [African Americans] have traditionally been misrepresented by standard social science" (Gwaltney 1980, p. xxii). Edmond Gordon (1990) and his colleagues state the problem bluntly:

> "Too many of us have been co-opted by the Euro-American male establishment traditions which render us unable to be sensitive to perspectives born of our own cultural traditions." (p. 17)

This criticism of biased social science knowledge challenges the hegemony, objectivity and neutrality of mainstream research and calls for "multiple ways of knowing." Some researchers suggest a "marriage between the arts, humanities, and social sciences" as an alternative "because the meanings of our behavior are often better explicated in our artistic and fictional work than are the mechanisms of such behavior explained by social science research, whether done by us or others" (E. Gordon et al. 1990, p. 18).

Although the ideological bias and normative commitments of scholars to the status quo have made an African American research perspective, or "way of knowing," in the human sciences and the humanities (Morrison 1992) all but invisible, a "distinctly African American mode of rationality" exists that has a long history (Childs 1989; Gordon 1990). This scholarly tradition, which reflects the collective African American cultural ethos and social thought that evolved out of our common heritage and struggle, is represented well in the scholarship of Carter G. Woodson (1933) and W.E.B. DuBois (1973). In one essay DuBois (1973) stated that his commitment was to the "possibility of black folk and their cultural patterns existing in America without discrimination; and on terms of equality," that is to say, without "getting rid of black folk." DuBois insisted that this requires the "preservation of African history and culture as a valuable contribution to modern civilization as it was to medieval and ancient civilization" (pp. 150–151). For DuBois education in all areas should be for service to humanity—not just for personal gain and profit making.

The values and purposes of education for African American people that DuBois articulated accord with human emancipation as a guiding principle of culture *Centered* transformative social research (Giddens 1979) and pedagogy (Giroux 1988). The *Centered* and *Congruent* perspectives discussed in this chapter recognize the distinctive needs of African American students and the transformative potential of African American cultural knowledge. This recognition is noticeably missing from cultural *Difference* and *Deficit* research on African American education and discussions about the teacher education knowledge base (Giroux 1992; Gordon 1984; Grant & Gillette 1987).

III. African American Cultural Knowledge

In contrast to the individualism inherent in Euro-American cultural traditions, African American cultural knowledge is grounded in a legacy of collective sociocultural identity, communalism and reciprocal social relations (Mbiti 1970; Nobles 1985; M. White 1987). This cultural knowledge also involves forms of social competence that are implied in the Songhay concept: *alasal-tarey*. This term, in the West African Songhay language and culture, literally means "the process through which one understands his or her origins as a human being."[3] For Songhay people, as in any traditional African culture, "one is not a human being except as he [or she] is part of a social order" (Dixon 1971, p. 128).[4] A person is *alasal*—a very high compliment indeed—who meets the highest Songhay ideals and expectations in terms of values, shared perceptions and behavior. One's identity is simultaneously personal and collective just as one's individuality, as a particular expression of one's personal uniqueness, expresses the unity and diversity of humanity.

Because African American cultural identity is also grounded in and expressed within this kind of communal tradition; identifying with one's race is not merely a self-defensive, boundary-defining reaction against racism and discrimination as some scholars maintain. The feeling of belonging many Black youngsters find in peer group allegiances and loyalties takes on a particular cultural significance. It is also understandable that African Americans experience a contradiction between our dual identities—being African and American. This is partly because the cultural differences between these two heritages—what DuBois called our "double consciousness"—are real. In many respects Euro-American culture is defined in opposition to qualities that are attributed to "blackness" (Boykin & Toms 1985; Prager 1982). Thus, it is not surprising that many educators continue to hold decidedly negative attitudes about African American cultural knowledge and the behavior of Black students (Cecil 1988; Gilmore 1985; Irvine 1991; Robinson et al. 1980; Rosenbaum et al. 1987; Solomon 1988; Winfield 1986).

It is simply wishful thinking to believe that these conceptions of the culture and background of African American students have disappeared from the popular imagination or the expectations of educators. "Blackness" is still silently devalued if not openly degraded (Steele 1992) and besides their suspicion that African American culture is just "lower class," some scholars continue to assert that there is little or nothing African about it. In an essay entitled, "Black Culture: Myth or Reality?" Robert Blauner (1970) noted that it was Myrdal's book, *An American Dilemma,* that set the tone for this skeptical outlook. Indeed, Myrdal concluded that the "Negro" is an "exaggerated American" whose values are "pathological." Later on, of course, Nathan Glazer and Daniel Moynihan (1963) resurrected the "Myrdal position" with their declaration that "the Negro is only an American and nothing else. He has no values and culture to guard and protect."

This conclusion persists in the perspectives of researchers and teachers. However, a body of scholarship indicates that the core values of traditional African American culture are not only different from those of mainstream Euro-America but that most African Americans "have common values that appear to transcend training and occupation" (Hollins 1983, p. 31). In comparison to Euro-American culture, Robert Staples (1976) finds that Black culture is more communal, emotional, person-oriented and flexible (including role flexibility), for example. Values commonly (but not exclusively) shared by African Americans also include mutual aid, compassion, adaptability, and racial loyalty. Likewise, Barbara Shade and Patricia Edwards (1987) reviewed research that finds a "greater attention to the social environment" among African American learners. In addition, another researcher (cited in Johnson, 1992) reported that "African American children tend to have an orientation and preference related more to persons than to objects and this preference is related to classification and analytical skills using person-versus-thing-oriented content" (p. 112).

The continuing study of Africanisms in African American culture (Asante & Asante 1985; Holloway 1990; Nobles 1977; Sudarkasa 1988) suggests that an essential quality of the African

American cultural ethos is its "African humanism" (Jenkins 1991; Richards 1985). Other traditional African cultural referents can be identified in personality and character attributes that African Americans value such as "coolness," a "relevant Black personality" (Ladson-Billings & King 1990) and cultural excellence (NABSE 1984). Richard Majors (1986) has studied the "cool pose" young Black males adopt and he likens it to the "coolness" that is considered a most excellent personal quality in many African civilizations (Majors & Billson 1992; Thompson 1983). Other researchers have identified values such as a strong sense of justice and a commitment to freedom, interdependence, reciprocal social relations, communalism, and a basic belief in a transcendent supreme power and the "oneness of being" of all humanity. Etta Hollins (1983) suggests that "although the values of communalism and humanism can be found in the African referent (and may have been brought from Africa), these values also appear to be a most appropriate response to an oppressive life condition" (p. 28).[5]

A number of scholars in different disciplines have identified links between positive aspects of African American children's cultural background, modes of communication and community socialization and their negative school experiences (Boykin 1979; Carter 1988; Garibaldi 1992; Gay 1975; Hale-Benson 1986; Heath 1983; Hollins 1982, 1983; Irvine 1991). This research suggests, for instance, that the intensely person-centered, present-orientation the children develop begins with their early language socialization experiences. Anthropologist Virginia Young (1974) concluded that through authority "contests" with their mothers pre-schoolers became experienced in "procedures of interpersonal interaction" not "rules of conduct" (p. 408). Other cultural knowledge children acquire through home and community socialization includes a strong sense of self-independence, assertiveness, and persistence. Early autonomy, family role flexibility and role reversal prepare children to care for younger siblings and to solve their problems with "sensitivity to the group" (Young 1974, p. 408). This type of family interaction, reported by several researchers (Heath 1983; Mitchell 1988; Ward 1971,1986), reflects the value African Americans place on "the interdependence of people" and the expression of emotion, intuitive feelings, and affect (Boykin & Toms 1985).

Furthermore, Charles Henry (1990) argues that "African orality" is the "dominant feature of Afro-American culture and that "oral thinking fosters skills of performance, listening, and remembering." He adds that the "limitations of orality are often offset by the use of proverbs, allegory, allusion, rite, music, dance, rhythm, sculpture, and art" (p. 8). These and other aspects of African American children's cultural knowledge and competence, that are either missing from or misinterpreted in the context of mainstream schooling, include the skills and the value placed on public performance, improvisation, emotional expression, spontaneity, verbal dexterity, as well as the dynamic interplay of body kinetics and words in oral communication (Hollins 1982). For example, other researchers report that African American "speech styles" result in negative teacher attitudes and evaluations of students and that conformity to school rules and values is an important factor in teacher judgments (Robinson 1980). Fortunately, research continues to identify ways teachers can use the unique cultural strengths of African American youngsters to form a bridge between the school, the home and the "street" (Lee 1991; MacLeod 1991; Mahiri 1991; Moses 1989).

IV. Research Perspectives and the Knowledge Base for Teaching

The Culture Centered Knowledge Base. The research in this section focuses on the parenting of Black mothers and the pedagogy of Black teachers from a culture *Centered* perspective; it illustrates links between autochthonous African American cultural knowledge and education for social transformation. King and Mitchell (1990) combined literary and social analysis to study mother-to-son relationships in Black literature and to examine the experiences, concerns, values and socialization practices of Black mothers raising sons. These include: character attributes such as, perseverance, compassion, and faith and behaviors such as, responsibility, family loyalty, and identification with the Black community and family ancestors. The mothers discussed using family lore—as a "healing power"—to help sons transcend their anger and limited societal conceptions of Black manhood. They also expressed concerns about protecting their sons from hostile forces in the larger society (e.g., schools) and within the Black community.

Similarly, several recent studies of the pedagogy of Black teachers (Ladson-Billings & Henry 1990; Mitchell 1988; King 1991b) and successful teachers of Black students (Ladson-Billings 1990) show how teachers use their knowledge of students' family and community socialization to teach responsibility and perseverance and ways

to transcend negative school and societal forces. Some of these
teachers explicitly stated their goal is to prepare children to change
the society rather than fit into it (King 1991b). These teachers also
recognized limiting factors in the community and the wider social
environment—or "street stuff"—that they prepared their students
to evaluate critically. Jay MacLeod (1991) describes instructional
processes he developed to engage Black high school students in
studying the local culture and history of their community to
"bridge" the school and the "street." This empowering instructional
strategy guides students in developing "tools of social analysis," and
as they begin to understand how inequities affect them, "this critical awareness" is a more powerful motivating force than the individualistic "achievement ideology" (p. 274).

   The Culture Congruent Knowledge Base. The prevailing
outlook in *Congruent* research is that African American cultural
knowledge and patterns are positive resources with which instructional processes can be aligned. Such cultural alignment, or congruence, is expected to make school learning more inclusive, culturally
responsive and thus, more effective. For instance, Shirley Brice
Heath's (1982, 1983) ethnographic research in a southern Black
working class community is one example. She re-examines "what it
means to be literate," as the title of one article, "What No Bedtime
Story Means," indicates. This "literacy event" did not take place in
the Black families she studied. In contrast to deficit-oriented research, in which "no bedtime story" presumably would indicate culturally deprived, inadequate parenting, Heath's analysis and
interpretation values the communicative behaviors and literacy
skills Black children learn in home and community settings, even
though these forms of literacy conflict with standard practices of
reading instruction. As a result of the particular language socialization practices in Black families and community oral traditions
that reflect a culture-specific world view, the children must learn to
adapt their cultural competence to mainstream ways of teaching
and learning that function as requirements for reading. Heath
(1983) reports success assisting teachers to modify their instructional mode to incorporate a Black cultural communication style.

   Heath (1989) also analyzes the congruence between Black oral
literacy traditions and the communication and social skills needed
in the changing workplace. These include "collaboration and numerous verbal forms of displaying knowledge, as well as taking multiple approaches to interpreting a wide variety of types of texts."
She concludes, however, that "formal schooling does not mesh well

with either nonmainstream communities or workplaces" (p. 371). Consequently, she regrets the erosion of traditional African American "socialization patterns that offered adaptability, persistence, and strong self-identification with a group" and the language skills, "keen interpretive talents," and group collaboration Black children typically learn at home but must abandon to "succeed" in school (p. 372). Organizational research on the increasing need for collectivism versus individualism in the workplace that documents such "potentially positive effects" of ethnic group cultural differences on work tasks support Heath's conclusions (Cox et al. 1991).

Janice Hale-Benson (1986) also pioneered an alternative interpretation of Black children's educational needs based on an analysis of their unique "cultural style." She emphasizes that the distinct culture Black children grow up in requires "an educational system that recognizes their strengths, their abilities, and their culture and that incorporates them into the learning process" (p. 4). She concludes that education should "complement rather than oppose Afro-American culture" (p. 104). Other studies that address the need to eliminate home and school discontinuities or social and cultural conflicts in classroom instruction suggest changes are needed in modes of student-teacher interaction, curriculum content, discipline practices, and teacher responses to students' different "ways of speaking" and learning, all of which negatively impact student social identity (e.g., Abrams & Gay 1972; Boykin 1979; Erickson 1984; Gilmore 1985; Irvine 1990; Rosenfeld 1971).

The Cultural Difference Knowledge Base. The prevailing outlook within this perspective regards the existence of different cultural groups with varying strengths and needs as the reality in a diverse society. Contrary to the view that such differences reflect *cognitive* deficits, it is expected that members of subordinate groups, like African Americans, can successfully adapt to school processes by becoming bi-cultural, that is to say, without either total assimilation or fundamental change in schools. Research within this *Difference* perspective includes studies of home environmental influences on school learning and examines what parents do to prepare their children for schooling (Johnson 1991; Slaughter & Kuehne 1989).

In one review of the literature on the "home environment and academic achievement" of Black children, Diana Slaughter and Edgar Epps (1987) note that researchers neglect to examine diverse "parenting styles" which could result in equitable educational outcomes. They criticize studies that stress "only changes in lower-

status Black families and children" without recognizing their
strengths and particular needs. They also oppose the prevailing assumption in "culture deficit literature" that families merely reflect
and mediate their social environment without "filtering and thus
protecting children" from its hostile forces (p. 11). For instance,
Shade and Edwards (1987) conclude that the interpersonal educative style or socialization process in working-class Black families
produces a "cultural filter" which teaches Black children "that people are important, that co-operation and group solidarity produce
effective results, and that it is important to examine both verbal
and non-verbal cues to assess the way to respond to complex and
unfamiliar situations."

Although cultural *Difference* research acknowledges certain
functional indigenous strengths of Black family life, the emphasis is
on schooling to enable students to acculturate and participate in
the dominant culture as it is. Whether or not Black students are enculturated within their own group, they are expected to "succeed"
only if they learn mainstream "cultural capital" and "culturally appropriate" ways of behaving in school settings (McDermott 1987).
This means learning the "culture of power" or cultural knowledge of
"elites" (Bourdieu & Passeron 1977; Delpit 1988; Erickson 1984).

The Cultural Deficit Knowledge Base. From the *Deficit* research perspective African American children appear to possess no
relevant cultural knowledge or competence that schools should necessarily build upon, transmit or preserve because their nonmainstream ways represent sociocultural deficits that are barriers to
school learning and success. The burden of ameliorative social
change, or individual upward social mobility, is placed on students
who must be re-socialized to adapt to mainstream school culture
and practices. In contrast to earlier *Deficit*-oriented research the
emphasis has shifted from students' presumed *cognitive* deficiencies
(Pai 1990, p. 67) to *sociocultural* deficits resulting from nonmainstream social development and socialization that is at odds with the
cultural ways of middle-class schooling. This perspective can be
identified in research on parent education and involvement programs that presume "cultural deficits in the home" and aim to re-
socialize children (Epstein 1985). Luis Laosa (1983) comments that
this kind of parent education has replaced earlier, cognitively-
oriented compensatory education strategies:

> ". . . poor and ethnic minority parents are taught child rearing
> techniques that are considered to produce children with intellec-

tual skills and attitudes necessary for successful academic competition with their middle-class peers." (p. 332)

Likewise, the objective of James Comer's School Development Program is to re-socialize poor Black children in order to increase their academic achievement and social adjustment—Comer's definition of "educational excellence." This involves making structural changes in schools and changing the behaviors of parents, teachers and other "school people" so they "again serve as surrogate parents" (Comer 1980, 1988a,b,c; Haynes et al. 1988). Comer's personal life story has certainly influenced his approach. The parents of his friends were "afraid to go to the library or to be around white people" but his parents gave him the "social skills and confidence" to take advantage of educational opportunities (Comer 1988c).[6] That his friends and the children in his program never read books (and presumably had "no bedtime stories") "frustrated and angered" their teachers (Comer 1988b, pp. 42–43). Such "sociocultural misalignment between home and school" must be resolved at the level of the "emotional bond" a child develops to "competent caretakers" and through a social skills intervention program that permits the school to become the child's adopted community. As parents come to trust the school and learn new skills, a consensus develops about the cultural knowledge parents need to impart and reinforce: middle-class language, "mainstream social skills" and certain "moral and psychological attitudes." Comer (1988a) acknowledges that a child's "decision to pursue academic achievement and to join the mainstream also exacts a heavy price: such a choice means rejecting the culture of one's parents and social group" (p. 46).

V. Variability in Black Student Academic Performance

The explicit re-socialization goals in Comer's program are implicit in studies by Reginald Clark (1983) and John Ogbu (1990). A critical question for Ogbu (1990) is why some minorities do well in school while others do not. Clark (1983) studied Black family life to better understand why some poor Black children succeed while others fail. His study of the "pedagogical environments" in families of high and low achieving poor Black students reveals substantial differences in family culture, support, and the social control processes parents provided regardless of family composition. Clark found that the family life of low achieving students lacked precisely the

"success-producing" expectations and patterns of organized parental contact that "sponsors" competent academic performance found
in the families of high achievers. These parents also engage in what
Clark calls "cognitive work to promote the development of a child's
interpersonal competence" in school encounters (p. 199). These
forms of socialization *for success* are present in some families but
missing in others, according to Clark.

Ogbu (1990) argues that, partly as a result of societal discrimination and partly because of their own cultural frame of reference,
"involuntary minorities have not developed a widespread effort optimism or a strong cultural ethic of hard work and perseverance in
pursuit of education" (Ogbu 1990, p. 53). He concludes that, unlike
"immigrant minorities," the values, attitudes and behaviors of
Black students and other caste-like "involuntary minorities" do not
support school success. Although he identifies structural inequalities that can play a role in Black students' educational failure, his
research is frequently cited as evidence of deficient socialization or
faulty "habits," cultural knowledge and "symbolic factors" that negatively affect students' "social adaptation" and school performance
(Custred 1990). For Ogbu (1990) factors like these do not "encourage
striving for school success": students' "oppositional" social identity,
cultural frame of reference, negative dual-status, [in]ability and
[un]willingness to "cross cultural and language boundaries," and
their limited-mobility frame of reference (p. 52).

Signithia Fordham (1988) and Ogbu (Fordham & Ogbu 1986)
have also advanced the thesis that Black high school students who
don't persist in academic tasks fear peer group alienation and believe that "learning certain aspects of White American culture, or
behaving according to White American cultural frames of reference
in certain domains, is detrimental to their own cultures, languages,
and identities" (Ogbu 1990, p. 53). Of course, Black students' apprehension about alienation from their peers is an important consideration. However, the Fordham-Obgu "burden of acting white"
thesis rests on a too literal interpretation of students' expressed
fears about being called names and teased about "acting white."
Nick-naming is a long-standing African American cultural practice
and other metaphorical meanings of "acting white" are plausible.
For instance, the term is used to denote the kind of "arrogance" that
Black people also call acting "stuck-up"—what schooling aimed at
re-socialization and competitive individualism apparently promotes. This interpretation is consistent with the way Black people

use language and is indicative of Black people's characteristic concern with how one *relates* to others.[7] Fordham (1988) is right, though, to insist that Black Americans "as a people" must address these issues. "If Black Americans . . . are willing to have their children evince behaviors and attitudes that suggest a lack of connectedness to the larger Black community," as she observes, then these (re-socialization) approaches will be acceptable (p. 82).

The alienating education process that African American students often experience is not a result of *their* faulty cultural frames of reference (Felice 1981; King 1991b; Steele 1992; Trueba 1988). On the contrary, as C.A. Bowers and David Flinders (1990) point out, the fault lies with the body of teachers' professional knowledge and its nearly "uniform silence on the importance of understanding cultural patterns that influence the manner in which the teacher and students think and communicate" (p. 14). For African American students the conceptually limited and faulty ways teachers think about culture and learning lead to lower expectations and erroneous conclusions about their ability based on prevailing assumptions about learning as an individualistic, culturally neutral process.

What African American students, especially males, experience in schools and consequently in the society is particularly compelling evidence that the education process is not working and that it is impervious to ameliorative, individualistic education strategies that do not question these assumptions.[8] It is unlikely that education aimed at re-socializing individual African American students will address these *systemic* problems or significantly increase upward mobility opportunities for the masses of African Americans. Given the retrenchment of such opportunities for more and more white Americans, the limitations of *Difference* and *Deficit* re-socialization approaches become increasingly evident.

A teacher's own self-awareness regarding matters of culture, ethnicity, educational purpose and societal injustice are all part of the *sociocultural context knowledge* that should be included in the knowledge base of teaching.[9] For example, Etta Hollins (1990b) and Wilma Longstreet (1978) recognize the importance of "helping teachers explore their own ethnicities" if they are to develop the "self-awareness" to go beyond ethnicity as ethnic "quaintness" (p. 16). What teachers know and believe about the relationship between culture and learning, about Black students' cultural background, for example, or the way these beliefs affect their pedagogy are other relevant aspects of sociocultural context knowledge teach-

ers need to understand. Teachers need sufficient in-depth understanding of their students' background to select and incorporate
into the education process those forms of cultural knowledge and
competence that facilitate meaningful, transformative learning. It
is not sufficient to acknowledge, for example that: "In their interactions with students, teachers should aim to maintain the integrity of the home culture while respecting the demands of the school"
(Hernandez 1989, p. 50). To discriminate between those school "habits" that do indeed respect the integrity of the home culture and
those that do not, teachers need specific sociocultural context
knowledge from a culture *Centered* or *Congruent* perspective. As
Heath points out, "mainstream ways" of acquiring school-type competencies "offer no universally applicable model of development"
(Heath 1982, p. 73).

VI. The Purpose of Schooling for
African American Students

Preparing teachers to educate African American children in
the context of their own cultural traditions requires in-depth knowledge of African American cultural knowledge and competence. Research and scholarship with a transformative perspective suggests
the following purposes of school learning for African American children. The content of schooling for African American children
should:

1. Enable children to recognize and affirm their collective identification with people of African descent.[10]
2. Give students an enhanced sense of mutual responsibility for
   their own learning and the learning of their peers; enhance
   their commitment to use their cultural knowledge and school
   learning for the benefit of their community, the society and for
   humanity.
3. Include a humanistic, personally meaningful focus in all areas
   of the curriculum. This requires use of traditional knowledge,
   values, and skills of the African American cultural ethos such
   as proverbial wisdom, metaphoric language and other skills
   of "African orality," public performance, artistic expression in
   music, dance, dramatic and visual art forms and humanistic
   values in math and science.
4. Enable children to recognize and maintain the world view, values, and cultural standards and practices of the African Amer-

ican ethos (and these may differ from and transcend both mainstream and "street" subculture values and expectations).

5. Enable children to discover, understand and use the strengths of their community's cultural patterns including peer group structures; relations with elders; interpersonal relatedness and authority relations; role flexibility and self-determination in the processes of instruction. This may involve the indigenous wisdom and socialization practices of parents, surrogates, and community elders.

6. Enable children to analyze and understand the strengths and weaknesses of their community's cultural patterns, inequities and opportunities in the society and global community in which we live. Instruction should also enable students to think critically about and act positively to support community and social transformation.

In conclusion, the expectation that African American cultural knowledge can and should contribute positively to school learning is missing from the knowledge base of teacher education. Nor is this perspective well-developed in multicultural textbooks for teachers (Hernandez 1989; Gollnick & Chinn 1990; Longstreet 1978; Sleeter & Grant 1988). Bennett's (1990) "comprehensive approach" and Banks's (1989, 1991) emphasis on socially transformative curriculum inclusion are two possible exceptions. Another text correctly suggests that teachers "must have specific knowledge about the varied ways of thinking, believing, learning, and communicating" that are influenced by culture and how they affect what schools do (Pai 1990, p. 69). Few teachers, teacher education students, or teacher educators have such an in-depth understanding of African American cultural knowledge and the sociocultural context of teaching and learning. The culture *Centered* and *Congruent* research perspectives presented here address this knowledge gap. More research and scholarship along these lines will certainly help to reconceptualize the professional knowledge base of teaching to make it more culturally inclusive and enhance its social relevance and transformative potential.

Notes

1. Space does not permit an in-depth examination of the literature that includes, for example, studies of Black family and community life (Gibson, 1980; Staples 1971; Willie 1985); child development and socialization

(Peters 1985; Spencer, et al. 1985) and parent's educational expectations (Seginer 1983).

2. "Urban youths hard to reach: Even black leaders can't get messages across, study finds." *San Francisco Chronicle*, May 28, 1992:A3.

3. Personal communication, August 1988. Hassimi Maiga, Regional Director of Education, Gao, Mali.

4. Several contemporary proverbs illustrate the community-family collective identity in the Songhay culture: "Zanka kul manti kala nga hugo diya."—Every child is a potential ambassador of a family. "Boro hugo ti ni seeda aduniara."—Your hometown is your witness in your lifetime. "Jeeri si sar izo ma gangama."—Don't ask a baby deer to crawl while mother deer is jumping along all alone. Field notes, H. Maiga, October 1991.

5. Recent ethnographic research shows both the oppressive conditions and the erosion of traditional African American cultural patterns in urban communities (Anderson 1990). These include socially integrative mentor/protege relations between youth and elders and surrogate parenting, for example, in contrast to the socializing power of "street peer groups" and "street culture."

6. Space does not permit a review of Comer's (1988c) autobiography. However, it most certainly includes his interpretation of the cultural knowledge and competence his mother imparted.

7. Fanny Haughton suggests this alternative interpretation based on her observations as a teacher and researcher and her understanding of African American values expressed in the term. Personal communication, May 1991. Michele Foster concurs and suggested the term "stuck-up." Personal communication, June 1991.

8. African American female students, who experience both gender and racial stereotyping, may receive more social support but less academic encouragement (Carter 1988; Scott-Jones & Clark 1986).

9. This is in contrast to "pedagogical content knowledge," for example. See California State University (1985) "The profile of the beginning teacher."

10. Elsewhere I have discussed the importance of "Diaspora literacy" as an important aspect of this global African identity and ethos in the context of oppression (King & Wilson 1990, pp. 18–20; King 1992).

Part I: References

Abrams, R. D. and Gay, G. (1972). Black culture in the classroom. In R. D. Abrams and R. C. Troike (Eds.). *Language and cultural diversity in American education,* (67–84). Englewood Cliffs, NJ: Prentice-Hall, Inc.

Allington, R. L. (1983). The reading instruction provided for readers of differing abilities. *Elementary School Journal, 83* (5): 548–559.

Anderson, E. (1990). *Streetwise: Race, class and change in an urban community.* Chicago: University of Chicago Press.

Asante, M. K. (1987). *The Afrocentric idea.* Philadelphia, PA: Temple University Press.

Asante, M. K. (1990). *Kemet, Afrocentricity, and knowledge.* Trenton, NJ: Africa World Press.

Asante, M. K. (1991). The Afrocentric idea in education. *Journal of Negro Education, 60* (2): 170–180.

Au, K. H., & Mason, J. M. (1981). Social organizational factors in learning to read: The balance of rights hypothesis. *Reading Research Quarterly, 17* (1): 115–152.

Au, K. H., & Mason, J. M. (1983). Cultural congruence in classroom participation structures: Achieving a balance of rights. *Discourse Processes, 6*: (2) 145–167.

Au, K. H., & Kawakami, A. J. (1985). Research currents: Talk story and learning to read. *Language Arts, 62* (4): 406–411.

Au, K. H., & Crowell, D. C., Jordan, C., Sloat, K. C. M., Speidel, G. E., Klein, T. W., & Tharp, R. G. (1986). Development and implementation of the KEEP reading program. In J. Orasanu (Ed.). *Reading comprehension: From research to practice.* Hillsdale, NJ: Lawrence Erlbaum Associates, pp. 235–252.

Au, K. H., & Kawakami, A. J. (1991). Culture and ownership: Schooling of minority students, *Childhood Education, 67* (5): 280–284.

Au, K. H. (1980). Participation structures in a reading lesson with Hawaiian children: Analysis of a culturally appropriate instructional event. *Anthropology and Education Quarterly, 11* (2): 91–115.

Banks, J. (1989). Integrating the curriculum with ethnic content: Approaches and guidelines. In J. Banks and C. A. Banks (Eds.). *Multicultural education: Issues and perspectives,* pp. 189–207. Boston: Allyn and Bacon.

Bell, D. (1987). *And we are not saved: The elusive quest for racial justice.* New York: Basic Books.

Banks, J. (spring 1991). Multicultural literacy and curriculum reform. *Educational Horizons,* pp. 135–140.

Barnhardt, C. (1982). Tuning-in to Athabaskan teachers and Athabaskan students. In R. Barnhardt (Ed.). *Cross-cultural issues in Alaskan education*, Vol. 2. Fairbanks: Center for Cross-Cultural studies.

Bennett, C. I. (1990). *Comprehensive multicultural education*. Boston, MA: Allyn and Bacon.

Blauner, R. (1970). Black culture: Myth or reality? In N. E. Whitten, Jr. and J. F. Szwed (Eds.). *Afro-American anthropology: Contemporary perspectives*, pp. 347–366. New York: The Free Press.

Boggs, S. T. (1972). The meaning of questions and narratives to Hawaiian children. In C. Cazden, V. John, & D. Hymes (Eds.), *Functions of language in the classroom*. New York: Teachers College Press.

Boggs, S. T. (1980). Summary of speech events involving part-Hawaiian children five years and older. Honolulu: Kamehameha Early Education Program, unpublished manuscript.

Boggs, G. L. (1974). Education: The great obsession. In Institute of the Black World (Ed.). *Education and black struggle: Notes from the colonized world*, pp. 61–81. Harvard Educational Review Monograph, 2.

Bourdieu, P. and Passeron, J. (1977). *Reproduction in education, society and culture*. London: Sage.

Bowers, C. A. and Flinders, D. J. (1990). *Responsive teaching: An ecological approach to classroom patterns of language, culture, and thought*. New York: Teachers College Press.

Boykin, W. (1984). Reading achievement and the social-cultural frame of reference of Afro-American children. *Journal of Negro Education, 53* (4): 464–473.

Boykin, A. W. (1979) Psychological/behavioral verse: Some theoretical explorations and empirical manifestations. In A. W. Boykin, et al. (Eds.). *Research directions of Black psychologists*, pp. 351–167. New York: Russell Sage.

Boykin, A. W. and Toms, F. D. (1985). Black child socialization: A conceptual framework. In H. P. McAdoo and J. L. McAdoo (Eds.). *Black children: Social, educational, and parental environments*, pp. 33–51. Beverly Hills, CA: Sage Publications.

California State University (1985). *The profile of the beginning teacher: Report of the CSU Committee to Study the Teacher Preparation Curriculum*. Fullerton, CA: CSU Fullerton.

Carew, J. V. and Lightfoot, S. L. (1979). *Beyond bias: Perspectives on classrooms*. Cambridge, MA: Harvard University Press.

Carrasco, R. L., Vera, A., & Cazden, C. B. (1981). Aspects of bilingual students' communicative competence in the classroom: A case study. In R. P. Duran, *Latino language and communicative behavior.* Norwood, NJ: Ablex.

Carter, C. (winter 1988). Black female students: Issues and considerations for teachers of teachers. *Educational Considerations, 15* (1): 31–36.

Cazden, C. B., Carrasco, R., Maldonado-Guzman, A. A., & Erickson, F. (1980). The contribution of ethnographic research to bicultural, bilingual education. In J. Alatis (Ed.). *Current issues in bilingual education.* Georgetown University Round Table on Language and Linguistics. Washington, DC: Georgetown University Press.

Cazden, C. B. (1988). *Classroom discourse.* Portsmouth, NH: Heinemann.

Cecil, N. L. (1988). Black dialect and academic success: A study of teacher expectations. *Reading Improvement, 25* (1): 34–38.

Childs, J. B. (1989). *Leadership, conflict, and cooperation in Afro-American Social Thought.* Philadelphia, PA: Temple University Press.

Clark, R. M. (1983). *Family life and school achievement: Why poor black children succeed or fail.* Chicago: University of Chicago Press.

Collins, J. (1988). Language and class in minority education. *Anthropology & Education Quarterly, 19* (4): 299–326.

Comer, J. (1988a). Educating poor and minority children. *Scientific American, 259* (5), November: 42–48.

Comer, J. (January 1988b). Is 'parenting' essential to good teaching? National Education Association: *Families and Schools,* pp. 34–40.

Comer, J. (1988c). *Maggie's dream: The life and times of a black family.* New York: New American Library.

Comer, J. (1980). *School power: Implications of an intervention project.* New York: The Free Press.

Cox, T. et al. (1991). Effects of ethnic group cultural differences on cooperative and competitive behavior on a group task. *Academy of Management Journal, 34* (4): 827–847.

Custred, G. (1990). Standard language in modern education. *American Behavioral Scientist, 34:*232–239.

D'Amato, J. (1988). "Acting": Hawaiian children's resistance to teachers. *Elementary School Journal, 88* (5): 529–544.

D'Amato, J. (1987). The belly of the beast: On cultural differences, castelike status, and the politics of school. *Anthropology and Education Quarterly, 18* (4): 357–361.

Delpit, L. (1988). The silenced dialogue: Power and pedagogy in educating other people's children. *Harvard Educational Review, 58* (3): 280–298.

Dixon, J. (1971). African-oriented and Euro-American-oriented world views: Research methodologies and economics. *Review of Black Political Economy, 7* (2): 119–156.

DuBois, W. E. B. (1973). *The education of black people: Ten Critiques 1906–1960.* [H. Aptheker, (Ed.)] Amherst, MA: University of Massachusetts Press.

Dumont, R. V., Jr. (1972). Learning English and how to be silent: Studies in Sioux and Cherokee classrooms. In C. B. Cazden, V. P. John, & D. Hymes (Eds.). *Functions of language in the classroom,* pp. 344–369. New York: Teachers College Press.

Epstein, J. (1985). Home and school connections in schools of the future: Implications of research on parent involvement. *Peabody Journal of Education, 62:*18–41.

Erickson, F., & Mohatt, G. (1982). Cultural organization of participation structures in two classrooms of Indian students. In G. B. Spindler (Ed.). *Doing the ethnography of schooling: Educational anthropology in action.* New York: Holt, Rinehart & Winston.

Erickson, F. (1984). School literacy, reasoning, and civility: An anthropologist's perspective. *Review of Educational Research, 54* (4): 525–546.

Felice, L. G. (1981). Black student dropout behavior: Disengagement from school rejection and racial discrimination. *Journal of Negro Education, 50:*415–424.

Fordham, S. (1991). Peer-proofing academic competition among Black adolescents: "Acting white" Black American style. In C. E. Sleeter (Ed.). *Empowerment through multicultural education.* pp. 69–93. Albany: State University of New York Press.

Fordham, S. (1988). Racelessness as a factor in Black students' school success: Pragmatic strategy or pyrrhic victory? *Harvard Educational Review, 58* (1): 54–84.

Freire, P. (1971). *Pedagogy of the oppressed.* New York: Herder & Herder.

Gallimore, R., Boggs, J. W., & Jordan, C. (1974). *Culture, behavior and education: A study of Hawaiian-Americans.* Beverly Hills: Sage.

Garibaldi, A. (1992). Educating and motivating African American males to succeed. *Journal of Negro Education, 61:*4–8.

Gay, G. (October 1975). Cultural differences important in the education of black children. *Momentum, 6:*30–33.

References{.hidden}

Gibson, W. (1980). The alleged weakness in the black family structure. In W. Gibson (Ed.). *Family life and morality: Studies in black and white,* pp. 55–73. Lanham, MD: University Press of America.

Giddens, A. (1979). *Central problems in social theory: Action, structure and contradiction in social analysis.* Berkeley, CA: University of California Press.

Gilmore, P. (1985). "Gimme room": School resistance, attitudes, and access to literacy. *Journal of Education, 167:*111–128.

Giroux, H. (1992). Educational leadership and the crisis of democratic government. *Educational Researcher, 21* (4): 4–11.

Giroux, H. (1988). *Teachers as transformative intellectuals: Toward a critical pedagogy of learning.* Granby, MA: Bergin & Garvey.

Glazer, N. and Moynihan, D. P. (1963). *Beyond the melting pot.* Cambridge, MA: M.I.T. Press.

Gollnick, D. and Chinn, P. (1990). *Multicultural education in a pluralistic society.* Columbus, OH: Merrill Publishing Co.

Gordon, B. (1985). Toward emancipation in citizenship education: The case of African-American cultural knowledge. *Theory and Research in Social Education, 12:*1–23.

Gordon, B. (1990). The necessity of African American epistemology for educational theory and practice. *Journal of Education, 172:* 88–106.

Gordon, E. W., Miller, F., & Rollock, D. (1990). Coping with communicentric bias in knowledge production in the social sciences. *Educational Researcher, 19* (3): 14–19.

Grant, C. and Gillette, M. (November/December 1987). The Holmes report and minorities in education. *Social Education,* 517–521.

Grant, C. (1989). Urban teachers: Their new colleagues and the curriculum. *Phi Delta Kappan, 70* (10): 764–70.

Gwaltney, J. L. (1980). *Drylongso: A self-portrait of Black America.* New York: Vintage Books.

Hale-Benson, J. E. (1986, 1982). *Black children: Their roots, culture and learning styles.* Rev. ed. Baltimore, MD: The Johns Hopkins University Press.

Harding, V. (1990). *Hope and history: Why we must share the story of the movement.* Maryknoll, NY: Orbis Books.

Harris, R. L. et al. (1990). *Black Studies in the United States: Three essays.* New York: The Ford Foundation.

Haynes, N. et al. (1988). The school development program: A model for school improvement. *Journal of Negro Education, 57*:11–21.

Heath, S. B. (1982a). Questioning at home and at school: A comparative study. In G. Spindler (Ed.). *Doing the ethnography of schooling: Educational anthropology in action,* pp. 96–131. New York: Holt, Rinehart and Winston.

Heath, S. B. (1983). *Ways with words: Language, life, and work in communities and classrooms.* Cambridge: Cambridge University Press.

Heath, S. B. (1989). Oral and literate traditions among Black Americans living in poverty. *American Psychologist, 44* (2): 367–373.

Heath, S. B. (1982b). What no bedtime story means: Narrative skills at home and school. *Language in Society, 11* (2): 49–76.

Henry, C. P. (1990). *Culture and African American politics.* Bloomington, IN: Indiana University Press.

Hernandez, H. (1989). *Multicultural education: A teachers' guide to content and process.* Columbus, OH: Merrill Publishing Co.

Holliday, B. (1985). Towards a model of teacher-child transactional processes affecting Black children's academic achievement. In M. Spencer et al., (Eds.). *Beginnings: The social and affective development of Black children,* pp. 117–130. Hillsdale, NJ: Lawrence Erlbaum.

Hollins, E. R. (July 1989). *A conceptual framework for selecting instructional approaches for inner city black youngsters.* Paper prepared for the California Curriculum Development and Supplemental Materials Commission, Ad Hoc Committee. Sacramento, CA.

Hollins, E. R. (1983). *An instructional design theory relating black cultural practices and values to instruction.* Ph.D. Thesis. University of Texas. Austin, TX.

Hollins, E.R. (1990). Debunking the myth of a monolithic white American culture; or, moving toward cultural inclusion. *American Behavioral Scientist, 7* (2): 119–126.

Hollins, E. R. (1982). The Marva Collins Story revisited: Implications for regular classroom instruction. *Journal of Teacher Education, 33* (1): 37–40.

Holloway, J. E. (1990). *Africanisms in American culture.* Bloomington, IN: Indiana University Press.

Irvine, J. (1991). *Black students and school failure.* New York: Praeger.

Jenkins, E. S. (1991). Bridging the two cultures: American black scientists and inventors. *Journal of Black Studies, 21* (3): 302–312.

Johnson, S. T. (1992). Extra-school factors in achievement, attainment, and aspiration among junior and senior high school-age African American youth. *Journal of Negro Education, 61:*99–119.

Jordan, C. (1985). Translating culture: From ethnographic information to educational program. *Anthropology and Education Quarterly, 16:* 105–123.

Karp, S. (June 1991). Is all black and all male right? *Zeta Magazine,* 86–89.

King, J. (1991a). Dysconscious racism: Ideology, identity, and the miseducation of teachers. *Journal of Negro Education, 60* (2): 1–14.

King, J. (1991b). Unfinished business: Black student alienation and Black teachers' emancipatory pedagogy. In M. Foster (Ed.). *Readings on equal education, 11:*245–271. New York: AMS Press.

King, J. (1990). *In search of African liberation pedagogy: Multiple contexts of education and struggle,* (Special issue). *Journal of Education, 172* (2).

King, J. (1992). The middle passage revisted: Diaspora literacy and consciousness in the struggle against miseducation in the black community. Paper presented at the annual meeting of the American Educational Research Association, San Francisco, CA.

King, J. and Mitchell, C. (1990). *Black mothers to sons: Juxtaposing African American literature with social practice.* New York: Peter Lang Publishers.

King, J. and Ladson-Billings, G. (1990). The teacher education challenge in elite university settings: Developing critical perspectives for teaching in a democratic and multicultural society. *European Journal of Intercultural Studies, 1* (2): 15–30.

King, J. and Wilson, T. L. (1990). Being the soul-freeing substance: The legacy of hope in Afro humanity. *Journal of Education, 172* (2): 9–27.

Labov, W. (1970). The logic of non-standard English. In F. Williams (Ed.). *Language and poverty.* Chicago: Markham.

Labov, W. (1966). Finding out about children's language. *Working Papers in Communication,* Pacific Speech Association, *1* (1): 1–30.

Labov, W., & Robbins, C. (1969). A note on the relation of reading failure to peer-group status in urban ghettoes. *Teachers College Record, 70:* 355–406.

Ladson-Billings, G. (1990). Like lightning in a bottle: Attempting to capture the pedagogical excellence of successful teachers of black students. *Qualitative Studies in Education, 3* (4): 335–344.

Ladson-Billings, G. and King, J. (1990). *Cultural identity of African-Americans: Implications for achievement.* Aurora, CO: Mid-continental Regional Education Laboratory.

Ladson-Billings, G. and Henry, A. (1990). Blurring the borders: Voices of African liberatory pedagogy in the United States and Canada. *Journal of Education, 172* (2): 72–88.

Laosa, L. M. (1983). Parent education, cultural pluralism, and public policy: The uncertain connection. In R. Haskins and D. Adams (Eds.). *Parent education and public policy,* pp. 331–344. Norwood, NJ: Ablex Publishing Corp.

Lee, C. D. (1991). Big picture talkers/words walking without masters: The instructional implications of ethnic voices for expanded literacy. *Journal of Negro Education, 60:*291–304.

Lipka, J. (1990). Integrating cultural form and content in one Yup'ik Eskimo classroom: A case study. Manuscript submitted for publication.

Longstreet, W. (1978). *Aspects of ethnicity: Understanding differences in pluralistic classrooms.* New York: Teachers College Press.

MacLeod, J. (1991). Bridging school and street. *Journal of Negro Education, 60:*260–275.

Mahiri, J. (1991). Discourse in sports: Language and literacy features of preadolescent African American males in a youth basketball program. *Journal of Negro Education, 60:* 305–313.

Majors, R. (1986 winter). Cool pose: The proud signature of Black survival. *Changing Men, 17:*5–6.

Majors, R. and Billson, J. (1992). *Cool Pose: The dilemmas of Black manhood in America.* New York: Lexington Books.

Mbiti, J. S. (1970). *African religions and philosophy.* New York: Anchor Books.

McCollum, P. (1989). Turn-allocation in lessons with North American and Puerto Rican students: A comparative study. *Anthropology and Education Quarterly, 20* (2): 133–158.

McDermott, R. (1987). Achieving school failure: An anthropological approach to illiteracy and social stratification. In G. D. Spindler (Ed.). *Educational and cultural processes,* pp. 173–209. Prospect Heights, IL: Waveland Press (2nd Ed.).

McDermott, R. P. (1987).The explanation of minority school failure, again. *Anthropology and Education Quarterly, 18* (4): 361–364.

Mehan, H. (1979). *Learning lessons.* Cambridge, MA: Harvard University Press.

Michaels, S., & Collins, J. (1984). Oral discourse styles: Classroom interaction and the acquisition of literacy. In D. Tannen (Ed.). *Coherence in spoken and written discourse.* Norwood, NJ: Ablex, pp. 219–244.

Michaels, S. (1981). "Sharing time": Children's narrative styles and differential access to literacy. *Language in Society, 10:*423–442.

Moll, L. C. & Diaz, S. (1987). Change as the goal of educational research. *Anthropology and Education Quarterly, 18* (4): 300–311.

Morrison, T. (1992). *Playing in the dark: Whiteness in the literary imagination.* Cambridge, MA: Harvard University Press.

Moses, B. et al. (1989). The algebra project: Organizing in the spirit of Ella. *Harvard Educational Review, 59* (4): 423–443.

National Alliance of Black School Educators (November 1984). *Saving the African American child.* Washington, D.C.: Author.

Nobles, W. W. (1977). African root and American fruit: The Black family. *Journal of Social and Behavioral Sciences, 20:*52–64.

Nobles, W. W. (1985). *Africanity and the Black family: The development of a theoretical model.* Oakland, CA: Black Family Institute.

Ogbu, J. (1990). Minority education in comparative perspective. *Journal of Negro Education, 59:*45–57.

Ogbu, J. (1987). Variability in minority school performance: A problem in search of an explanation. *Anthropology and Education Quarterly, 18:* 313–334.

Ogbu, J. U., & Fordham, S. (1986). Black students' school success: Coping with the "burden of 'acting white.'" *The Urban Review, 18* (3): 176–206.

Ogbu, J. (1978). *Minority education and caste: The American system in cross-cultural perspective.* New York: Academic Press.

Ogundipe-Leslie, M. (1984). African women, culture and another development. *Journal of African Marxists, 5:*77–92.

Pai, Y. (1990). *Cultural foundations of education.* Columbus, OH: Merrill Publishing Co.

Peters, M. (1985). Racial socialization of young black children. In H. P. McAdoo and J. L. McAdoo (Eds.). *Black children: Social, educational, and parental environments,* pp. 159–173. Beverly Hills, CA: Sage Publications.

Philips, S. (1972). Participant Structures and communicative competence: Warm Springs children in community and classroom. In C. Cazden, V. John, & D. Hymes (Eds.). *Functions of language in the classroom.* New York: Teachers College Press.

Piestrup, A. M. (1973). *Black dialect interference and accommodation of reading instruction in first grade.* Monographs of the Language-

Behavior Research Laboratory, No. 4. Berkeley, CA: University of California.

Prager. J. (1982). American racial ideology as collective representation. *Ethnic and Racial Studies, 5:*99–119.

Ramirez, A. G. (1981). Language attitudes and the speech of Spanish-English bilingual pupils. In R. P. Duran (Ed.). *Latino language and communicative behavior.* Norwood, NJ: Ablex, pp. 217–235.

Richards, D. (1985). The implications of African-American spirituality. In M. K. Asante and K. W. Asante (Eds.). *African culture: Rhythms of unity,* pp. 207–231. Westport, CT: Greenwood Press.

Robinson, S. et al. (1980). Desegregation: A bibliographic review of teacher attitudes and black students. *The Negro Educational Review, 31* (2): 48–59.

Rosenbaum, J. E. et al. (1987). Low-income black children in white suburban schools: A study of school and student responses. *Journal of Negro Education, 56* (1): 35–43.

Rosenfeld, G. (1971). *"Shut those thick lips!": A study of slum school failure.* New York: Holt, Rinehart and Winston.

Scollon, R., & Scollon, S. B. K. (1981). *Narrative, literacy, and face in interethnic communication.* Norwood, NJ: Ablex.

Scott-Jones, D. and Clark, M. L. (1986). The school experiences of black girls. *Phi Delta Kappan, 67:* 520–526.

Seginer, R. (1983). Parents' educational expectations and children's academic achievements: A literature review. *Merrill Palmer Quarterly, 29:*1–23.

Shade, B. J. and Edwards, P. (1987). Ecological correlates of the educative style of Afro-American children. *Journal of Negro Education, 56,* (1): 88–99.

Singer, E. A. (March 1988). *What is cultural congruence, and why are they saying such terrible things about it?* Occasional paper no. 120. East Lansing, MI: Institute for Research on Teaching, College of Education, Michigan State University.

Slaughter, D. T. and Epps, E. G. (1987). The home environment and academic achievement of Black American children and youth: An overview. *Journal of Negro Education, 56* (1): 3–20.

Slaughter, D. T. and Kuehne, V. S. (1989). Improving Black education: Perspectives on parent involvement. In W. D. Smith and E. W. Chunn (Eds.). *Black education: A quest for excellence,* (59–75). New Brunswick, NJ: Transaction Publishers.

Sleeter, C. and Grant, C. (1988). *Making choices for multicultural education: Five approaches to race, class, and gender.* Columbus, OH: Merrill Publishing Co.

Solomon, R. P. (1988). Black cultural forms in schools: A cross national comparison. In L. Weiss (Ed.). *Class, race, and gender in American education,* pp. 230–248. Albany: State Universtiy of New York Press.

Spradley, J. P. (1972). Foundations of cultural knowledge. In J. P. Spradley (Ed.). *Culture and cognition: Rules, maps, and plans,* pp. 3–38. Prospect Heights, IL: Waveland Press.

Staples, R. (1971). *The black family.* Belmont, CA: Wadsworth. Steele, C. M. (April 1992). Race and the schooling of black Americans. *The Atlantic Monthly, 269* (4): 68–78.

Steele, C. M. (1992). Race and the Schooling of Black Americans. *The Atlantic, 269* (4): 68–78.

Sudarkasa, N. (1988). Interpreting the African heritage in Afro-American family organization. In H. McAdoo (Ed.). *Black families* (2nd Ed.) 27–43). Newbury Park, CA: Sage Publications.

Thompson, R. F. (1983). *Flash of the spirit: African and Afro-American art and philosophy.* New York: Random House.

Trueba, H. (1988). Culturally based explanations of minority students' academic achievement. *Anthropology and Education Quarterly, 19:* 270–287.

Van Ness, H. (1981). Social control and social organization in an Alaskan Athabaskan classroom: A microethnography of "getting ready" for reading. In H. T. Trueba, G. P. Guthrie, & K. H. Au (Eds.). *Culture and the bilingual classroom: Studies in classroom ethnography.* Rowley, MA: Newbury House, pp. 120–138.

Vogt, L. A., Jordan, C., & Tharp, R. G. (1987). Explaining school failure, producing school success: Two cases. *Anthropology and Education Quarterly, 18* (4): 276–286.

Vygotsky, L. S. (1978). *Mind in society.* Cambridge, MA: Harvard University Press.

Ward, M. (1971/1986). *Them children: A study in language learning.* New York: Holt, Rinehart & Winston.

Watson-Gegeo, K. A., & Boggs, S. T. (1977). From verbal play to talk story: The role of routine in speech events among Hawaiian children. In S. Ervin-Trip & C. Mitchell-Kernan (Eds.). *Child discourse.* New York: Academic Press.

Weiler, K. (1991). A feminist pedagogy of difference. *Harvard Educational Review, 61* (4): 449–474.

Weiler, A. (1981). Robert Coles reconsidered: A critique of the portrayal of Blacks as culturally deprived. *Journal of Negro Education, 50:* 381–388.

Weisner, T. S., Gallimore, R., & Jordan, C. (1988). Unpackaging cultural effects on classroom learning: Native Hawaiian peer assistance and child-generated activity. *Anthropology & Education Quarterly, 19* (4): 327–353.

White, M. M. (1987). We are family! Kinship and solidarity in the black community. In G. Gay and W. L. Baber (Eds.). *Expressively black: The cultural basis of ethnic identity,* pp. 17–34. New York: Praeger.

Wilcox, P. (1970). Educating for black humanism: A way of approaching it. In N. Wright (Ed.). *What black educators are saying,* pp. 3–17. San Francisco, CA: Leswing Press.

Willie, C. V. (1984). *Black and white families: A study in complementarity.* Bayside, NY: General Hall Press, Inc.

Winfield, L. (1986). Teacher beliefs toward academically at risk students in inner urban schools. *The Urban Review, 18* (4): 253–267.

Wynter, S. (1992). *Do not call us Negros: How multicultural textbooks perpetuate the ideology of racism.* San Francisco, CA: Aspire Books.

Young, V. H. (1970). Family and childhood in a southern Negro community. *American Anthropologist, 72:*269–288.

Young, V. H. (1974). A Black American socialization pattern. *American Ethnologist, 1* (2): 405–413.

*Developing a Holistic View of Schooling
for Diverse Populations*

Introduction

Developing a holistic view of schooling for diverse populations requires an examination of their particular educational needs. Part II begins by examining the needs of one culturally identifiable group that is usually overlooked in research on how schooling fails many minority students: Appalachian mountain children. The following chapters examine the educational success and failure of African-American, Native American, Mexican American and Puerto Rican/Latino students and the implications of their schooling experiences for teacher education.

In chapter 3, "Teaching for Change in Appalachia," Rebecca Eller-Powell argues that the Appalachian population is a distinct minority subculture for whom historically inferior schooling has resulted in marginalization, alienation and resistance in school. Eller-Power's review of the literature relates the low education attainment of Appalachian students to ways that schools serve as a "homogenizing force," adopting policies and structures, including textbooks, that ignore the Appalachian experience, as well as students' needs, cultural traditions and values. By examining and questioning the interests being served by recent educational reforms in the region, Eller-Powell concludes that a different "vision for education" is needed—one that includes culturally relevant curriculum and teaching practices that use students' cultural knowledge and literacy experiences and respects them as learners. This, Eller-Powell argues, is needed if students and teachers are to work together for change.

In the next chapter, Cornel D. Pewewardy describes the implementation of culturally responsible pedagogy in an American Indian magnet school in Saint Paul, Minnesota. According to Pewewardy, culturally responsible pedagogy "involves providing the best education for American Indian children that preserves their own cultural heritage, prepares them for meaningful relationships with other people, and for living productive lives in the present society without sacrificing their own cultural perspective." This "practice into theory" approach shares some features in common with culturally congruent pedagogy that Au and Kawakami discuss in chapter 1 and attributes of effective instruction for groups that other authors describe in this section.

For example, in chapter 5, "The Attributes of Effective Schools for Language Minority Students," Eugene E. Garcia explores the "state-of-the-art" in language minority education and reviews research related to "linguistic, cultural and instructional variables." In his examination of "commonalities in the organization and content of effective classroom instruction for language minority students," Garcia finds that in addition to instructional attributes "common to effective classrooms in general," such as clearly specifying task outcomes, communicating high expectations, and active teaching, monitoring and providing feedback, "the particular use of two languages" and instructional practices that "take advantage of the students' cultural background" are important. Moreover, Garcia notes that instructional strategies effective teachers of Mexican American language minority students use "build on the socialization factors" that are relevant to this student population, including: using an integrated curriculum approach; minimal individualized work tasks; student-to-student instructional opportunities; and a "highly informal, almost familial, social and collaborative relationship between teachers and students." As other authors affirm, these findings have direct implications for teacher preparation.

The authors of chapter 6, "Teaching and Learning in Puerto Rican/Latino Collaboratives: Implications for Teacher Education," describe their work in five university-school partnerships which focus on transforming the practice of professors, researchers, and classroom teachers. All the authors belong to a consortium of researchers, teacher educators, and practitioners, the Intercambio Research Project, that developed collaborative, ethnographic research-based interventions which changed classroom instruction and curriculum in New York City, Arizona and Puerto Rico. The Intercambio researchers helped teachers integrate the experience, language and culture of students and their communities into the learning process. Collaboration requires new ways of doing and documenting research on teaching and learning, as this collectively written chapter that preserves the multiple perspectives and diverse voices of the authors demonstrates.

The success of the research-based collaborative interventions and collective action suggests to these authors that "schools can become the vehicles by which teacher educators, practicing teachers, and prospective teachers learn to integrate theory, methods and practice." Moreover, theory about "why and how students succeed or fail" and changing educational practice in the knowledge base for teacher preparation must emerge from interdisciplinary university-school partnerships. The authors conclude that teacher education should prepare teachers to: (1) learn from experience and test their theories through reflection and action; (2) transform the isolated work of teaching into collective activity; and (3) education professors must model the integration of theory, methods and practice in their own work.

Chapter 7, "Who Will Teach *Our* Children: Preparing Teachers to Successfully Teach African American Students," concludes Part II. In this chapter, Gloria Ladson-Billings observes that at least four things need to happen to improve the knowledge base for preparing teachers for African American learners. She suggests that prospective teachers need: (1) to know the history of African American education; (2) more and better explications of African American culture; (3) researchers and teacher educators need to examine the pedagogy of successful teachers of African American learners; and (4) a more extensive advocacy network on their behalf is needed. Like the preceding authors, Ladson-Billings advocates using students' culture to make teaching "culturally relevant," that is, student-centered and empowering, and not only in order to counteract negative expectations teachers may hold about students but to dispel negative judgments about African American culture as well.

In conclusion, the chapters in Part II describe forms of classroom organization, such as "culturally relevant interactional strategies," and content like the community-focused "environmental science" course and other ways of incorporating students' home and community culture into classroom life that enable teachers, students and researchers to work together as a "community of learners." Eller-Powell contrasts such transformative education with "training" to fit into society as it exists; other authors agree that the latter approach is inadequate. They argue that students should gain knowledge and skills in the academic subjects and use the intellectual and cultural resources of their families and communities to face real problems in their lives and communities. In other words, students need empowering activities that affirm their self-worth, build a positive cultural identity, and enhance their confidence as learners.

CHAPTER 3

Teaching for Change in Appalachia

REBECCA ELLER-POWELL

Questions to Think About

1. The author maintains that the Appalachian population is a distinct ethnic minority culture. Why do some scholars contend that what exists in the Appalachian population is merely a matter of social class differences?
2. How does defining a population as a racial or ethnic minority influence social status and schooling?
3. How are the issues associated with the educational failure of Appalachian children similar to or different from those of other minority groups?

Appalachia has often been overlooked in studies dealing with the educational failure of minorities. Yet the failure rate of mountain students has been well documented. When compared to the non-mountain counties in the central Appalachian states (Kentucky, Tennessee, Virginia, West Virginia), Appalachian counties continue to have proportionately higher numbers of students who drop out before completing high school. Recent statistics show that 52.1 percent of central Appalachian residents over the age of 25 have not completed high school, compared with a national average of 33.5 percent (Tickamyer & Tickamyer 1987). Research also shows that students in the mountain counties tend to score lower than their non-Appalachian counterparts on tests of reading, language, and other basic skills (Bagby et al. 1985; DeYoung 1985; DeYoung, Vaught, & Porter 1981).

This chapter addresses a number of critical issues in educating mountain children. First, I will argue that the Appalachian population represents what John Ogbu (1987) has classified as an involuntary minority, and therefore, as with other minority groups, there are problems inherent in the system of schooling in Appalachia that must be confronted. I will then examine the ways in which schools in Appalachia have functioned to marginalize certain segments of the population, which has led to alienation and resistance. Finally, using the data from interviews with Appalachian teachers, I will offer a number of suggestions for educators and educational policymakers for combatting the widespread educational failure that exists in the region.

Defining Appalachians as a Minority Group

Perhaps because minorities typically are defined in terms of race, Appalachia has generally been omitted in discussions about minority populations. Nevertheless, Appalachia has long been regarded as a distinct subculture in the American mind (Precourt 1983; Shapiro 1978), and the "Appalachian image" has been perpetuated by the media through television programs such as "Hee Haw" and "The Beverly Hillbillies." Linguistic studies show that mountain speech is characterized by a number of distinct features which differentiate it from other dialects (Wolfram 1984; Wolfram & Christian 1976).

In an attempt to explain the variability in the educational attainment of particular minority groups, Ogbu (1987) distinguishes between "immigrant" and "involuntary" minority populations. Immigrant minorities are groups that have moved voluntarily to the United States in search of greater political freedom and/or economic opportunities; involuntary minorities are groups who "were originally brought into United States society involuntarily through slavery, conquest, or colonization" (p. 321). Thus, contrary to immigrant minorities, who "strive to play the classroom game by the rules . . . because they believe so strongly that there will be a payoff later" (p. 328), involuntary minorities have experienced a cumulative history of discrimination and inequality.

Because involuntary minorities traditionally have been denied opportunities to advance in the labor market and often have been subjected to inferior schooling, they tend to distrust educational institutions and the dominant ideology they represent. Further, these

groups tend to develop alternate responses to schooling and to society in general by establishing a social or collective identity that
is generally in opposition to the dominant group. These responses
frequently take the form of differences in linguistic/communica-
tive style (Christie 1985; R. G. Eller 1989b; Jordan 1988; Michaels
1981, 1986; Piestrup 1973) and differences in attitudes and behavior (Gilmore 1987; Willis 1977). In fact, frequently these differences
become cultural "markers" that serve to distinguish individuals
as members of a particular group, and therefore they become reinforced in an effort to avoid "acting white" (Gumperz 1985; Mc-
Dermott 1974).

In order to understand the current educational dilemma in the
region, it is important to examine the historical developments leading to the "making of Appalachia" (Shapiro 1978). With a history of
exploitation and deprivation, Appalachians possess many of the
characteristics associated with involuntary minorities. Prior to the
late 1880s and 1890s, Appalachia was a self-sufficient society that
was not unlike other rural areas of the United States. With the coming of industrialization, however, Appalachia became a haven for
outside capitalist interests. Within a few short decades, the region
was transformed from a primarily agrarian economy dominated by
an independent mode of production (Banks 1980), to a market economy dominated by a capitalist mode of production.

In the years after the Civil War, outside investors descended on
the mountains and began acquiring vast mineral and timber re-
serves (Caudill 1963; R. D. Eller 1982). Between 1900 and 1930,
over six hundred company-controlled coal towns were created in the
Southern Appalachians. Most of these companies eventually were
sold to absentee owners, who often had little concern for the local
inhabitants. In addition, by the 1920s, sixty-two percent of the pri-
vately owned timber acreage in the region was held by industry, and
this figure does not include the more than two million acres of public timberland owned by the federal government. Because land ownership was so tightly controlled, there was little opportunity for
diversification, making the region dependent upon the fluctuations
of the national economy. Even today, absentee land ownership remains a critical problem (Appalachian Land Ownership Task Force
1983).

Along with this industrial onslaught came contrasts in values.
Entrepreneurs, missionaries, and others who came to the Appalachian region in the late 1800s and early 1900s brought with them
their own set of cultural norms which often tended to conflict with

those of the native population. Lewis, Kobak and Johnson (1978) write that ". . . always the mountain people were compared with 'back home': the educated and professional middle-class, the urban homes and situations from which they came" (p. 19). Today, discussions about Appalachia invariably invoke images of backwardness, poverty and deprivation. Shapiro (1978) documents the making of the popular image of Appalachia, which sometimes has been characterized as "a strange land inhabited by a peculiar people."

Precourt (1983) argues that the development of this image emerged not from actual deprivation, but rather from the imposition of capitalist standards upon a precapitalist society. He states that ". . . the market defines existing needs and constantly generates new needs oriented toward the survival and perpetuation of the market system per se" (p. 95). Those who are not able to participate fully in the market economy tend to be stigmatized, and negative stereotypes emerge which are propelled by culturally-defined differences in behavior. Thus, accompanying the lack of relative wealth was an image of the mountaineer as being culturally and intellectually inferior.

The modernization of the Appalachian region has been compared to the colonization process elsewhere (Lewis & Knipe 1978). Certainly many of the components of the colonization model apply to the modernization of Appalachia, e.g., involuntary entry resulting from technological superiority in order to obtain valuable resources; rapid changes in values and social patterns among the colonized; domination by the group gaining entry, with an accompanying denigration of the native population (i.e., the "hillbilly image"). The colonization hypothesis has been amended to suggest that Appalachia represents a peripheral region within an advanced capitalistic society, and thus can be compared to Third World countries that similarly suffer from underdevelopment and dependency (Walls 1978).

Today, poverty in the region continues to be widespread. With the "rediscovery" of Appalachia in the 1960s and the initiation of anti-poverty programs, the incidence of poverty declined (Tickamyer & Tickamyer 1987). During the 1980s, however, this trend was reversed, largely resulting from increased mechanization in the mining industry and the scarcity of other available employment opportunities. As of May 1986, 176 counties in the Appalachian region reported unemployment rates of over one-and-a-half times the national average, and sixty-five counties reported unemployment rates that were more than double the national average; only ninety counties had rates that were below the national average (Kublawi 1986). A recent report by the Appalachian Educational Laboratory indicates that thirty percent of the "persistent poverty counties" in the United States, i.e., counties that have repeatedly ranked in the lowest per capita income quintile since 1950, are located in Central Appalachia (AEL Interim Report 1988). Surely the schools in the region have a major responsibility in reversing this trend (Miller 1977).

To summarize, it has been argued that the mountain population possesses many characteristics of an involuntary minority as defined by Ogbu (1987). They were invaded by capitalist interests and have experienced a history of exploitation, resulting in a cycle of deprivation and dependence (Batteau 1983); they have established a somewhat distinct language and culture which tends to differentiate them from other subcultures, and these differences have prevailed despite efforts to "bring them into the mainstream" (Beaver 1986; Hicks 1976; Wolfram 1984; Wolfram & Christian 1976). In addition, employment opportunities have been limited, and hence Appalachian residents have been skeptical of middle-class values that advocate upward mobility.

Finally, it should be noted that, like other minority groups, Appalachians have historically received inferior schooling. A 1915 report of educational expenditures in the region shows that the annual per capita expenditure in eight Appalachian states surveyed was $6.60; in the most mountainous counties, the average amount was $4.79. These figures can be compared to a national per capita expenditure of $16.09 (Frost 1915). A 1933 report of education in Kentucky and Tennessee shows that there were fewer opportunities for secondary education in the mountain counties, and consequently there tended to be a "ceiling effect" that resulted in proportionately larger numbers of students enrolled in elementary school in the mountain counties in contrast to the non-mountain counties. Further, teachers in the mountain counties were paid considerably less and tended to be less educated (Gaumnitz 1933). More recent data reveal that in the central Appalachian states of Kentucky, Tennessee, Virginia, and West Virginia, the mountain counties continue to spend less per pupil for instruction and depend more heavily on federal and state sources than do the non-Appalachian counties (De Young 1985). At the time of this writing, in at least two states in central Appalachia, the method for funding education has been determined to be inequitable by the state supreme court (Hazi 1989; Roser 1988).

"Blaming the Victim". With the coming of the missionary schools during the late 1800s and early 1900s (Whisnant 1983), and continuing today through public schooling, the educational institution has been seen as a means for socializing the mountaineer into the mainstream culture (Branscome 1978; Schwarzweller & Brown 1971). Schwarzweller and Brown (1971) write that, while schools in the region are reflections of the local community, each school is also "a reflection of the greater American society of which it is an instrumental part reflecting national norms, teaching more universal patterns of behavior, and diffusing national and even international cultural values" (p. 130). Thus, a primary role of schools in the region has been to "Americanize" the mountain population.

One way in which the educational institutions in Appalachia have been a "homogenizing force" is through the adoption of urban policies and structures. School systems in the region often have been quick to embrace what Boyd (1987) has called the Urban-Idealistic Consciousness, i.e., the belief that "urban forms of human association and urban institutions" are synonymous with progress (p. 34; also see Sher 1977). This policy is evident in a statement made at a 1968 NEA conference by former Kentucky Governor Edward T. Breathitt, who suggested that "a child's education must prepare him to be a first-class citizen in tomorrow's urban world and prepare him for a lifetime of occupational change" (Sixth NEA Conference 1968, p. 4). The Urban-Idealistic Consciousness has been carried out largely through concerted efforts to consolidate many of the small rural schools, and through an emphasis upon a unified, centralized curriculum.

Both of these reform efforts have brought their own set of problems. School consolidation has led to significantly higher transportation costs, long bus rides for students, and more frequent school closings during the winter months. Further, it has been found that student participation in extra-curricular activities has decreased, and there has been less parent involvement in the local schools (Boyd 1987; Boyd & De Young 1986; Smith 1988). The use of standardized textbooks has been problematic in that these texts often either ignore the Appalachian experience altogether, or they present a distorted image of the region (Keefe, Reck, & Reck 1987; Miller 1975; Oxendine 1989).

A second way in which Appalachian schools have served as a homogenizing force in the region is through reinforcing dominant patterns of behavior. In addition to structural reforms, the urban model has imposed a certain ideology that is consistent with dominant norms. In a study of one rural Appalachian school district, Reck, Keefe, & Reck (1987) found that students tend to be differentiated according to certain symbolic identifiers, such as dress, speech patterns, behavior, and general attitudes and lifestyles. These factors are used by both teachers and students to sort students into certain classifications. Poor, rural students are frequently labeled as the "lower group," the "mountain kids," or the Rednecks," while the middle- or upper-class students from town are given favorable labels such as the "upper group," the "popular group," or the "college prep group." The researchers found that students in this latter classification are more apt to win awards and participate in extra-curricular activities, and are typically found in the upper academic tracks; those in the lower-status group tend to enroll in vocational courses and generally are not involved in extra-curricular activities.

This research supports other investigations on the educational failure of minorities which indicate that students who are "more like the teacher" are more likely to receive favorable treatment (Gilmore 1987; Oakes 1985; Page 1987; Rist 1970; Spindler 1974). As a result, students in the lower tracks have been described by their teachers as being shy, less confident, insecure, and with feelings of inferiority (Reck, Keefe, & Reck 1987). These findings are consistent with earlier research on students' self-concepts in the region (Reck 1982). In contrast, teachers described upper-track students as being more confident and self-assured.

Attempts at homogenizing the Appalachian population through schooling have had other ramifications as well. Through the propagation of the dominant belief system and the simultaneous marginalization of minority values, schools in the region have tended to alienate the very population they have been commissioned to serve. This alienation has resulted in high drop-out and illiteracy rates that are commensurate with those of other minority populations (Crew 1985; Tickamyer & Tickamyer 1987). In their interviews with Appalachian families, Reck et al. (1987) found that students in the low-status group and their parents perceive that they are being treated unfairly by the schools. Cultural and/or class conflict in the schools is also felt to be a factor in recent textbook controversies and school consolidation struggles in the region (Billings & Goldman 1983; Boyd 1987; Clement-Brutto 1987; Weaver 1977).

Educators and the general public traditionally have tended to "blame the victim" for the high incidence of educational failure in Appalachia. Publications in the 1960s and 1970s suggested that mountain families did not value education, and lacked a sense of responsibility for the education of their children (Ford 1962; Weller 1975). A more recent study sponsored by the Appalachian Regional Commission revealed that many school officials still believe that the high drop-out rate in the region is directly linked to the limited expectations of parents (Brizius, Foster, & Patton 1988).

In addition, it has been found that even teachers who are natives of the Appalachian region are likely to exhibit bias toward their lower-class "mountain and hollow" students. In keeping with their professional status, these teachers tend to identify more with the middle-class (Reck, Reck, & Keefe 1987). In reporting their findings, Reck et al. state that "Appalachian teachers typically did not identify overtly with the rural, Appalachian group that they perceived. Despite their shared origin—the mountains—they distanced themselves from that group. In fact, only one Appalachian teacher volunteered a positive identity with Appalachia" (p. 12). Thus, it is apparent that educators still tend to attribute educational failure to factors associated with the mountain culture, despite evidence to the contrary (Bagby et al. 1985; Duncan 1987).

While schools in the region have traditionally failed to take full responsibility for the low educational attainment of mountain students, there nevertheless have been positive trends in recent years. Many school systems have established drop-out prevention programs for at-risk youth. Some have devised innovative ways for offering a more diversified curriculum (Brizius, Foster, & Patton 1988). One of the more exciting movements is the grassroots reform effort being initiated by teachers in the region (R. G. Eller 1989a).

Given the bleak economic outlook in Appalachia, however, it is evident that schools generally have failed to take the initiative in helping to solve the region's problems. In fact, patterns of outmigration in years past show that there historically has been a drain of local leadership. Thus, rather than providing the region with an enlightened populace, the educational system often has promoted an attitude of compliance that has supported, rather than challenged, the status quo (Branscome 1974). By legitimizing the dominant rationality and simultaneously devaluing the belief system of nonmainstream populations, schools in the region have encouraged the better educated to leave for greater economic opportunities, thereby helping to perpetuate the cycle of poverty and dependency.

Improving the Educational System:
Moving Beyond Traditional Reform

During the past decade, all of the Appalachian states initiated changes aimed at improving education. These reforms generally included increasing accreditation and graduation standards; instituting various changes in the curriculum; enhancing the certification requirements and professional development of teachers; upgrading the leadership and management skills of school officials; providing additional programs for special populations; and increasing state monetary aid to local districts (Brizius, Foster, & Patton 1988).

While the full impact of these changes cannot yet be determined, a 1988 study published by the Appalachian Regional Commission shows that thus far these reforms have had both positive and negative effects. The researchers report that public support for schools, particularly among community leaders, has increased. Nevertheless, many small, rural school districts have experienced financial strain in an effort to implement the state mandates, and the general lack of parental involvement continues to be problematic (Brizius, Foster, & Patton 1988). In addition, the authors state that "[f]or all their sweeping effects on school districts, teachers and students, few of the first wave of education reform measures have had deep and far reaching impacts on the classroom itself or on the process of teaching and learning" (p. 71). Suggestions for future reform efforts included (1) targeting resources to more rural districts; (2) changing schools and classrooms by providing incentives for effective restructuring efforts and instructional innovations, and by using computers and technological aides to enhance learning; (3) changing district governance policies and re-evaluating state school aid formulas; (4) expanding early childhood and after-school programs; and (5) initiating efforts to change parental attitudes toward schooling.

While these reforms will undoubtedly improve education in the Appalachian region, it can be argued that they do not go far enough. Given its history of poverty and exploitation, it seems imperative that schools in the region begin to have a different vision for education—one that addresses the problems that confront Appalachia, and challenges its students to work for change. In the words of Martin (1987), "the key lies in the difference between training and education, *training* as that constant maintenance of the status quo, versus *education*, the creative process of enabling growth that can be the process of transformation" (p. 63). The reforms initiated thus far are aimed at training students to fit into society as it now exists, hoping that we can somehow persuade mountain students and their parents to "buy into" the system—a system that traditionally has created limited job opportunities and has tended to stigmatize their Appalachian heritage. To reverse the trend of educational failure, teachers and administrators must be encouraged to reassess their role as educators in an economically deprived region and to begin to see themselves as change agents.

Schools should implement material forms and structures that are culturally relevant to mountain children, and that enhance students' self-worth. A recent study reveals that one of the features of effective schools of language-minority students is that the students' language and culture are valued (Lucas, Henze, and Donato 1990). Like other minority groups, mountain children must begin to develop a pride in "being Appalachian." Too often children who live in the more rural areas of the region are labeled early as underachievers and potential dropouts. A "transition" teacher in one Appalachian elementary school tells about the negative self-concepts of her students, and how, through her commitment to the children in her classroom, they eventually came to see themselves as learners:

> [S]ome of those little kids were repeaters. They were losers. They knew it, honey. They were in second grade but they had already failed. And when they realized that more was expected of them than just being at school every day and just filling up a desk, why it was just beautiful to watch them blossom. (R. G. Eller 1989a, p. 192)

Positive experiences such as this, in which students begin to develop a sense of self-worth and of "belonging," will continue to be rare unless schools in the region are willing to initiate both structural and pedagogical changes.

Changes in Structure. In recent years, there has been a wealth of evidence suggesting that labelling and separating students through grouping and/or tracking practices can result in differential treatment of certain students. Further, students from middle- and upper-class homes, who are more readily able to adapt to the expectations of the school, tend to be placed in upper ability groups. (See, for example, Bennett 1991; Grant & Rothenberg 1986; Goodlad 1984; Oakes 1985; Rosenbaum 1976). Recently educators have even begun to question the expediency of using terms such as "at risk students" (Harris 1989). Despite evidence documenting the negative effects of such practices, however, schools still tend to sort students into the "more able" and the "less able," thus reinforcing and legitimizing a system of social stratification. One Appalachian teacher describes her frustration with this system:

> It's common for people [I work with] to make fun of the names of other kids, and of the parents, especially if they taught them and they were poor students. Occupation is real important; what you do—who your parents are and what you do is real important—definitely where in the county you live... I think there's just no equality because of the status and lack of it. And I think that the mountain concept is definitely lower-class. The people who live in town really draw lines around themselves. (R. G. Eller 1989a, pp. 178–179)

Solving the problems of Appalachia and elsewhere will require a cooperative effort. Thus, rather than dividing students along class (and consequently symbolically ethnic) lines, students and educators in the region need to be encouraged to work together to realize mutual goals emerging from a common heritage. Practices that tend to separate students should be re-evaluated, and should be replaced by structures that allow students to learn from one another and to engage in collaborative dialogue. Toward this end, teachers should be encouraged to experiment with various grouping procedures that allow students to discover the unique talents of others. One example can be found in eastern Kentucky, where three teachers combined their sixth grade classrooms and undertook a local history project that culminated in the publication of a magazine. The teachers reported that, through this project, the children began to develop an interest in and respect for one another's abilities. Local school boards and school administrators can encourage such innovations by allowing teachers to take risks and by providing financial support.

Changes in Curriculum. In addition to structural changes, Appalachian schools need to initiate material forms that are culturally relevant to mountain children. As discussed above, textbooks that are currently on the market generally either ignore the region altogether or present a distorted image. In addition, teachers have reported that their curriculum does not include literature written by Appalachian authors, and that there is a scarcity of Appalachian literature books in their school libraries (R. G. Eller 1989a). In order to help students learn about their Appalachian identity, it is important that school systems in the region take the initiative in developing a curriculum that speaks to the Appalachian experience.

Too often, however, the implementation of a culturally-relevant curriculum has been confined to learning about local handicrafts and folklore. While such experiences are useful and certainly help to promote group pride, they represent only one small segment of Appalachia's unique heritage. In order to prepare students to face regional and national problems, it is critical that both students and teachers have an understanding of the region's history, and that they be allowed to compare their own experiences with those of others, both within the United States and throughout the world. As an example, one seventh grade classroom in eastern Kentucky decided to learn where the coal goes after it leaves their county; this investigation triggered a year-long study on environmental pollution which resulted in a classroom recycling project (R. G. Eller 1989a). This same classroom undertook a project on the "hillbilly image" the previous year. In other classrooms, computer modems are being used to communicate with teachers and students throughout the country on various issues and current affairs. (Examples of other innovative projects such as these can be found in *Hands On,* a publication of Foxfire, Inc.)

Finally, the idea of a "culturally-relevant" curriculum needs to be expanded to incorporate the background experiences of Appalachian youth. Appalachian children come to school with particular linguistic and cultural backgrounds, and schools in Appalachia must build upon the unique experiences of the children they serve (Heath 1983; Sleeter & Grant 1991; Taylor & Dorsey-Gaines 1988). Moll and Diaz (1987) state that "the problems these working-class children face in school must be viewed primarily as a consequence of institutional arrangements that constrain children and teachers by not capitalizing fully on their talents, resources, and skills" (p. 302). The authors go on to suggest that there is reason for optimism, because "just as academic failure is socially organized, academic success can be socially arranged."

Appalachian teachers need to be encouraged to discover and to use the literacy and other experiences that children bring with them to school, in order to "arrange" opportunities for success. For instance, teachers could ask children to bring in various print forms found in their homes—magazines, calendars, notes, cereal boxes. They could allow students to write about their own experiences. They could incorporate Appalachia's rich oral tradition into their language arts instruction by recording mountain tales and folk-songs. In math and science instruction, teachers could use local economic indices for teaching math concepts, explore mountain rock formations, and examine the pollution of mountain streams. The opportunities for a more culturally-relevant curriculum are limitless (Stumbo 1989).

Schools ought to adopt pedagogical practices that enable both teachers and students to have a voice in their own learning, so that they might become agents for change. In addition to initiating a culturally-relevant curriculum, students and educators alike must be led to question their own ideological perspectives and to acknowledge their power to work for change. In other words, schools ought to be promoting what Strike (1985) refers to as the "Jeffersonian ideal," whereby the Appalachian people themselves become advocates for their own interests. Thus, schools in the region must be seen as "democratic public spheres" which are committed to social empowerment and transformation and where "students learn the knowledge and skills necessary to live in an authentic democracy" (Giroux 1988, p. xxxii).

What tends to occur in schools, however—not only in Appalachia, but elsewhere—is that students are conditioned to become passive recipients of information, rather than active creators of knowledge (Brown 1991). One Appalachian high school teacher uses the word "robots" as a metaphor to characterize students who have been trained through traditional education models:

> My kids are familiar with my phrase, "well, this is not an assembly line where we're sending out robots." We talk about what is education? What is it? And they realize that those facts will be in those books . . . But a true education is being able to think about a problem that needs to be solved and possibly coming up with one solution, or two or three. (R. G. Eller 1989a, pp. 166–167)

What is needed in the region is not "more of the same"; rather, we need to be offering experiences to students that will enhance their confidence as learners and will encourage them to take risks. Students need to see themselves as active participants in the learning process; they need to be allowed to challenge information being presented to them; they must be encouraged to debate issues and seek solutions. Further, they need to be given numerous opportunities to develop communicative competence by providing meaningful activities in reading, writing, speaking and listening.

Students' voices in Appalachia typically have been silenced within the educational institution. Rarely have they been given the opportunity to write about their own experiences, or to learn about their history and culture. In fact, like other minority groups, their experiences have often been ignored in classrooms (Delpit 1988), creating what Freire (1978) has called a "culture of silence." A high school English teacher, who now writes professionally, shares her experiences:

> I have always wanted to write. I have written for as long as I can remember. But by the time I got through college, I really didn't want to write anymore because everything had been corrected. People had . . . it just took the heart out of it for me . . . The kids here, I see them writing all this fantasy stuff. And fantasy is part of their development, but to write about every place except here, and to not see value in here. And when you give words to somebody, you give them an awful lot. (R. G. Eller 1989a, pp. 150–151)

This same teacher describes her own realization of the learning potential of her students:

> I have never believed that kids can do what I know they can do. The thing that limits them is the structure of education—the very structure of education. It keeps them from being creative. It keeps them from being problem solvers. I mean they have so much that they can think of and that they can do and we require that they sit in a seat and they answer yes and no, and fill in the blanks . . . I did not know that students were this intelligent. The school system simply doesn't call on it, doesn't demand it, or allow it to happen. (R. G. Eller 1989a, p. 173)

By promoting passivity in the classroom and by marginalizing the Appalachian experience, students in the region often have been taught to acquiesce in the face of severe economic challenges. Yet, it is only by valuing their thoughts and opinions and encouraging them to reflect critically upon their own experiences that these students will begin to take an active role in reversing the cycle of poverty and dependency.

Teachers and Administrators Need to Confront Their Own Biases and Encourage Positive Expectations for All Students. Coming to grips with our own biases is perhaps the most difficult task that we as professional educators must face. Yet, as was noted previously, many teachers in the region—even those who are natives—do not consider themselves to be "Appalachian." Because the Appalachian culture traditionally has been stigmatized, teachers and other professionals are inclined to deny their ethnic heritage (Borman, Meuninghoff, & Piazza 1988). Consequently, they are unable to identify with their mountain students, and tend to see these students as part of the problem, rather than as part of the solution.

In a recent study on grassroots educational reform in eastern Kentucky, one of the major findings was that those teachers in the region who have been able to transcend their position as members of the middle-class and have come to accept their own Appalachian identity have begun to relate to their students in a new way (R. G. Eller 1989a). They now see their primary role as one of creating a sense of self-worth in their students, so that these children might come to realize their own potential. In the words of one teacher: "I have to instill in them that they can do it, that they have the will-power and the brain power, even when the world says they have all these things marked against them" (R. G. Eller 1989a, p. 156).

Further, in re-examining their relationship with their students, these teachers have begun to respect their students as learners. As a result, they now give their students more control in the classroom, and see the teacher-student relationship as a collaborative one. As one teacher explains, they have become more appreciative of their students' knowledge and capacity for learning:

> [Before] I would like them or hate them. They were either annoy-ances or special cases or wonderful kids, but I didn't really respect their brains . . . I didn't really have a sense that they were learners who could also teach me something, and we could teach each other. I never thought of it that way . . . I saw this real split, and now I feel like I'm a part of it, and they're a part of me as a teacher. (R. G. Eller 1989a, p. 172)

When teachers begin to respect their students as learners, they begin to have higher expectations for them. In fact, it seems that a primary characteristic of effective teachers is that they simply refuse to allow their students to fail (Goldenberg 1989). Thus, rather than harboring negative assumptions about certain children and essentially blaming the students for their own educational fail-ure, exceptional teachers have a strong commitment to educate *all* of the children placed in their charge.

Conclusion

One of the primary ways in which schools in Appalachia can confront educational failure is to begin to recognize that they are significant institutions within the region, and as such, they must take the initiative in confronting the region's problems. Beyond basic state-mandated reforms, what is required is a fundamental *philosophical* change whereby teachers and school officials acknowledge that they provide a critical link in working for the betterment of the region. As institutions for promoting change, school systems in Appalachia need to provide the necessary materials, resources, and opportunities for individuals to learn about their distinct history and culture, and to use that knowledge as a basis for local and regional reform.

In addition, in order to reverse the trend of educational failure in the region, schools and classrooms must become places where students' experiences are affirmed and legitimated. All students should leave our Appalachian schools with feelings of self-worth, knowing that they are capable of making contributions to their communities. Classrooms must become places where students' voices are heard; where they are challenged to examine critically the issues confronting the region; and where every child is expected to succeed. If change is to occur in Appalachia, it must come from within, and schools must provide the necessary leadership.

In essence, the system of schooling in the region must be examined within a larger sociopolitical context in which educational goals are determined and assessed in relation to whose interests are being served. Accepting the school's norms should not require that students reject those of their own community; rather, schools need to become an integral part of that community, working to change conditions that perpetuate poverty and dependency. Instead of merely accepting the status quo, educators must begin to question the validity of mainstream values for the students they serve, in a region where there are few opportunities for upward mobility. By coming to grips with their own Appalachian identity, those responsible for educating mountain youth might begin to provide needed leadership in creating a new vision for the region. Transforming Appalachia will require a collaborative effort, and schools must be at the forefront.

CHAPTER 4

Culturally Responsible Pedagogy in Action: An American Indian Magnet School

CORNEL D. PEWEWARDY

Questions to Think About

1. Many Native Americans strive to maintain the integrity of their cultural values and practices in thought and behavior. Why should the schooling process support this effort?
2. In what ways might integrating aspects of Native American culture into the total schooling process improve the education of all children?
3. How might the issues and challenges in implementing culturally responsible pedagogy for American Indian children differ from that for other ethnic minority groups?
4. How does the vision for the education of American Indian children described in this chapter compare with that for African American children described by King?

The United National Indian Tribal Youth proclaimed the national agenda for American Indian/Alaskan Native youth will be "The Healing Generation's Journey to the Year 2000." Indian youth across the country are reclaiming their hope for the future through challenging the modern educational practices in schools. As the country embarks upon the "Healing Generation's Journey to the Year 2000," the progress of science can lead to a rebirth of human values and the education of children can become the highest priority of the nation. Today, the age of technology competes with the age of communication with major consequences for America's youth. For many Indian youth who confront this situation, the consequences mean either forfeiting cultural heritage for academic achievement or enriching culture, thus de-emphasizing quality learning experiences. At the newly established American Indian Magnet School in the Saint Paul, Minnesota Public School District, we attempt to address this issue through quality learning experiences that "place education into culture rather than continuing the practice of placing culture into education." The mission is to integrate American Indian methodology and ideology across all curriculum areas through effective teaching and sensitivity to learning styles of all students. As a result, students realize the value of being capable, knowledgeable, productive and caring members of a free and global society.

American Indian Magnet School

In recent years, attention has been focused upon processes which emphasize equity and schools of choice. This is especially true in large public school districts like the St. Paul, Minnesota Public Schools where magnet schools are made so educationally attractive because their particular emphasis is designed to meet the needs and interests of students and parents. They have become "magnetized" to draw voluntary student enrollment. Moreover, magnet schools often provide a setting for teacher-generated reform initiatives and are an important component of the Saint Paul District's commitment to quality educational and social experiences.

Society today tends to espouse educational experiences that are primarily didactic. Many children in America are instructed in textbook learning, lectures and filmstrips; however, still many more children rarely experience this method of learning. American Indian education may reveal some answers to the paradigm shift to holistic education. Indian education has always been experiential and holistic and seen as preparing the young to be productive citizens in the world in which they live.

The American Indian Magnet School (K–8) opened its doors to three hundred Indian and non-Indian students for the first time in September 1991. With fifty-four percent Indian enrollment, the new magnet school becomes the first of its kind in Minnesota and second in the entire nation. The Native American Magnet School in Buffalo, New York was the first Indian magnet school in the country and was used as our model.

An important reason for students to attend the American Indian Magnet School is the intrinsic interest. Indian cultures provide a rich and varied tapestry of approaches to life. Ancient tribal cultures possess a myriad of myths and tales that are culturally diverse. Many of these traditions contain beliefs and ideas about the world that achieve high levels of sophistication, as in the notions about the beginning of the world, the concepts of a lofty Supreme Being, and the elaboration of cosmic harmony. In ritual and ceremony, American Indian philosophy and thought presents a rich and varied cultural heritage of dramatic beauty and spiritual force, primarily expressed in dancing and repetitive movements, prayers, and songs.

Through careful screening, selected and shared literature, students learn to understand and appreciate a literary heritage that comes from an American Indian worldview. Students learn to identify diverse cultures who created stories, both past and present. They learn from the past that story telling, folktales, myths and legends attempt to clarify the values and beliefs of diverse cultures. They learn great stories on which whole cultures were founded. The present explores the threads that weave the past with the present, as well as pursues themes that we deem appropriate to diverse cultures.

Equally as important are the personal gains acquired by students when they read great works of people of their own cultural backgrounds. Students gain understanding about different beliefs and value systems. They develop social sensitivity to the needs of others and realize that people have similarities, as well as differences.

Significant aspects of the instructional environment of our school include the absence of bells and clocks. Teachers and students are not constrained to set "periods" of time in which to "teach" reading, math or any other subject. Student journal writing reflects critical thinking skills and provides teachers feedback on their projected lesson plans. Scope and sequence planning allows all culturally responsible teachers to align their overall "theaters of learning" for the school year.

Each teacher has the flexibility to establish and alter his/her instructional schedule to address the specific needs of the students. Classrooms are self-contained in "family-style" rooms, linked to another class by connecting doors. Team teaching and cross-age grouping approaches to instruction capitalize on the strengths of teachers and students alike. These cooperative methods ensure the highest degree of social and academic success with the least frustration possible. Whole language instruction utilizing a wide variety of multicultural literature is employed across the curriculum to strengthen the thinking and communications skills of all students, from kindergarten through eighth grade.

The use of student portfolios and parent-teacher meetings are methods used to assure the district's outlined-specific Outcomes Based Education (OBE) per grade level based upon year-long goal setting conferences. Our students achieve the desired learner outcomes because American Indian sports, games, music and crafts are incorporated across the curriculum, therefore, learning is relevant to the students' knowledge base and culture.

Practice Wisdom. In the same mode of thinking, there continues to be growing interest in building theories from successful practice rather than just trying to put theory into practice. In higher education the academy has many times formulated an "ivory tower" attitude that permeates many multicultural conferences and consultants of Indian educational programs, many of which are a result of "instant" Indian education experts or specialists.

It's ironic that Indian people are not allowed to be experts on themselves, it's usually someone else "defining" the Indian. For example, there have been scores of contributors profiting from Native American education, more so in the area of spirituality, and most have been tendered some measure of credibility by the "certified scholars" of American universities and the academy. So pervasive are these "scholars" that scarcely an Indian in this country has not been confronted by some "New-Age" like apparition wishing to teach crystal-healing methods to recovering Elders, many of whom claim to be a pipe-carrying reincarnation of a seventeenth century Lakota warrior with an assumed "Indian name" such as "Chief Thundercloud" or "Princess Pale Moon."

Of late, there are signs of renewed respect for the importance of "practice wisdom" toward building a cultural knowledge base of professional child and youth work. Educational researchers are investigating characteristics of exemplary schools throughout the country in order to develop models for effective practice. The American Indian Magnet School is attempting to provide "action research' toward refining culturally responsible pedagogy in its challenge to bringing about a new future for Indian youth by the year 2000.

Children have always been a challenge for Elders, thus, there seem to be few novel ideas in how to deal with Indian youth. The

American Indian Magnet School attempts to rediscover the pedagogy practiced by traditional Native peoples. Macroculture philosophies of education and child care have been heavily influenced by European tradition. The intent of this chapter is to present the challenge of providing new ways to design the future, develop this agenda—this *Journey to the Year 2000*. The healing generation is composed of families, friends, tribes and communities taking their rightful place and contributing to the economic and cultural prosperity of all Americans. The intent is to use "practice wisdom" and reclaim the untapped heritage of American Indian philosophies of child rearing practices.

Culturally Responsible Pedagogy. Beliefs and values learned from society and the educational system may provide us far less freedom to choose than we realize. Paulo Freire's (1970) text, *Pedagogy of the Oppressed,* warned us that a major danger of any successful revolution results from the oppressed becoming oppressors when they assume positions of power. For those in power positions only the names and faces have changed. For whatever reasons many systems resist change and the educational system has shown this pattern. If this basic principle holds true, designing culturally responsible pedagogy may amount to nothing more than a change of names and faces of those who decide how and what will be learned by Indian students.

To combat this pattern the American Indian Magnet School was created. The traditional American Indian philosophy and thought provides the knowledge base for designing our school. Traditional holistic approaches to teaching and learning represent a rebalancing of educational practice, moving away from its more than half-century old behavioral and reductionist bent (Komoski 1990). Such a view is that of American Indian philosophy and thought. That is, both the Western and Native methodologies recognize the interrelatedness of the physical, psychological, emotional, social, spiritual, and environmental factors that contribute to the overall quality of a person's life. No part of the mind, body, or environment is truly separate and independent. "We are all related."

The pedagogy used for learning is based on the traditional American Indian belief that children learn and retain knowledge better through experience, touching and active participation in educational activities. This process involves field trips, activities, and a comprehensive understanding of how things grow and can be used. This learning experience allows for a national emergence of respect for nature, self-reliance, and understanding of the values and significance of American Indian people.

Theoretical foundations of a culturally responsible pedagogy many times rest upon strong cultural variables that are often overlooked in explaining factors in the demise of Indian education. Indian children bring to Indian magnet schools a unique set of cultural forms and behaviors that include tribal history, language dialect, traditional values, cultural norms, rituals, symbolism, imagery and spirituality. Thus, school culture soon becomes a tribal environment conducive to feeling good about being Indian. This is incongruous with many non-Indian schools that Indian children attend, especially public schools.

Most Indian students today attend public school. When Indian students are confronted with white, middle-class cultural norms and behaviors within many public schools, the result is usually "cultural discontinuity" or "lack of cultural synchronization" between students and their school. When there is a cultural mismatch between students and their school, Irvine (1990) contends that the inevitable occurs: miscommunication and confrontation among the student, the teacher, and the home; hostility, alienation, diminished self-esteem and eventual school failure.

Cultural conflicts can be minimized and cultural continuity maximized by restructuring teacher training programs to promote the concept of culturally responsible pedagogy. Teachers of Indian students in the year 2000 must be conduits through which culturally encapsulated monocultural, minority youth become multicultural and multilingual.

Craft Wisdom. Teachers of Indian students should be knowledgeable, sensitive, and comfortable in working with Indian students' languages, code switching, style of presentation and tribal community values. Whether Indian students come from reservation areas or urban settings, the element of obtaining "craft wisdom" is critical to maximizing learning for all students. Obtaining craft wisdom many times takes years to acquire. Some teachers have almost a natural instinct in adapting and working successfully with diverse populations, while others may take a lifetime.

Craft wisdom comes from acquiring the element of being "street smart," "reservation smart," and/or the ability to adapt to culturally diverse populations and geographical locations. It also brings together all the personal qualities of classroom leadership. Like "OJT" (on-the-job-training), classroom leadership is something to be learned over time, not simply by completing a teacher training program. Basic leadership is an art—more tribal than scientific. It's more a weaving of relationships than an amassing of information, and in that sense encompasses all the elements of craft wisdom.

Issues that Challenge the Implementation
of Culturally Responsible Pedagogy

Culturally responsible pedagogy involves providing the best possible education for children that preserves their own cultural heritage, prepares them for meaningful relationships with other people, and for living productive lives in the present society without sacrificing their own cultural perspective. There are several issues that pose both challenges and threats to the implementation of culturally responsible pedagogy. The remainder of this chapter will discuss those issues.

Language Difference. Tribal differences are very real and tribal affiliations are quite important to Indian youth today. One of the main tribal connections to Indian identity is tribal languages, many of which are still spoken. Many historical Indian tribes were wiped out (particularly by Europeans) and other groups have no one left who remembers the tribal language. In what is today the continental United States alone there lived hundreds of aboriginal groups speaking some two hundred and fifty distinct languages. In that connection, decades ago, perceptive teachers of Indian students saw the advantages of using Indian languages and recognized the gap between what Indians wanted and what was forced upon them in mission and government schools.

Most Indian students across the country attend public school. Therefore, if Indian parents and tribal agencies advocate language preservation programs, it appears that greater attention needs to be given to the implementation phase of language preservation programs and/or Indian studies programs in order for students to learn their tribal languages and culture. Marginal programs will fail to attract Indian students who have few tangible connections to tribal culture (Pewewardy 1989).

Advocates of the "English Only" movement say that a common language is the glue that holds a country together. It enables people to understand each other and work toward common goals. Granted, few can disagree with that logic. It is difficult for citizens to make

responsible decisions if they cannot read or write, or even understand the primary language of their country. However, laws are not
needed to force people to speak English.

Change comes slowly with time and real time is still needed to
assess all the languages that compete for primacy in any given marketplace. To acknowledge that English is the language of primacy in
the academic marketplace is not a problem for most people, but to
acknowledge English as the language of primacy in first world
trade—or North America is becoming more and more problematic.
The academy may be able to adjudicate language usage in the classrooms, but certainly does not have the final say over what languages are retained by specific cultural groups.

Not only is the United States diverse today because there are so
many different language groups, but more so because there may be
as many as fifty-seven different varieties of American English. It all
depends upon the demographic region in which one lives. And Indian people are no different, as Indian communities across the
country have formulated their own type of "Indian English." The
concept of Indian English suggests a combination of American English and their tribal language[s].

Tribal Language Instruction Debate. There seems to be
some confusion about the direction tribal language programs
should take. For instance, some tribal communities want language
immersion programs to occur in elementary education, while others
want a set of selected courses to be instructed only in the later
grades (or even higher education), once the student first learns the
basic English reading and writing skills. Many Indian parents and
educators are hesitant to promote these types of programs because
as mentioned previously, they fear it will be detrimental to their
child's mastery of regular school subjects. Moreover, the linkage of
several tribally controlled community colleges is making great
strides in promoting, as well as articulating the post-secondary
tribal language development programs.

While the debate continues as to the degree of tribal language
instruction that is needed to preserve our languages, most of us can
agree that more tribal language instructors are needed in schools.
Therefore, it is up to the Indian people (and concerned non-Indian
people) to preserve tribal languages in school.

Legislation like the Native American Language Act (S. 1781,
which passed April 3, 1990) will help to establish as the policy of the
United States the preservation, protection, and promotion of the
rights of American Indians to use, practice, and develop American

Indian languages, to take steps to foster such use, practice and development, and for other purposes.

Cultural Literacy. The whole matter of relevant education for American Indians is still unresolved. Today there is danger on several fronts to a culturally appropriate curriculum for minority group children in the United States. The "English Only" movement, as promoted by groups such as "U.S. English" which advocates the adoption of English as the official language, jeopardizes the early education of non-English speaking American children (Crawford 1989).

The "cultural literacy" movement that received a lot of media attention a few years ago is reflected in E. D. Hirsch, Jr.'s two books on cultural literacy: *Cultural Literacy: What every American needs to know* (1987) and *The dictionary of cultural literacy* (1988). A related book is Alan Bloom's *The closing of the American mind* (1987). These books call for a return to the "classics" and a Eurocentric tradition; these critiques bemoan the relativism and "nihilism" of the 1960s and the multicultural movements which, in the name of tolerance, have supposedly left our culture in shambles. Reyhner and Eder (1989) advocate that both Hirsch and Bloom jeopardize the teaching of non-Western, non-European and non-Judeo-Christian heritages in American schools.

Simonson and Walker (1988) have since come out with a book refuting the Hirsch/Bloom argument for educational reform in American schools. The theme of their new book is *Opening the American mind.* It is ironic that Hirsch and Bloom never really question the political and historical bases of cultural response. Americans could do well to become acquainted with the literature and cultures of American Indians, as well as other minorities and women.

Researchers and teachers of minority literature (especially American Indian literature) have in recent years been among the foremost critics of the traditional literacy canon, and many have attacked the very idea of a standard list of great works to be read and taught. According to Coughlin (1990), teaching and research on minority literature is more prevalent and the formation of minority canons are inevitable.

Cognitive Learning Styles. Banks (1988) contends that researchers who rejected the cultural deprivation paradigm created a conception of the cultural and educational problems of lower-income and minority youths based on a different set of assumptions. Banks continues to point out that researchers argue that these students, far from being culturally deprived, have rich and elaborate cultures. Their rich cultural characteristics are evident in language and communication styles, behavioral styles, and values. Ramirez and Castaneda (1974) advocate that cognitive, learning, and motivational styles of ethnic minorities such as African Americans and Mexican Americans are different from those fostered in the schools. These students, like American Indian students, achieve less academically because the school culture favors the culture of white mainstream students and places students from other backgrounds and cultures at a serious disadvantage. The school environment consequently needs to be reformed substantially so that it will be sensitive to diverse learning, cognitive, and motivational styles.

Huber and Pewewardy's (1990) learning styles research suggests that all students will come to the classroom with many kinds of differences, many of which may be related to their ethnic group. This research suggests that teachers will need to work with minority students to help them to see the relationship between their effort and their academic performance. Moreover, teachers and the academy should use a variety of teaching styles that appeal to diverse students. Concepts should be taught when possible with different strategies so that students who are relational and/or analytic in their learning styles will have an equal opportunity to learn.

Many arguments surface when confronting cognitive learning styles research and strategies surrounding the advisability of matching teaching styles and learning styles (e.g., Dunn & Dunn 1979; Gephart, Strother, & Duckett 1980). Central to this argument is whose responsibility is it to change; should teachers change to accommodate students or should students change to accommodate teachers? In that connection, an additional question could be: Should students be taught using their preferred learning styles or should students be encouraged to develop skills associated with non-preferred learning styles? Perhaps one way to address these issues is to pose the question differently: Is the student presently learning successfully? For students who are not currently demonstrating successful achievement, such as many American Indian and other minority students, it might be reasonable to ask teachers to be as flexible and adaptable as possible in addressing student needs and to specifically teach to student strengths. On the other hand, if students are being successful, then one might challenge students to develop non-preferred learning strategies.

It is important for teachers to understand that the characteristics of ethnic and socioeconomic classes can help us understand groups but not individual students (Banks 1988). All types of learning styles are found to varying degrees within all ethnic groups, as well as social classes. We need to assess learning styles and how they match learning situations, not just in the academy, but in the everyday classroom in American schools.

Indian Studies Programs. The 1960s and 1970s saw ethnic groups assert their cultural identity and traditions. Native Americans have been at the forefront of the movement to preserve ethnic identity. The late 1960s saw several student protests that evolved around the establishment of Indian studies programs. Indian youth took action such as the take-over of Alcatraz Island where students from the colleges and universities of the San Francisco Bay area wanted to use the abandoned island for a cultural studies center.

Deloria (1974) contends that there were nearly sixty Indian studies programs established in colleges and universities during this period of time throughout the country. The most popular in the period were the University of Minnesota, University of California at Los Angeles, University of Arizona and Montana State University. Now, we can see many more Indian studies and special interest support system programs starting at Pennsylvania State University, Arizona State University, the University of Oklahoma, Harvard University, Cornell University, Stanford University, and the list goes on. Many of these programs were integrated into the regular curriculum, providing extensive course offerings which enrolled both Indian and non-Indian students. The idea of an Indian and Chicano group took form at Davis, California; however, the college did not attract many Indian students.

The attention given Indian Studies in higher education affected the attitudes of Indian people toward the education of their own people. In the Twin Cities, Indian groups formed "survival schools" to teach their children about their cultural traditions, ceremonies and languages. Tribal languages courses were started in almost every urban Indian center. Interest in these schools and formulating a cultural knowledge base grew among Indian people of every political persuasion—from activists to conservatives.

Tribally controlled community colleges were seen as vehicles for preserving cultural traditions. Early on, the Navajo Community College and other colleges in North and South Dakota offered major courses in cultural traditions. Prior to the establishment of these programs, macroculture asked Indian people how they expected to preserve their culture in a "high-tech" world. No one ever seemed to have an answer to the question before the introduction of Indian

Studies programs. The question at hand is not how to preserve tribal culture and languages, but rather how non-Indian culture should be taught in the Indian schools in order to enable Indian students to understand and live in white society.

The Academy and the Community. Higher education is essential to schools that educate Indian students toward sharing the objective of self-determination. Planning and implementation of educational operations on all levels requires the professional research and skilled guidance of qualified personnel.

There seems to be a critical need for Indian teachers who have experience teaching Indian students, as well as working in Indian schools. Within schools that have high populations of Indian students, Indian teachers are needed as positive role-models to encourage students and provide incentives for students to pursue teaching as a career. Aside from direct involvement in the field of education, special programs are needed to train Indian teachers in the area of socioeconomic development, tribal government, and tribal leadership.

As for higher education institutions which certify Native languages, there are only a few. We can learn much from Canadian First Nations toward obtaining federal acknowledgement and recognition of Native languages in order to justify formalized development in higher education. The academy needs to offer more intensive studies of Native languages and reconstruct curriculum that will extend Native studies teaching to other levels. Suggestions for such development include accrediting courses for Native language teachers, providing equal pay with other professionals in the academy; recognition of Elders as professional Native language instructors and resource personnel; establishment of Native language institutes and cultural research centers both at regional and national arenas; offering adult Native language instruction classes to school personnel and community members; the use of technology to enhance survival and evolution, allowing the academy to facilitate the use of Native languages as a second language entrance requirement; and accreditation of Native language courses in higher education. Unlike many other languages officially used in this country, Native languages have their roots and resources in the tribal communities.

Teacher Education Curriculum. Teacher training programs must develop culturally responsive curriculum for teachers of Indian students. Pewewardy (1990), contends that prominent white institutions have impacted Indian students in Oklahoma higher education institutions, and that there seems to be a lack of culture-specific understanding (i.e., identity and values) of communities, culturally responsible pedagogy, parent-teacher communication methods, and relating the concepts of tribal sovereignty to self-determination. Teacher training programs should include "cutting-edge" culturally relevant research on learning styles of diverse learners, teaching pedagogy, community participation, open communication, and evaluation strategies. Higher education curriculum must be designed to meet the needs of the students and communities (both urban and rural).

The teacher education curriculum that espouses a culturally responsible pedagogy for Indian children must address the following needs:

- require preservice teachers to gain classroom experience with Indian children before their student teaching internship.
- train teachers to understand and respect students' cultural knowledge base.
- require preservice teachers to study the history and culture of Indian children including their values, stories, music and myths, as well as racism/sexism from both cognitive and affective worldviews.
- train teachers to be reflective practitioners and develop observational, empirical and analytical skills necessary to monitor, evaluate and revise continually their respective teaching styles.
- help teachers learn to acknowledge the cognition-worldview of Indian children.
- teacher education must include Indian parents and respective communities in the decision-making process.
- teachers should understand the cultural code switching, dialect and/or language of their students.
- train teachers to understand students interpersonal skills: body language, eye contact, silence, touch, public space, facial expression.
- teacher education must assist preservice and inservice teachers with their fear, apprehension, and overreaction related to Indian childrens' styles of personal presentation.
- supervise student teachers' clinical experiences in strong support system schools.

Treatment of Indian Students. Although there are no universal characteristics that one can study to understand American

Indian students, a few common behaviors may seem to be demonstrated by most Indian children. Classroom teachers need to be aware of the following:

1. Indian students should not be stereotyped or all placed in the same category. In some cases, ethnic background is the only constant. Many Indian students have middle-class backgrounds. Therefore, they may demonstrate many of the same behaviors as other students who hold middle-class values. The major difference is these students may receive more peer pressure to "act Indian" than middle-class whites do to "act white."
2. Students should not be referred to as a boy or girl. some teachers will contend that the students are boys and girls and see nothing wrong with an apparently appropriate reference. This belief is probably correct, yet the very words boy or girl can cause students to make mental reference to past experiences of minorities, and some students will become very hostile.
3. Students should not be reprimanded publicly. If there is a need to reprimand a student, it should be done in private. Even the most mild-mannered students are likely to fight back when embarrassed in front of their classmates.
4. Whenever possible, ignore foul language, especially if it occurs in jocular, good-natured ribbing sessions. These sessions are often an important rite of passage in Indian culture and critical to the development of peer and social relationships.
5. A lack of involvement should not be assumed to mean that the families are not interested in the welfare of the student. Many Indian families will not become involved in the school because they do not know what to do; they feel that they do not have the appropriate skills, they work several jobs, or they feel uncomfortable in the area of intervention or in the presence of what may be perceived as a white authority figure.
6. Teachers should not take everything personally. There are times when things will not proceed as planned. At times, teachers may feel that it is their fault that students are demonstrating certain behaviors. In such cases, teachers feel that the negative behaviors are directed toward them, rather than the situation. Consequently, the relationships between the teacher and student may begin to deteriorate. If it is allowed to continue, this relationship will most likely develop into a negative situation.
7. Teachers should not try to take on the behaviors of the students. It is important to understand the students and make every attempt to help them. In other words, teachers must respect others if they are to be respected.

8. Students should not be corrected each time they use nonstandard English. The goal is to assist Indian students in understanding that the usage of standard English is important if they wish to become successful in society.

Conclusion

The Holistic Circle of Learning emerges from American Indian "craft wisdom," wherein the education of children is viewed as the responsibility of the whole tribe. The American Indian Magnet School's effort is to blend "practice into theory," as well as draw from the enduring wisdom of diverse cultures and traditions of other Nations.

Teachers of Indian students need pedagogical skills that will develop their diverse teaching styles. They need to discover the craft wisdom of seasoned teachers who have refined methodologies for teaching diverse student populations. To maximize learning, Indian students have to define on their own terms, "success" and "winning" from an American Indian worldview. For Indian students, the feeling that they have to "act white" should not be a requirement for achieving their prescribed learner outcomes. The alternative is found in learning environments based on "culturally responsible pedagogy."

Thus, the intent of this chapter has been to provide a description of the American Indian Magnet School in Saint Paul, Minnesota (which is in its beginning stages) and to describe the issues and challenges associated with implementing culturally responsible pedagogy that remain to be confronted and resolved. Whether or not a teacher works with Indian students, it is important to consider the circumstances of the students. However, the issues that affect Indian students are special and different from those of other students because of cultural, linguistic, and historical factors.

Practice into theory like theory into practice has generated only fragmentations of research on ethnicity, social class, and cognitive styles. This type of research is scarce, however, we can screen through a variety of guidelines for practice into theory. Teachers and the academy could learn to select content from diverse ethnic groups so that students from various cultures will see their respective images in the curriculum.

Understanding language differences and cognitive learning styles is critical in pursuit of culturally responsible pedagogy as well as understanding the role of cultural transmission in the process of enculturation, the lifelong learning of one's own culture beginning from infancy—*"Journey to the Year 2000."*

For many Indian students much of this journey includes learning aspects of their own school culture, as well as their student subculture. The close network of Indian families permits this learning to occur. Until recently, little of this enculturation process was reinforced in reservation schools. In contrast, macroculture students are firmly enculturated through schooling because the formal school culture is designed for and represents their culture. Potentially, culturally responsible pedagogy could alter this rigid model in American schools.

Actually, the bottom line becomes a matter of seeking the answer to this question: How can we make education work for, not against Indian children? Practice into theory through culturally responsible pedagogy is providing some answers for educators, students, and parents in the American Indian Magnet School in Saint Paul, Minnesota Public Schools. Coupled with multicultural education, it is another way to educate our future generations toward a process of educational equity. It will exist for all students when teachers become culturally responsible in their professional practice, vary their teaching styles to match diverse student learning styles and modify their curriculum to include authentic cultural content.

Thus, practice into theory with an American Indian worldview provides a holistic approach in education. The basic concepts and issues discussed in this chapter provide a starting point for building the foundation for a cultural knowledge base supporting the healing generation's "journey to the year 2000" for American Indian and Alaska Native Youth.

CHAPTER 5

Attributes of Effective Schools for Language Minority Students[1]

EUGENE E. GARCIA

Questions to Think About

1. Garcia's review of the research suggests that language minority students *can* be effectively served in schools. What obstacles to their success must be overcome?
2. How might the practices of schooling be changed to better serve the needs of language minority students?
3. How might teachers of language minority students incorporate features of students' home and community culture into the instructional process?

It is almost universally accepted that language and social repertoires have their origins in early childhood years. It seems that almost all of the basic linguistic skills (phonology, morphology, syntax) of adult language, as well as important personal and social attributes (self-concept, social identity, social interaction styles), are significantly influenced during these years. Consequently, one motive for early educational intervention has been the potential removal of barriers related to the development of these important linguistic, psychological, and social attributes. With respect to language minority children, children who come to school with limited

This article is reprinted with permission from *Education and Urban Society, 20* (4), 1988 (August): 387–398.

proficiency in English, recent research and program attention has resulted in a knowledge base related to the enhancement of educational success. Programs for this population have taken on many forms (for a more detailed topology of such programs, see Ovando & Collier 1985, and Ramirez 1985). Moreover, in the last decade language minority education has received a large dose of systematic program evaluation attention (Sandoval-Martinez 1982; Hakuta 1985). Findings from these evaluations suggest that at the program level of analysis, conclusions regarding specific effectiveness of program type remain difficult (Willing 1985; Hakuta and Gould 1987). Rather than emphasizing differential program type effects, the following discussion will explore the recently developed knowledge base with a concern for identifying specific program and instructional features that have shown promise with the growing number of language minority students in this country. Such a discussion will necessarily focus on issues related to language minority education "state-of-the-art" and a review of research directly related to linguistic, cultural and instructional variables.

Program Attributes

Research and theoretical contributions related to language minority education and specific educational initiatives have generated several sets of general assumptions that have guided program development and implementation and are of specific importance to early childhood educators. The California State Department of Education (1984, p. 4) identifies the following guidelines:

(1) Under optimal schooling conditions, on the average, students realize the full academic benefits of their bilingualism only after four to seven years of appropriate instructional treatment.

(2) Bilingually schooled students, at times, even under the very best conditions, may initially lag behind their monolingually schooled counterparts in some literacy-based skills. After three or four years, they begin to catch up; by six or seven years, they equal and commonly surpass their monolingually school counterparts.

(3) When the instructional treatment is adequately designed and appropriately matched to local sociolinguistic realities, native speakers of a majority language may be schooled in a second language for an average of approximately 50% to 75% of the time from kindergarten through the twelfth grade, with no

detrimental effects on their academic achievement and native language development. Conversely, it may also be predicted that many language minority students in the United States could be schooled in their native language for an average of 50% to 75% of the time from kindergarten through the twelfth grade as an appropriate means to promote their normal academic achievement, high levels of English language proficiency, adequate psychosocial adjustment, and satisfactory native language development.

(4) To avoid cognitive confusion and greatly increase learning efficiency, program staff should provide initial literacy instruction in bilingual settings in a sequential manner. That is, basic literacy skills should be developed through one language before reading instruction is introduced in the other language.

(5) Underachievers and students with learning disabilities seem to experience no detrimental effects from bilingual instruction. When such children receive bilingual schooling, their academic achievement and native language development are similar to those of their counterparts in monolingual programs.

(6) Formal second language instruction, even when provided under optimal conditions, appears to be insufficient to develop all of the language skills needed by those who acquire a second language. Some amount of exposure through natural social interaction is also required.

Enumerations of program assumptions related to educational programming for language minority students remain significant only if some notion of actual program implementation is available (see Garcia 1986, for a detailed discussion of program implementation issues in U.S. language minority education). Carter and Chatfield (1986) provide a more focused picture of specific educational program attributes and their effects on language minority students.

Carter and Chatfield (1986) report on a series of studies attempting to isolate the attributes of schools that are academically successful with language minority students. Their work draws upon a growing concern for identification of "effective" schools and instruction (Purkey & Smith 1983; Anderson, Hiebert, Scott & Wilkenson 1985; U.S. Dept. of Education 1986).

Carter and Chatfield (1986) report similar attributes to those reported by Edmonds (1979) and Purkey and Smith (1983) in their study of effective language minority elementary schools serving Mexican-American students in California. Their analyses suggest that processes are most closely linked to effectiveness, not structures and particular curriculum attributes. There was a common thread regarding curricula, pedagogy, administrative arrangements and classroom organization. The effective bilingual elementary school was characterized by:

A. A well-functioning, total system producing a school social climate that promotes positive outcomes
B. Specific characteristics crucial to the development of effectiveness and thus to a positive school climate were:
   1. A safe and orderly school environment
   2. Positive leadership, usually from the formal leaders
   3. Common agreement on a strong academic orientation
      a. Clearly stated academic goals, objectives, and plans
      b. Well-organized classrooms
   4. Well-functioning methods to monitor school inputs and student outputs
C. A positive school social climate
   1. High staff expectations for children and the instructional program
   2. Strong demand for academic performance
   3. Denial of the cultural-deprivation argument and the stereotypes that support it
   4. High staff morale
      a. Strong internal support
      b. Consensus building
      c. Job satisfaction
      d. Sense of personal efficacy
      e. Sense that the system works
      f. Sense of ownership
      g. Well-defined roles and responsibilities
      h. Beliefs and practices that resources are best expended on people rather than on educational soft- and hardware (Carter & Chatfield 1986, p. 205).

A close examination of one particular effective school, serving more than fifty percent Mexican American students with limited English proficiency and low socioeconomic status indicated that goals and objectives along with grade-level expectations were clear. In most curricular areas, rich Spanish-language materials were utilized on a continuum of Spanish-to-English instruction. The school was in the lowest quartile of district schools in SES but in the top quartile in achievement as measured by district proficiency tests. As opposed to other findings of language minority program and staff segregation (Halcon 1981), all the school staff worked together in an ongoing effort to improve instruction, with teachers actively involved in studying the possibility for and strategies to change programs. The emphasis on the need for continual instructional improvement pervaded the planning processes. Collaborative instruction between bilingual and monolingual teachers allowed the maximal contact of fully qualified bilingual teachers with students and led to a sense of total school ownership of the program. In addition, one-third of student participants were non-Hispanic, furthering an adoption of program ownership by non-Hispanic parents (Carter & Chatfield 1986).

Instructional Attributes

Are there any commonalities in the organization and content of effective classroom instruction for language minority students? The most systematic attempt to answer that question comes from Tikunoff (1983) in the report of the Significant Bilingual Instructional Features Study (SBIF). The fifty-eight classrooms observed in this study come from six sites and include a variety of non-English languages. All were considered "effective" on two criteria: first, they were nominated by members of four constituencies— teachers, other school personnel, students, and parents; and second, the teaching behaviors produced rates of "academic learning time" (ALT)—a measure of student engagement on academic tasks, as high or higher than reported in other effective teaching research.

An initial set of instructional features identified in the fifty-eight SBIF classrooms pertaining to the communication and organization of instruction were common to those reported for effective classrooms in general:

- Successful teachers of Limited English Proficient (LEP) students specify task outcomes and what students must do to accomplish tasks competently. In addition they communicate (a) high expectations for LEP students in terms of learning and (b) a sense of efficacy in terms of their own ability to teach.
- Successful teachers of LEP student, like effective teachers generally, exhibit use of "active teaching" behaviors that have been found to be related to increased student performance on academic tests of achievement in reading and mathematics including (a) communicating clearly when giving directions, specifying

tasks, and presenting new information; (b) obtaining and maintaining students' engagement in instructional tasks by pacing
instruction appropriately, promoting involvement, and communicating their expectations for students' success in completing
instructional tasks; (c) monitoring students' progress; and (d)
providing immediate feedback whenever required regarding the
students' success.
- When students worked on instructional tasks that involved the
  creating of a product, the form and content of the product was
  described by the teacher over ninety percent of the time.

A number of instructional classroom features unique to language minority student education have been reported by various researchers. These unique features include the particular use of two
languages, special activities for teaching a second language, and instructional practices that take advantage of students' cultural
background.

In SBIF classroom, averaged across the fifty-eight classrooms
in the SBIF study, English was used approximately sixty percent of
the time, and L1 or a combination of the two was used the rest of the
time, with the percentage of English increasing with grade level. An
additional significant instructional feature was the particular way
in which the two languages were often combined:

- Successful teachers for LEP students mediated instruction for
  LEP students by the use of the student's native language (L1)
  and English (L2) for instruction, alternating between the two
  languages whenever necessary to ensure clarity of instruction.
- Students learned the language of instruction when engaged in
  instructional tasks using that language. This integrative approach to developing English language skills during ongoing instruction in the regular classroom contrasts with the more
  traditional, pull-out procedures where LEP students leave the
  regular instructional setting to receive ESL instruction.

The SBIF study reports that the use of information from the
LEP students' home culture can promote engagement in instructional tasks and contribute to a feeling of trust between children
and their teachers. The SBIF researchers found three ways in which
home and community culture is incorporated into classroom life:
cultural referents in both verbal and non-verbal forms are used to
communicate instructional and institutional demands, instruction
is organized to build upon rules of discourse from the L1 culture,

and values and norms of the L1 culture are respected equally with those of the school. The cultural appropriateness of teaching practices was identified as important as the language of instruction in achieving students' maximum attention to the task at hand.

Wong-Fillmore, Ammon, McLaughlin, and Ammon (1985) provide a detailed analysis regarding the influence of classroom practices on the development of oral English in Hispanic and Chinese background language minority students. In their study, seventeen Hispanic and Chinese language minority student classrooms (thirteen third grade and four fifth grade) served as sites. These students were in classrooms that either used both the native/home language during instruction or used only English instruction. Specific measures of English language production and comprehension were obtained over a year's period. In addition classroom observation documented the character of teacher-student interaction, student-student interaction as well as the organizational features of instruction. A companion study evaluated the effect of classroom practices on students who had minimal (0–1 years) exposure to English.

These authors report a series of potentially significant observations:

- Instructional practices that were related to English language development were dependent upon the students' initial level of English proficiency. Therefore, the instructional practice of high level teacher/peer interaction were more highly related to enhanced English development for nonproficient speakers of English.
- The instructional variables that were related to enhanced English development were different for Hispanic and Chinese background students. Chinese students seemed to do best under classroom conditions in which they received independent help on English language learning and in classrooms where the instructional style was characterized by teacher-directed instruction. Hispanic students demonstrated enhanced English oral language development under classroom conditions in which there were more opportunities to interact with English speaking peers.

In addition, these researchers report that growth in English production and comprehension was related to several attributes of student-teacher interaction. Classrooms in which teachers adjusted the language level of their interaction based on student feedback were more likely to produce English language gains. Allowing and encouraging student participation as well as calling attention to the structure of language while using it were reported as additional enhancing characteristics.

In recent research that focused on Mexican American, language minority, elementary school children, Garcia, Flores, Moll, and Prieto (1988) report several findings related to instructional strategies utilized in schools whose students score at or above the national average on Spanish and/or English standardized measures of academic achievement in the Phoenix, Arizona metropolitan area.

More specially, activities of students in instructional school contexts as well as in home and community contexts were systematically sampled over a two-year period. Data were collected on

- instructional processes in literacy and math
- parental attitudes related to educational materials
- education assistance provided to students, teacher and principal attitudes
- student performance on standardized language, cognitive, and metacognitive measures academic achievement

Results of these data can be summarized as follows:

"Macro" Description of Community, Schools, and Classrooms. The findings indicate several types of classrooms, each with individual linguistic and organizational characteristics, yet a high degree of commonality with each other in several significant domains. It was evident that in each classroom the key emphasis on ensuring functional communication between teacher and students and between students and students. Classrooms were characterized by an integrated curriculum emphasizing thematic organization of instructional objectives with (1) student collaboration in almost all academic activity, (2) minimal individualized work tasks, and (3) a highly informal, almost familial, social and collaborative relationship between teachers and students.

Instructional Discourse. Analyses of audio/video taped classroom instruction during literacy and math lessons were conducted biweekly. Results of these analyses indicated that for instruction related to literacy, teachers organized sessions in a manner that led students to interact with each other about the instructional topic. It was during these student-student discussions (occurring more than fifty percent of the time) where higher order cognitive and linguistic discourse was observed. These data also indicated a trend to English language instruction, with lower grades emphasizing Spanish and upper grades emphasizing English concomitantly with a clear commitment to "self-transitioning" strategies, such as the utilization of student-teacher and student-student dialogue journals.

Literacy Development. Analysis of literacy in grades K–6 was conducted utilizing daily journal entries that allow students to "discuss" topics of their choice with teachers on a daily basis. Results of these analyses indicate (1) a systematic progression of writing in the native language in the early grades, (2) writing in the second language "emerged," (3) generally a high degree of conventional spelling was observed even at early grades (even when spelling was not an independent "target" in these classrooms), and (4) the quantitative and qualitative character of student journal entries was directly related to the cognitive and linguistic nature of the teacher's responses.

Academic and Cognitive Achievement. Several cognitive and academic achievement measures were administered to students, and teachers were asked to rate academic success. Results indicate (1) teachers at early grades did not assess academic achievement (as measured by academic achievement tests) as proficiently as teachers in later grades, (2) average academic achievement in reading and math for students in these classrooms was at or above grade level. However, students scored higher on math measures, and (3) there was a positive predictive relationship between cognitive measures and math academic achievement measures and between Spanish language proficiency and English reading achievement.

Professional Staff, Parental, and Student Perspectives. Interviews with classroom teachers, school site principals, parents, and students were conducted to determine their own perspectives and roles regarding education. Classroom teachers (with average teaching experience of 6.7 years) were highly committed to educational success of all their students; perceived themselves as instructional innovators utilizing new psychological and social theories to guide their instructional approaches (all were highly articulate regarding theory-to-practice issues); continued to be involved in professional development activities including participation in small-group teacher networking; had a strong and evidenced commitment to student-home communication (three teachers had developed a weekly mechanism for informally communicating student progress with parents); and each felt they had the autonomy to create and/or change the curriculum implemented in their school even

if it did not meet with the letter of the guidelines established by local or state education agencies. Principals (with an average of 11.7
years of administrative experience) tended to be highly articulate
regarding the curriculum and instructional strategies undertaken
in their classrooms, were highly supportive of their instructional
staff, and recognized the importance of teacher autonomy while recognizing the pressures to conform to district policies regarding the
"standardization" of the curriculum and the need for academic ac-
countability. Parents (with 7.1 average years of schooling completed) expressed a high level of satisfaction with the educational
experience of their children, indicated their active support for the
educational endeavors of their children and strongly encouraged
student academic success as a pathway to their children's economic
betterment. The strategies for support by non-literate parents were
particularly interesting (ensuring sibling/peer assistance for homework, "reading" to young children by inventing prose to match
storybook pictures, etc.).

The general impressions of investigators as they shifted
through these data and interacted personally with the school's various constituents was that these schools indeed served all students
well, academically and otherwise. That such schools exist is not so
surprising; however, viewing their success with students who have
historically been significantly underserved, such effective schooling
was reported as a particularly exhilarating experience (Garcia,
et al. 1988).

Conclusion

The preceding discussion has focused on aspects related to enhancing language minority student academic success. However, it is
important to note that the major issues facing the education of language minority children pertain to the large number of such children failing in school, differing explanations for their failure, and
the kind of evaluation and basic research necessary to help educators and policymakers determine how best to structure programs to
meet the needs of these students. Based on reading tests given in
1983 and 1984, the National Assessment of Educational Progress
(1986) reported that, on the average, language minority students,
especially Hispanic children, were considerably below the national
average at grades 4, 8, and 11. Furthermore, they were likely to be
older than the typical student, were less likely to have taken ad-

vanced science and math classes, and were more likely to expect that they will not graduate from high school. Unfortunately, individuals from non-English-language backgrounds drop out nearly twice the rate of people from English-language backgrounds and at four times the rate if they themselves do not speak English. As might be expected, language minority education is working hard to address this crisis situation (Garcia and August 1988).

School failure may result in part from the low enrollment of language minority students in bilingual ESL classes. Data from the same national assessment indicate that among Hispanics with limited proficiency in English, less than forty-five percent were in programs specifically designed to address the language difference. Among the non-Hispanic, language minority children, less than twenty-five percent were in such classes. This finding is indeed unsettling, since the U.S. Supreme Court, in the 1974 *Lau v. Nichols* decision, ordered school districts receiving federal funds to take affirmative steps to overcome the English-language deficiencies of students with limited English-speaking ability.

However, it seems clear that language minority students can be served effectively by schools. They are served by schools that are organized and have developed educational structures and processes that take into consideration broader attributes of effective schooling practices and specific attributes relevant to language minority students (Tikunoff 1983; Wong-Fillmore et al. 1985; Carter & Chatfield 1986; Garcia et al. 1988). These classrooms exemplify instructional strategies that seem to build on socialization factors relevant to the student population. For Mexican American students, effective instruction is characterized by student-to-student instructional opportunities related to academic material. Such instruction builds on culturally relevant interactional strategies. Moreover, it allows engagement of students during instruction that promotes higher order (process and metaprocess) linguistic and cognitive functioning.

It is important to conclude that language minority education is in a developmental period, immersed in a crisis situation, and in need of further clarifying research. But it is clearly not in its infancy. A serious body of literature addressing its instructional practices, organization, and effects is emerging. The challenge for the educational practitioner is to consider this emerging data and to examine critically its implications for the classroom.

CHAPTER 6

Teaching and Learning in Puerto Rican/Latino Collaboratives: Implications for Teacher Education

MARÍA E. TORRES-GUZMÁN, CARMEN I. MERCADO,
ANA HELVIA QUINTERO, AND DIANA RIVERA VIERA[1]

Questions to Think About

1. Students are frequently subjects of educational research, but seldom are they actually trusted informants. How might researchers employ students as trusted informants or collaborators in identifying the effects of specific instructional approaches and teacher behaviors?
2. How might ethnic minority communities be used as resources for teaching?
3. Should community or socially based changes in schooling incorporate achievement and individual upward social mobility that encourages students to leave the community? How does this relate to Garcia's finding that Mexican American parents view schooling as a path to economic betterment?

The continued educational failure experienced by many Puerto Rican children and the unsuccessful attempts of educational reforms in dealing with the situation has prompted five research collaborators from the United States and Puerto Rico to work together. The result is the Intercambio Research Project, a consortium of researchers, teacher educators, and practitioners bound by a common goal of seeking alternative ways of seeing and acting upon the social reality of schooling of Puerto Rican/Latino children.

All five projects employ ethnographic procedures. This approach captures the richness of the context and the nuances of the cultures, and allows for the transformation of relationships among the participants. In addition, these projects use ethnography as a powerful instructional tool and a vehicle for teacher development.

Through direct involvement in the research process, teachers reflect on their practice by examining the unexamined and questioning the unquestioned. As a result, they gain confidence and extend the possibilities of organizing instruction in ways that validate and empower action in their classrooms and beyond. Similarly, the researchers and teacher educators are enabled to encode and reconceptualize what constitutes a successful educational experience for Puerto Rican/Latino youth by engaging in reflection. Together, both practitioners and researchers are discovering new conceptions of teaching and learning and new ways of engaging in the activity of research. New roles for students, teachers, for teacher educators, and for researchers are also being explored. Promoting these conceptual shifts is not easy, but we are inspired to continue because of the successes encountered in our individual projects, the solidarity that collective activity engenders, and the sense of belonging that reflects our common history.

In the next section, we describe our individual projects. They were initiated in different settings and under different conditions. These serve to illustrate the common threads that create our tapestry of diversity and how we believe our conceptions of teaching and learning should be changed. We, the members of the Intercambio, found that sharing our work enabled us to move out of the isolation of the individual projects and to reflect on and develop further our ideas about teaching, learning, and research. In particular, the activity of collaborative writing has been a significant means for explaining ourselves to each other and for realizing the contributions we can make to the knowledge base for teaching and for teacher preparation.

In the spirit of presenting our multiple perspectives, we have decided not to impose a uniformity of style. We want our voices and their written expressions to show our diversity. The projects are presented in the following order: the Bronx Middle School Collaborative (Mercado with Torres), the Alternative High School Project (Torres-Guzmán with Pérez), the Afterschool Research Project (Pedraza and Ayala), the Arizona Community Project (Moll), and the University of Puerto Rico Partnership (Quintero and Rivera Viera).

Descriptions of the Collaboratives in the
Intercambio Research Project

The Case of the Bronx Middle School Collaborative. Our collaborative partnership began in the spring semester of 1989 as a result of the graduate course on reading and language arts that Carmen Mercado teaches at Hunter College. We were both excited and curious about the application of research to practice for the purposes of improving "reading comprehension." The relationship we started has now evolved into a significant personal and professional one in which we work together with our research colleagues, the students of an intermediate school. It is this relationship, which has been nurtured and strengthened with time, that is at the core of what we have been accomplishing together for the past two years.

What we have been doing is as simple and as complex as initiating multi-ethnic students, two-thirds of whom are Latino and who come from homes with low or subsidized incomes in the northwest "South" Bronx, into the world or research as practiced by educational ethnographers. Students in a Chapter I school, whose ethnicity, family income, and academic histories make them prime candidates for the type of low level curriculum that characterizes instruction in "inner city schools," are learning about the work of educational ethnographers and conducting original research which goes beyond the type of library work they are typically assigned.

In light of Heath's (1985) pioneer work in this area, these activities no longer appear to be unusual. Yet, this project is distinctive in that sixth graders have been entrusted with the responsibility for organizing and conducting our local and national conference presentations. It has been exhilarating to see the students gain confidence in their own abilities as they share their work in academic settings where others usually do the speaking for them. The experience has been a truly transforming one for those of us involved as well as those who have witnessed it. Through our work together, we are demonstrating that our students are capable of great accomplishments, and that by "being seen and heard" our students are in fact having a direct influence on the academic/research establishment.

Creating a Student-Centered Curriculum. Our collaborative efforts have sought to give students increased responsibility in the teaching-learning process in a number of ways. One, students study or research topics of personal interest and significance. It is instructive, but not surprising that students favor topics such as "drugs," "teen pregnancy," "AIDS," the "homeless," and "children's illnesses." When given a choice of what to research, students tend to focus on trying to understand their lived experiences. For example, they ask some of the following questions: "How does it feel to be a teen parent?" "Why does this happen?" and "What can I do about this?" Explanations and insights of complex social phenomena, particularly from the perspectives of those who are most affected by them, are not typically forthcoming in school, and neither are the means for addressing them. In different ways, we—the teacher, the students, and the researcher—are driven by a commitment to understand and assume responsibility for doing something about situations or conditions that affect the education of our youth and the quality of life in our community. It is this common mission the binds us and gives us strength to persevere despite the occasional tensions, conflicts, and contradictions that are inherent in the collaborative process.

Second, students are encouraged to learn with the assistance of more capable others, and to understand that they can learn from their peers, their parents, and other authorities (Vygotsky 1978). Angel, a student in the AY1989–90 groups, has willingly given up his lunch period and seizes any other opportunity that presents itself to work with us as a research assistant. He shares his knowledge of research through formal presentations as well as through group and individual consultations. He has also had a major role as organizer and moderator of our research presentations, a role he has truly mastered.

As their adult collaborators, we have played a key role in helping students (1) remain focused, (2) explore and take advantage of the many opportunities that present themselves naturally to create sources of data, and (3) reflect on what they have done and what they are learning from their research activities. A train ride to Boston on our way to make a presentation at a literacy conference became a five hour adventure during which we experienced how students were beginning to make the research process their own. They interviewed and engaged in conversations with a soldier and a school teacher, passengers on the train ride who provoked a student's curiosity or whose curiosity was provoked by the way they saw us relating to one another. We took this spontaneous occasion to encourage students in their quest to understand their world. We have also made students aware of the especially rich, but usually unrecognized, sources of information that exist outside the library and the classroom, beginning in their homes.

These collaborative activities have been an essential means of accomplishing tasks students initially characterized as challenging ("hard") and beyond their individual capabilities. Students have become aware that they are capable of doing "college work" that is also more interesting ("fun") than the "boring board work" usually assigned. As some students have expressed, we have let them "discover on their own" real life, "the life of a teenager." We have not lectured to them or told them what to do. As an educational ethnographer, Carmen had not anticipated the ethnography would be the powerful instructional tool that it has proven to be with these young adolescent learners.

Learning from Ethnographic Research on Social Issues. First year data, derived from field notes of observations and conversations with classroom participants, and written products developed by the students, yield rich insights about the power of ethnography as a process for inquiry, a process for teaching and learning, and as a mechanism for instituting change.

Students are learning a great deal about learning through their research activities. That is, they are learning (1) to take notes for different purposes, (2) to elicit information orally, (3) to organize and synthesize information in different formats, and (4) to make oral presentations.

By engaging in the literate practices of researchers, students have produced an impressive variety of written documents. For example, students have produced notes of our sessions together (scribe notes), of their group meetings, and of their research plans. They have transcribed interviews, written abstracts of their projects, and developed speeches for conference presentations. Throughout, a great deal of reading, discussion, and thought have accompanied the presentation of these documents. Gordon Wells (1986) refers to this as "literate thinking" preferring to emphasize the *practices* of literacy, particularly the *primacy of writing* and its relationships to reading, talking, and thinking, aspects not captured by the more popular term "reading comprehension."

Through these activities, students have also learned a great deal about the power of writing as a tool for learning. We have developed portfolios of students' written work as a means of documenting more carefully their progress. We are beginning to see that not only is the quality of their written expression becoming increasingly detailed and clear, but that students are also expressing enjoyment of writing. As Peilian, one of the students, said, "I can't stop writing!"

Students are also enjoying talking, particularly during the conference presentations. They have been most affected by the interest and responsiveness of their audiences—that people really listen to them and view them as authorities.

Some students have also movingly described how these activities are bringing them closer to their families. They have told of conversations with relatives and friends about the realities of being a teen-parent. Conversations and interviews with a variety of authorities have also been an important means of gaining insights on issues that concern these young adolescent students.

However, ethnographic documentation is not the only form of documentation that we have relied on. Analysis of scores on the Degrees of Reading Power (DRP) test administered in the spring of 1990 revealed dramatic gains in reading, in some cases by as much as sixteen points (a four point increment is considered significant).

Perhaps the most surprising finding to date is that students are learning to be caring, compassionate individuals through their research activities, a finding which Angel and John first called to our attention. That is, these and other students have voiced the need to care about the homeless, to care about their communities "even if at times you want to get away from it."

It is difficult to reduce an organic, dynamic process to a few simple words. This description is but a pale representation of the "real thing." However, it is an important means for reflecting on past accomplishments and for planning for what lies ahead. At this time, one of our most pressing challenges is to create a narrative which captures more fully our individual voices, a difficult though not impossible endeavor. We need to continue telling *our* story to ourselves and to others.

The Alternative High School/Teachers College Collaborative Project. The initial intention of the university-community collaborative was to document the development of a bilingual/bicultural, empowerment-oriented alternative high school. The specific focus proposed was on parental involvement in curriculum development and the cultural underpinnings of such curriculum. The collaborative began in the fall of 1987 and within a period of three months experienced a change in focus. For the remaining school year, the data collection period, the collaborative focused on documenting and examining how empowerment was manifested in a variety of domains—instruction, curriculum, and organization.

The collaborative was composed of researchers, graduate students, teachers, high school students, and staff of a community-based organization. One of the researchers, one of the graduate students, one of the teachers, and the majority of the students and the staff of the agency grew up in, or were members of the Williamsburg, Brooklyn community. While the data gathering and analysis of the project findings for the final report occurred from July 1987 through February 1989, the principal investigator and the teachers are still engaged in analysis of and reflection on classroom processes.

The research was ethnographic in nature. Members of the research team observed classrooms and "hung out" at the agency once or twice a week and on special occasions. Students, teachers, staff, and parents of the youth were interviewed formally and informally, in groups and individually. School site, agency, and community documents were also gathered. An explicit agreement of the collaborative, from the very beginning of the project, was that the data gathered was the "property" of its producers—the teachers, the students, the parents, and the staff. The interpretations, however, were mutual undertakings.

The relationships initially established in the collaborative unintentionally followed fairly traditional roles; there were clear distinctions between teachers and researchers. Breaking with these distinctions was a goal of the type of research collaborative proposed. The differences in interpretation about what was observed among the researchers led to establishing mechanisms for eliciting the teachers' perspectives. The dialogue established between researchers and teachers took on the "collaborative" and "reflective" nature originally proposed for the project.

The theme had also changed. The teachers had directed the dialogue toward empowerment. By asking teachers to define their concept of empowerment and by examining how they went about integrating their conceptions with what they did, we came to understand that empowerment had as many definitions as there were teachers—one definition was centered on enabling students as learners and another on developing community leadership. Even the students of the school, through the organizing of a school strike, made known what empowerment meant to them—participation in organizational decisions affecting their lives. The school events illustrating how the participants in the school negotiated the concept of empowerment in the classroom, in the organization, and in the community were numerous: the integration of students' lived experiences and language and culture, the lived curriculum developed around environmental science, and the students' organizing around governance. These events became vehicles for examining the relationships between language, culture, instruction, power, and social change. The following are but "key incidents" (Erickson 1977, p. 61) that highlight our findings.

The 'Student Experience Approach.' Our discovery of the 'student experience approach' occurred early in the fall of 1987. The university research team observed that the way one of the teachers organized instruction altered the relationship between the learner and the text. The suggested order of instruction provided by the text had been changed. Instead of reading the selection, followed by the identification of the vocabulary and follow-up activities, the teacher did the reverse. She began by introducing the vocabulary, relating the vocabulary to the students' lived experiences, and then proceeded to read the text.

Understanding that they had some knowledge of the concepts discussed positioned the students in a lateral relation to the text. The unit was about civil rights and the vocabulary included concepts such as racism, discrimination, segregation, emancipation, ghetto, freedom, among others. Elaboration of concepts was first embedded within the experiences known to the students. The teacher elicited an affective and cognitive response to the topic by using the examples provided by the students. By validating the voices of students through the retelling of their experiences in the form of examples, the teacher was altering the relationship between text and reader. Traditionally, the text is viewed as the authority; here the student was also an authority. The interaction of the student with the text could be transformed into a critical one; the reading of the text could be seen as the process of negotiating truths established by the collective discussion between the teacher and the students and in contrast to, or complimented by, what was presented in the text.

Close examination of the classroom practices of this teacher repeatedly demonstrated how she used the students' language, lived experiences, and culture as pedagogical tools to legitimize new social relationships of power (Torres-Guzmán 1990, 1992). What she did in the civil rights lesson is only illustrative.

Leadership for Community Development as Empowerment. The environmental science curriculum was developed by a teacher who was intent on developing a pedagogical approach incorporating, in his words, "a process of action-reflection-action." It is an example of an integrated curriculum aimed at building leadership for community development and empowerment.

Early in the fall, the class had a series of field experiences: a walk through the neighborhood, a visit to a tri-state storage facility for toxic and radioactive waste, and a nearby park preserved as a "natural environment." Students with photographic skills became the visual recorders. The class, soon to be known as the Toxic Avengers, observed, analyzed, read, and wrote about what they saw and experienced. Contrasting environments within the discussion of individual and community rights to healthy environments set the stage for future action.

A lot four blocks away from the school, which was used by an adhesive factory to store barrels of residue, became the target of their investigation. Daily visits permitted the students to count the barrels and determine the traffic flow in and out of the lot. Getting close enough was creatively approached by staging an accidental throwing of a football onto the premise. Establishing a faintly disguised excuse to trespass on private property and their continuous presence in front of the lot had its effect. The number of barrels stored began to decrease (from two hundred barrels to thirty), the liquid of some of the drums was spilled into the gutter, one of the students and the teacher were "bullied" by one of the adhesive plant employees, and a high sheet metal fence crowned with barbed wire was erected. The counting came to an end. But the students had taken some samples of the spillage. They sent the sample to a chemical lab that confirmed the presence of hazardous and toxic waste.

Meanwhile, in the classroom, the students learned about cell structures, chromosomes, mutants, chemicals, toxicity, and so forth. They distinguished between the different categories of hazardous material and the specific effects these could have on an individual's health and on the environment. Their experience with the lot helped them frame their social studies learning. They studied about government structures and lines of authority. In trying to determine which authorities would be helpful with their cause for a better, healthier environment, the students learned about zoning laws, the Environmental Protection Agency, and the role of the fire chief, the mayor, and the governor. Although they never found a need to send the letter they collectively wrote to the fire chief, they experienced the writing process—determining audience, purpose, message, and editing—as part of their learning.

The environmental science curriculum embodied many principles of a pedagogy that promotes transformation. Students were not passive recipients of knowledge, but active creators. The students and the teacher assumed the posture of active co-participants in the process of learning/teaching. The task was sufficiently complex so as to require that they rely on each other's strengths and engage in collective action. The experiential and abstract learning were facilitated by the integration of classroom learning and community action. The learner had to apply what was learned in the classroom to what happened in the community, and their community action informed and gave meaning to the classroom learning. The students' actions were embedded in the passion, morality, and caring they felt for what happened to their family and friends in the community. Reflecting on the significance of what occurred permitted the students to distance themselves sufficiently so as to gain understanding of the political, social, and scientific complexity of their work. They entertained multiple perspectives on what occurred as well. For example, while they felt victorious, they understood why they were to, in their presentation of the events, cautiously refrain from claiming a causal relationship between their daily presence at the chemical lot and the eventual clean-up.

Reflections. The teachers and students were involved in change in various domains. Teachers were reflecting on their conception of teaching as they examined what empowerment looked like in their classroom and in the school. They were involved in establishing alternative relationships with the students and positioning student learning so that the students themselves were creating change within the school and in the community. While there were many occasions in which the interactions described above were far from being the norm, the school was a positive experience for many of the students as it provided the support, love, and safety of a *familia* or *un segundo hogar* (Carrasco 1984) for the youngsters involved. What the teachers did to create this positive environment for students had much to do with understanding that the language and culture of the students, their parents, their community were valuable tools for organizing instruction (be it through the use of cultural images, lived experiences, or through the use of the neighborhood as a learning site).

Incorporating students' lived experiences, cultural background, and language as a way of validating student voices changed the relationship of power and collaboration in the classroom. Students became active participants in molding their own lives. The content became accessible and the learning process became meaningful and purposeful. Furthermore, the learning environment created in this alternative school provided spaces for the students to explore their own relationships as individuals in the broader societal context.

The stories also say something about research and the relationship of theory and practice. Research on teachers' conception of learning and teaching practices can be incredibly powerful in bridging the gap between theory and practice that so often makes the research process and research findings so alienating for the practitioners. The students, the teachers, and the researchers became partners in molding the direction of the research and the interpretation of the findings. Martín-Baro (1989) sums up how we came to see our work—research that is centered on what is important to and at the service of those it proposes to serve. We know that research that aims at change can be transformative.

Afterschool Research Project The Centro de Estudios Puertorriqueños at Hunter College has over the last two years conducted an intervention research program at a community-based site in East Harlem. The program works with an afterschool elementary grade level African American and Puerto Rican student population. The children live in the surrounding low income housing projects and range between seven to twelve years old.

The purpose of this intervention program is to improve the literacy, math, and science skills of the children in a learning environment that emphasizes participation in schools and society in general.

Experts in mathematics and science education acknowledge that children's negative attitudes and low motivation for learning could be major hurdles in these fields. They also propose that teaching elementary school children the process of scientific investigation and introducing elementary school children to the principles of mathematical and scientific reasoning is more important than having the students memorize scientific facts and/or acquire mechanical skills.

Furthermore, our approach to curriculum development has been guided by a socio-historical, cultural perspective. As an approach to cognitive development, this effort seems promising, particularly with school children who have often been treated as subjects of remediation. The perspective we take views cognitive development as emerging from the nature of social interactions that occur in educational activities that are motivated by goals derived both from the content domain and from the culture and interests of the communities to which the learner belongs.

A feature of this approach is that the content around which the curriculum is organized is primary. First, the development of intellectual skills depends on working with the relationships and contradictions in the subject matter. Second, the content must be carefully selected. The objective is to focus on questions that are fundamental to the children and their position in society. Third, the effective use of content in educational activities requires careful planning. And, fourth, the approach is activity-based. Intellectual development comes from working directly with the relationships in the subject matter.

In addition, we want to develop a critical consciousness in our children. We define this critical consciousness as containing an historical and socio-economic understanding and knowledge of the community. The development of such consciousness gives students a sense of their potential human agency, and potential for action, by providing them with a perspective of continuity and possibility not afforded by explanations that ascribe the cause for poor community conditions on cultural, racial, linguistic, or personal factors. We have assumed that a person's knowledge about their past could help them understand the present in ways that could connect to future solutions of social problems.

Two aspects of such a learning process which we have not explicitly developed but are intrinsically important to our approach is the role of positive self-esteem and strong cultural identity. They are important to our theoretical approach for two basic reasons. One is related to the issue of self-determination and the right of people to maintain their identity and culture. (In the case of Puerto Ricans in the United States this has a particularly legal constitutional basis as well since we are born American citizens.) The second reason is related to our implicit analysis of society and the strategies for social change that derive from this analysis. Essentially, unlike the schools, we believe that the strategies for change should be community or socially-based (the schools focus on individual achievement and upward social mobility as the way out of the community). If collective response and action are needed to change social reality, then we must begin preparing children at an early age. Good and effective citizenship needs to be nurtured rather than expected to arrive magically with the coming of voting age.

Our general approach is to help children build an identity as a Puerto Rican minority group member so that they become integrated, as opposed to assimilated, into the city where they live. Through a knowledge of the history and background of the Puerto

Rican culture, the children could develop self-respect. The children could reflect on cultural practices; that is, they could gain an understanding of the factors that affect the origin or maintenance of particular practices. In short, we would like to help the children develop a theoretical approach to understanding their identity.

A theoretical approach is important for the following reasons. Done properly, the children will have a deeper, richer understanding of cultural practices. They will be able to understand them as reflecting solutions and adaptations to particular material conditions in which their ancestors lived. By understanding their culture in this historical way, they will start to appreciate the processes that generate cultural practices. Consequently, in their own lives, they can help to adapt and extend their culture, examining what practices can and should be maintained in an urban environment, and maintaining the spirit of other practices, even if the forms are changed to accommodate present conditions.

The Arizona Community Project The design of this project consisted mainly of three main, interrelated activities. First, it included an analysis of the use and communication of knowledge and skills within and among households in a Latino community in Tucson, Arizona. Second, the researchers and teachers examined classroom practices and used local resources to experiment with literacy instruction in an after school site. And, finally, classroom observations were conducted to examine methods of instruction and to explore how to apply what was learned at the after school site.

During the first year a study was undertaken in twenty-eight households in which data on literacy practices in Spanish and English and on the structure and functions of social networks within the community were collected. Self-report questionnaires, literacy checklists, and ethnographic field notes were used to gather information during prearranged visits to these homes by the members of the research team. The instructional component occurred in two distinct settings: an after school lab and in school-based classrooms in two districts.

Households are Repositories of Knowledge. Particularly important in our work has been our analysis of households, how they function as part of a wider, changing economy, and how they obtain and distribute their material and intellectual resources through strategic social ties or networks (Vélez-Ibañez 1988). In contrast to many classrooms, households never function alone or in isolation; they are always connected to other households and institutions through diverse social networks. In our sample of primarily Mexican working class families, these social networks facilitate different forms of economic assistance and labor cooperation that help families avoid the expenses involved in using secondary institutions, such as plumbing companies or automobile repair shops. For families with limited incomes, these networks are a matter of survival. They also serve important emotional and service functions, e.g., in finding jobs and in assisting with child-care and rearing so that mothers may enter the labor market. In brief, these networks form social contexts for the transmission of knowledge, skills, information, and assistance, as well as cultural values and norms (Vélez-Ibañez 1988; Greenberg 1989).

The knowledge exchanged through these types of social ties or networks refer to as funds of knowledge. Greenberg has defined funds of knowledge as an "operations manual of essential information and strategies households need to maintain their well being" (p. 2). Our analysis shows that funds of knowledge are related to the social and labor history of the household members and the participants in the networks. With our sample, much of the knowledge is related to the rural origins of the households and, of course, the current employment or occupation of the household members, such as soils, cultivation of plants, seeding, and water distribution and management. Others know about animal husbandry, veterinary medicine, ranch economy, and mechanics. Many of the families know about carpentry, masonry, electrical wiring, fencing, and building codes; to maintain health, often in the absence of doctors, some families employ folk remedies, herbal cures, midwifery, and first aid procedures. And the list goes on. Needless to say, not every household in our sample possesses knowledge about all of these matters. But that is precisely the point. It is unnecessary for individual persons, households, or classrooms to possess all this knowledge. When needed, such knowledge is available and accessible through social networks of exchange.

Clearly, the idea that these families are somehow devoid of abilities and skills is simply erroneous. The common view that their children suffer from a deficit of "funds of background experience" is seriously challenged by our work. From our perspective, these families represent a major social and intellectual resource for the schools. The extent of their funds of knowledge justifies our position that the community needs to be perceived by others, especially educators, and probably by the community itself, as having strength or power, as having resources that schools cannot ignore.

In an important sense, the schools are in an analogous situation to the households we are studying. All schools consider that they need more resources in addressing the needs of students, especially if these students are minority children and from poor neighborhoods. It is common for teachers to bemoan the scarcity of resources. Dealing with scarcity of resources, however, is an everyday issue in the households. The exchange of funds of knowledge, as we have explained, is a major strategy to deal with the lack of resources, a strategy developed to harness, control, and manipulate resources. The idea is to do the most with what you have.

Accessing Funds of Knowledge for Academic Learning. Ina, the sixth grade bilingual teacher, had a classroom that contained all of the elements necessary to experiment with literacy instruction. Although she followed the assigned curriculum, she deviated often to implement supplementary activities. For example, she supplemented the basal reader with novels, newspaper and magazine stories, and poems. She also had the class write often, including poems, short stories, narratives, and descriptions. Ina joined the after school setting already sharing the group's belief that the use of outside, community resources could give more meaning to the learning experiences of the students.

Ina introduced the theme of construction, which had been discussed in the teacher study group, to her class. She discussed with the students possibilities for research on this topic. She believed that the work required conducting a unit would be more in depth and extensive than anything they had done before.

Ina started by asking the students to visit the library to look for information on building or construction. The students obtained materials in both English and Spanish on the history of dwellings and on different ways of constructing structures. Through her own research in a community library and in the school district's media center, the teacher identified a series of books on construction and on different professions, including volumes on architects and carpenters, and decided to use them as part of the module. The students built a model house or other structures as homework and wrote brief essays describing their research or explaining their construction.

In short, the teacher was able to get the students to write about their experiences and, in the process, she improved the activities she had learned about at the afterschool site.

The teacher, however, did not stop there. She proposed that the class invite parents as experts to provide information on specific aspects of construction. The teacher reported that the children were surprised by the thought of inviting their parents as experts, especially given some of the parents' lack of formal schooling, and were intrigued by the idea. She invited a father who was a mason to describe his work. She was particularly interested in having the father describe his use of construction instruments and tools, and how he estimated or measured the area or perimeter of the location in which he works.

The teacher also invited other people in the community to contribute to this unit. The teacher invited parents and others in the community to contribute substantively to the development of lessons, to access their funds of knowledge for academic purposes. Theirs was an intellectual contribution to the content and process of classroom learning. The parents came to share their knowledge, expertise, and experiences with students. This knowledge, in turn, become part of the students' work or a focus of analysis. These visits helped create a new instructional routine in this classroom that helped the teacher and students exceed the curriculum, stretch the limits of their writing, and expand the knowledge that formed lessons. In total, about twenty persons visited the class during the module implementation and the teacher used different sources of funds of knowledge: the students' own knowledge, that of the students' parents and relatives, the parents and relatives of other students, the teacher's own network, the school staff and other teachers, the community members who did not have school age children, and university faculty and graduate students.

Establishing social networks to access funds of knowledge for academic learning generated many important secondary activities that went far beyond the initial module and the activities around the theme of construction became more central to the classroom activities. The teacher started to generalize the module by incorporating the "core" curriculum within the module's activities. This generalization illustrates the extent to which the teacher and her class had appropriated the initial model's activities and created something new to address the needs of this specific classroom.

Concluding Vision. We started the project convinced that there were ample resources in the students' community that could be used to help improve literacy instruction. We set out to document these resources in terms of the funds of knowledge found in the households and were struck by the breadth of the knowledge and by the importance of social ties in making this knowledge available to others.

We soon realized that the insights gained from studying households held special relevance for the study of education. But we also realized that household funds of knowledge could not simply be imported into classrooms, especially as currently organized. We needed to work closely with teachers to figure out how to create circumstances where these funds of knowledge would become legitimate resources for teaching and learning. We formed an after school setting where we could develop innovations and soon learned that any initiative for change, and the bulk of the work to make it happen, had to come from teachers. The afterschool site became a teachers' study group, where teachers could share their funds of knowledge about teaching and create a social network among themselves.

Meanwhile we observed in classrooms, and realized that under the best conditions, those classrooms where the children were eagerly using literacy to explore and understand issues of interest to them and the teacher served as good analogues to the households: very different settings but both using social processes and cultural resources of all kinds to get ahead. It is here, in the strategic combination of resources to help students learn and develop, that we see the greatest potential for change.

University of Puerto Rico's Partnership with the Schools. The University of Puerto Rico's Partnership Project with Schools was initiated in February 1987 with the participation of school personnel at different levels—teachers, school directors, supervisors, the district superintendent, representatives from the Puerto Rican Department of Education Central Office—as well as university professors from different disciplines, including Sociology, Psychology, Planning, Public Administration, Mathematics, Science, Language, History and Education. The project's main objective was to identify alternatives for dealing with major educational problems of the school district. The school district selected was the San Juan II School district, which with ninety-seven percent of its families below poverty level it has one of the lowest income levels in the Island and is one of the most problematic districts. The project was initially organized around a seminar. Participants from the district and the University met on a monthly basis to identify the multiple variables that are interwoven in the educational problems affecting the area.

During the initial months of the project the forty project participants met to develop a socio-economic and educational profile of the district. In this process, we found that educational passivity and disengagement among students in the upper elementary grades and high school were frequently cited as symptomatic of the educational problems. In order to deal with this situation, a smaller group of seminar participants met during the summer of 1987 to develop specific projects that would make school work more relevant to the students' needs and potentials. It was our hope to transform teaching into a more active process.

We will describe one of the many projects that took place as a result of the University of Puerto Rico Partnership Project with Schools. It is important to point out that the project involved people from the school and the University that were not part of the original forty seminar participants. Similarly, some of the initial participants in the partnership were not directly involved in the specific projects that were eventually developed. While the individual projects developed, the seminar meetings continued. They became a vehicle for sharing the difficulties and successes of the various projects and for exploring ideas and analyzing experiences.

History of the Project. The Resource Center Project at the Manuel Elzaburu Middle School was initiated in October 1987. The goal was to improve students' writing and reading skills using their interests, potentials, and community resources as the basis for learning. It involved a group of twenty seventh graders receiving services through the Chapter I program. While this program proposes to help students get back into the regular group, our experience was that students never left the program because their work remained below the expected performance level.

The project was viewed as a demonstration using an innovative interdisciplinary approach and involving professors from the University of Puerto Rico, mainly from the Laboratory High School of the School of Education who worked together integrating theater, visual arts, and language arts through an enrichment program.[2] The University professors met weekly with the seventh graders (El grupo de los 20) using the amount of time usually allotted to the regular Chapter I services. Traditional teaching hadn't been successful with these students, so new avenues were needed.

The Barrio Obrero Community surrounding the school is overridden with socio-economic problems, but it is also very rich in its popular culture. Some of the most well-known singers of popular music in Puerto Rico were born and raised in Barrio Obrero. Thus, we decided to build around the history of the popular music and performers of Barrio Obrero. Students became involved in diagnostic reading and writing activities by reading and discussing a newspaper article about Ismael Rivera, a famous "salsa" musician who had died several months before. Ismael Rivera was born and raised in the neighborhood and had been buried in the local cemetery just a few blocks away from the school. The students shared information regarding the musician, his music, his involvement with drugs, details of the burial and so forth. As a result of these discussions, we thought about what other things we wanted to know about his life and what sources of information we could use. Among them were interviews. The group developed questions to include in interviews with community members. Students read different portions of the newspaper article and took turns answering questions about the article. The reading samples were taped. Afterwards they wrote brief paragraphs summarizing what they had read. These initial activities provided valuable reading and writing samples to be examined as our work progressed. While some of the professors worked with the students, others observed them and took notes of their reading and general classroom behavior.

We were aware that these students did not find academic activities interesting and that they experienced low achievement and frustration in school. Several were very uncomfortable reading aloud and made fun of one another's poor reading ability. We were committed to working with their reading and writing skills in an environment that made them feel secure in their abilities, using the strengths they brought into school and recognizing their community as a source of knowledge useful to their school learning. We needed to modify their view of teachers as authority figures who corrected their mistakes continuously and viewed their community as problematic. This was not an easy task. We decided that reading and writing mistakes would not be corrected by the professors. Students were asked to use self-corrections whenever their reading didn't "sound right" or "make sense." A great deal of collective writing production occurred, thus requiring small efforts from each participant. At the very beginning students were either very loud, exhibiting unacceptable classroom behaviors such as disrupting activities or were extremely passive, unable or unwilling to judge their own work. A great deal of time was spent discussing what behaviors the group thought necessary to observe in order to work productively.

We also used semantic mapping activities to encourage the expression of their thoughts about a particular idea or word. Several significant activities occurred around a single word such as "ambiente." We found that the group initially expressed very few positive views about the "ambiente" in their neighborhood. As time progressed and with some prodding, the students began to view positively, among other things, their music, their sense of family, and their concern for community.

Group writing activity evolved around experiences they had as group participants, and through theater exercises they began to explore the use of their body, voice, and facial expressions as creative outlets for their ideas, feelings, and stories. An experimental theater group known as the Teatreros Ambulantes worked with the students during several sessions. Photostatic theater was particularly exciting as a means to express the stories they were writing. A trip to a well-known mascaras (masks) artisan in the city of Ponce helped the group see how crafts can be made from materials such as newspapers. Consequently, art activities involved the use of materials available in their environment. Each student selected the artistic means they wished to explore in order to represent different milestones in Ismael Rivera's life which resulted from their research. They became involved in art or theater activities according to their own interests and strengths.

The professors met weekly to assess what was occurring, the students' interest and development of their language art skills, and changes in student behavior. They planned accordingly. These meetings became a means for reflecting on pedagogical theory and practices. It helped develop a sense of cohesiveness among the professors who in the school setting were deeply involved in examining what teaching strategies were useful and successful in working with students who had almost given up on school. For this group of professors, these weekly activities and the work with the students also affected their own teaching at the School of Education.

Throughout the project, collaboration was a key issue. Collaboration among teachers, among students, and between teachers and students was stressed. Collaboration promoted genuine collective work and created a very strong bond among all participants strengthening their individual self-esteem. Looking back on this project, we find that change in student and teachers' perceptions of learning, schooling, and the power of collaboration were among the most significant gains of the project. Our commitment to students empowering themselves by acknowledging that they are part of a resourceful and rich community that should be present in their schooling proved to be a powerful tool in bringing about change in students attitudes and behaviors in school and in our own teaching.

Implications for Teacher Preparation Programs

The Intercambio projects suggest ways of improving teacher preparation programs at the university level through collaboration, through the integration of theory and practice, and through a focus on educational and social change. In each of the collaboratives, the nature of teaching and learning is conceptualized as an open system, one that allows for contingencies and surprises, that is highly interdependent with its environment and context, planning and implementation go hand in hand and are always incomplete. In other words, the planning and implementation processes are not linear but exploratory, they do not assume that the territory to be covered has yet been conquered or mapped, nor that all the unknowns have been vanquished. On the contrary, the process is open to the unexpected and to the discovery of the unknown. Stemming from these premises, we feel teacher preparation programs should focus on developing the students' ability to learn from experience, to test their theories through reflection and action, to learn how to cope with uncertainties, and to connect this learning to other academic learning.

Furthermore we believe that colleges of education cannot teach to learn from experience if they themselves are not teaching this way. How we teach is what we teach (Elmore 1989). Professors must take an active role in bridging the gap between educational theory, methods, and practice. They must model the integration of these elements and provide insights on how they enrich each other. To do so means working together with school personnel on the task of improving education. Schools can become the vehicles by which teacher educators, practicing teachers, and prospective teachers learn to integrate theory, methods, and practice.

This working together can also serve to help prospective, novice, and experienced teachers develop strategies to transform their individual and isolating work into collective activity. As Shulman (1989) points out "the difficulties of learning from experience are characteristic of the limitation of any individual trying to make critical sense of a complex world while working alone." Thus, our emphasis on collaboration.

Collaboration. Any attempt to study education in connection to the complex social relationships and cultural practices of human beings, be it in classrooms or in community settings, requires the participation of different colleagues. This emphasis on collaborative activity implies the need to create new arrangements for research on teaching and learning.

Our projects are collaboratives within schools and outside. The levels of collaboration differ. The UPR-San Juan II Project brings together the most varied groups of people and the greatest number of institutions. They bring together professors, administrators, school administrators, support personnel, teachers, community agencies, and students and their families. Both the Arizona Project and the alternative high school actively bring together three distinct groups: the school (including administrators and bilingual teachers), the community (parents and/or entire networks of exchange), and the university researchers and graduate students in an attempt "to combine basic research and educational intervention in a single project that arranges for a two-way flow of information between the school and other social institutions" (Cole and Griffin 1987, p. 90). The East Harlem Afterschool Project was housed in a community-based organization, like the alternative school, but does not deal directly with schools. The collaborative in the middle school was initially more focused on the collaboration between the teacher, her students, and the researcher, but the research interests of the students that grew out of their concerns and connectedness with the life and soul of their community, have brought the parents and community resources, other school staff, and other students into the project.

The collaboratives embody three elements proposed by Tharp and Gallimore (1988). The first is how we have established joint projects. In most cases university personnel have initiated joint projects, some of the projects were encouraged by individual teachers (as in the middle school) or by members of the community (as in the alternative high school). A second element is the interdisciplinary research posture that all our projects have taken. This interdisciplinary nature of our work promotes a more holistic interpretation of what is occurring and takes into account the complexity and interrelationships of the issues involved. The third element is how each of the projects has connected what happens in schools and in communities to other contexts (e.g., the students' concern with homelessness in the East Harlem After School Project and with city policies, the chemical lot with the Environmental Protection Agency, and so forth).

Theory and Practice. The educational reform movement is calling for university-school collaboratives to deal with the tensions mounting around the need for school improvement and teacher preparation. The premise is that "there are differences in purpose between the practice of the academy and those of the practitioners"

(Popkewitz 1987, p. 13). Bridging those purposes or dealing with the associated organizational tensions created by the differences so that the definitions and categories borne out in educational research can be translated into practice has become part of the educational discourse. This formulation is bothersome because it does not change the relationships between experts and practitioners, but instead reaffirms it. Moveover, it does not challenge current thinking about the organization and production of knowledge and its relationship to the social reality of those who produce it.

Educational research on teaching and learning must not only analyze the different contexts of education, but must focus on creating fundamentally new and challenging instructional activities and environments. This transformation of practice invariably results in the transformation of the contexts of research. Traditional research paradigms can be misleading because the shortcomings of theories of teaching and learning, in terms of their potential for changing practice, have been largely left unexamined.

Changes in educational practices, and theories about changing practice, must legitimately emerge from the collaborative attempts with teachers and others to modify and improve practice within specific social and historical circumstances. Just as there are no quick fixes in education, there are no grand theories that helped accomplish or circumvent the painstaking work that is represented in the joint efforts described in this chapter. *Why* and *how* students succeed or fail, we would argue, are inseparable questions whose answers must be found in social attempts to produce educational change.

Notes

1. The authors of this chapter base the text on the work of *La Colectiva Intercambio,* a consortium of Puerto Rican/Latino youth of which they are members. This subgroup is comprised of those of us working directly in teacher education. We would like to acknowledge the support provided by our respective institutions and, in particular, we are grateful for the assistance and financial support provided by the Intercambio City University of New York-University of Puerto Rico Academic Exchange Program and its director, Dr. Antonio Lauria Perricelli.

2. The participants were: William Padín (theatre), Carmen Rodríguez (art), Jorge Cruz, María del C. Curras and Diana Rivera Viera (language arts) from the University of Puerto Rico and Ileana Quintero from the Universidad del Sagrado Corazón.

CHAPTER 7

Who Will Teach Our Children? Preparing Teachers to Successfully Teach African American Students

GLORIA LADSON-BILLINGS

Questions to Think About

1. What is culturally relevant teaching and how does it differ from one cultural group to the next?
2. What is the relationship between "culturally relevant" teaching and effective instruction for language minority students as identified by Garcia?
3. To what extent should teacher preparation include a study of the history of ethnic groups other than the mainstream middle class?
4. What is the relationship between "culturally responsible" pedagogy as discussed by Pewewardy and "culturally responsive" pedagogy as discussed in this chapter?

The condition of education in the United States has been a paramount issue at every level of public life (Cuban 1990). The purpose of this chapter is to address one of the many issues educators are confronting in this period of rapid demographic, economic, and technological change—preparing teachers to successfully teach diverse students. In particular, this chapter looks at the literature concerning the preparation of teachers for African American students.

Although the 1960s produced a huge body of literature on preparing teachers for the "disadvantaged" (for examples see, Bloom et al. 1965; Bettleheim 1965; Ornstein & Vairo 1968) and the 1970s produced a body of "effective schools" literature (Austin 1979;

Brookover & Lezotte 1979; Edmonds 1979), none of this literature specifically recognized the culture of African Americans as a useful tool for preparing teachers for successfully teaching African American students. Even though some instructional strategies such as cooperative learning and whole language approaches to literacy were developed and refined as ways to improve achievement for "disadvantaged" students, their relationship to African American learners is rarely made clear.

This chapter begins with a brief discussion of diversity and education and is followed by a discussion of past and current teacher education responses to African American students. It concludes with some suggestions for promising practices for future study and programmatic change.

Diversity and Demographics

Three issues dominate discussions about diversity in education: (1) the student population is becoming increasingly diverse (*Education Week* 1986); (2) many of the racially, culturally and linguistically diverse are not faring well in schools (Cuban 1989) and (3) in the midst of growing student diversity, the teaching population continues to be largely monocultural (Haberman 1989). Statistical data substantiates each of these assertions.

Students of color comprise almost thirty percent of the student population. In the twenty largest school districts, students of color comprise seventy percent of the total school enrollment (Center for Education Statistics 1987). Demographic projections suggest that by the end of the decade, students of color will represent close to forty percent of total school enrollment nationwide (Hodgkinson 1985). These students of color are more likely than their white counterparts to be poor, live with one parent and drop out of school (Kennedy, Jung & Orland 1986).

Paradoxically, the nation's teaching force has changed inversely in relation to these shifting demographics. Our teachers are overwhelmingly white and mostly female and will continue to be so for the foreseeable future (Grant 1990; Haberman 1989). These demographic and educational trends have a particularly potent impact on the education of African American students.

Although nationwide the high school dropout rate is about twenty-eight percent, cities with high concentrations of African Americans, such as New York and Chicago, have dropout rates of over forty percent (Goodlad 1990a). African American students, compared to whites, are two to five more times likely to be suspended from school (Irvine 1990). Although African American students make up seventeen percent of the public school population, they are forty-one percent of the special education population (Kunjufu 1984). Indeed, a black male child who was born in California in 1988 is three times more likely to be murdered as he is to be admitted to the University of California (Fortune Magazine 1990, p. 18).

The news is no better concerning African American teachers. At one time, African American teachers made up eighteen percent of the nation's teaching force. Today they comprise approximately five percent of all teachers and their numbers are shrinking (Haberman 1989; Whitaker 1989). Irvine (1990) cites several factors that contribute to the declining numbers of African American teachers: the decline in the number of African American college students, the decline in the number of students who major in teacher education, and changes in certification requirements that more often than not require some form of competency testing.

This information about demographic trends helps us to see more clearly the magnitude of the change that is occurring in our schools. However, it does not explain fully what that change means and how educators can best be prepared to adapt to and meet the challenges of change. For instance, what difference does it make that our students are becoming more diverse and our teachers more monocultural? What is the impact of the teacher's cultural background on students' achievement? Unfortunately, most of the data concerning the declining numbers of African American teachers deals only with issues of employment equity and fairness for teachers. Little or no empirical evidence suggests that more African American teachers means higher academic performance for African American students (Ladson-Billings 1991). What, then, is the role of teacher education in this era of demographic change? What has been done in the past? What are the prospects for change? This chapter attempts to address these issues in the subsequent sections.

The Futile Search: The Literature on Preparing Teachers for African American Learners

The literature review for this chapter began with a search of the ERIC database from 1980 to 1990 with teacher education and Black education as descriptors. This generated twenty-seven citations that included seven journal articles, ten conference papers, six reports, one book and three teaching guides. Nine of the twenty-seven citations were based on empirical research. The substance of these citations was as follows: effective instructional programs (7), increasing the supply of Black teachers (5), teacher attitudes and perceptions concerning Black students and racism (4), school improvement for minority students (3), the impact of integration (2), the impact of standardized tests on prospective teachers (2), demographics and status of African American students (2), improving higher education (1), and one citation on Black South African students' perceptions of the goals of education.

A second search that included the descriptor multicultural education generated two hundred and forty-nine citations. Thirty-nine of these citations concerned educating teachers for diversity. None of the two hundred and forty-nine dealt solely with preparing teachers for teaching African American students. Grant and Secada's (1990) more extensive search covering the period from 1964 to June 1988 revealed twelve hundred journal articles and ERIC citations. However, when their criteria were limited to citations using empirical research the citations were reduced dramatically to twenty-three. Of these, seventeen were concerned with multicultural education. These computer searches indicate that the research on preparing teachers for teaching African American students is virtually non-existent. One book entitled, *Education by, for, and about African Americans,* (Daniels 1972) was actually a compilation of descriptions of several African American community schools. It did not contain information about preparing teachers to teach African American learners effectively.

The history of the educational mainstream's approach towards educating African American students has been discouraging. One of the primary reasons for this ineffectiveness may be found in the language that surrounded public school attempts to educate African Americans. The literature of the 1960s and 1970s is replete with works on teaching the culturally "deprived" (Bloom et al. 1965) and "disadvantaged" (Bettleheim 1965; Ornstein & Vairo 1968; Ornstein 1971; Doll & Hawkins 1971; Hyram 1972). Even if this literature was motivated by the best intentions, such as improving both student and teacher effectiveness, it contributed to a perception of African American students as deprived, deficient, and deviant. Consequently, many proposed interventions were designed to remove the students from their homes, communities and cultures in an effort to mitigate against their alleged damaging effects (Mitchell 1982). These compensatory programs were based on a view of African American children as substandard to white children.

By the 1980s the language had changed somewhat but the con-
notation remained the same. According to Cuban (1989), the new
term "at risk" is being used to describe certain students and their
families in much the same way they have been described for almost
two hundred years. Cuban further suggests that "the two most popular explanations for low academic achievement of at-risk children
locate the problem in the children themselves or in their family" (p.
781). It is interesting to note that the 1990 edition of the *Education
Index* continues to cross-reference issues concerning Black students
with the phrase "culturally deprived."

The primary reason for this continued focus on what's wrong
with African American learners has to do with the ethic of equality that underlies American culture. Educational theorists, policy
makers, and practioners balk at the notion of recognizing and cel-
ebrating the difference. Thus, a view of African American learners
as "just like us (white children)" justifies longstanding compensatory and remedial approaches. The one genuine effort at institutional change vis-à-vis cultural difference came in the form of
multicultural education.

The resurgence of multicultural education is testimony to the
impact of changing demographics and changing student needs.
However, there is confusion over what is meant by multicultural education (Sleeter & Grant 1987). While Sleeter & Grant (1987) identify five major approaches to multicultural education, McCarthy
(1988) argues that multicultural education is merely a "curricular
truce" (p. 267) to appease the demands for political and educational
change by African Americans as part of the Civil Rights Movement.
Thus, this view of multicultural education does not hold much
promise for fully meeting the educational needs of African American learners. However, Sleeter (1989) argues that despite all the
confusion surrounding multicultural education, it still stands as a
viable means for fighting oppression. The multicultural picture is
further muddied by conservative scholars who seek to embrace and
redefine multiculturalism as a new version of the melting pot (Ravitch 1990). Unfortunately, the impact of multicultural education
course work on teacher education students is neither profound nor
lasting (Santos 1986).

Capitalizing on the Culture

Almost sixty years ago Carter G. Woodson (1933) wrote persua-
sively about the unwillingness and inability of the American edu-

cational system to educate African Americans. This unwillingness and inability stems from the fact that the typical school experience for African American learners lacks the "validation and affirmation of their culture that would enable them to transcend the conflict between African American culture and those aspects of mainstream American culture that, in effect, devalue and denigrate blackness and alienate black students from themselves and from their own learning" (King 1991).

Fortunately, African American teachers and scholars have a long history of looking at African American learners as a group and have developed an alternative, although not widely disseminated, body of literature. During the early 1900s the American Teachers Association (ATA) was formed to "provide an outlet and encouragement to teachers in Negro schools" (Perry 1975, p. 7). Although it may be argued that the ATA was organized as an assimilationist organization hoping to parallel the role of the all white National Education Association, the fact that it did exist and recognized the need for specific training for teachers of African American learners is important. An emphasis on racial pride and uplift was a recurring theme of the ATA.

> There (in the South) the Negro teachers stressed to their pupils the rise and contribution of prominent black people . . . They tacked or pasted pictures of Negroes of accomplishment on the walls of the schoolrooms. The children were exposed to black preachers, doctors, small businessmen, lecturers and artists. In those completely segregated, educationally and physically inadequate schools, the principal motivation to press on came from the example of Negroes, dead and living, who had persisted and achieved. (Perry 1975, p. 42)

During the 1960s African American scholars and writers began to address the societal and systemic problems that African American learners confronted (Baldwin 1963; Brown 1966; Clark 1965). Much of this literature was used to shape an equal opportunity paradigm that was aimed at improving the academic and economic status of African Americans in relation to their white counterparts. However, by the 1970s there appeared to be a shift away from scholarly investigation and writing that merely sought to have African Americans achieve educational and economic parity with whites. This scholarship began to assert the integrity of a distinct African personality that would require new strategies for educational success (Banks 1973; Boykin 1978; Nobles 1974; Sizemore 1972). By the 1980s a line of inquiry directed at explicating the strengths of authentic African American culture began to emerge. This scholarship was aimed at describing African American learners as normative and capable and urged changes in curriculum, instruction and school organization. (Asante 1989; Hale-Benson 1986; Shade 1982). (See also, Boykin in chapter 13.)

Hollins' (1990a) investigation of what works for inner city African American students suggests that there are three categories of educational approaches that have demonstrated some level of effectiveness. These categories include strategies designed to remediate or accelerate with no attention being paid to students' social or cultural needs, strategies designed to re-socialize African American students to mainstream ways along with imparting basic skills, and, strategies designed to facilitate student learning by employing students' social and cultural backgrounds. Hollins identifies Chicago's Westside Preparatory School founded by Marva Collins as an example of an instructional program that employs students' social and cultural backgrounds and does not include implicit or explicit attempts at re-socializing African American learners. This third category is consistent with other examples anthropologists have considered effective in diverse cultural settings.

Culturally congruent, (Au & Jordan 1981;), culturally appropriate (Cazden & Leggett 1981; Erickson & Mohatt 1982, Jordan 1985;), culturally responsive (Mohatt & Erickson 1981;) and culturally compatible (Vogt, Jordan & Tharp 1987) are terms used to describe how the curriculum of the schools can be made more accessible to culturally diverse learners (See also, Au & Kawakami in chapter 1 and Pewewardy in chapter 4 of this volume). In a challenge to these sociolinguistic analyses Villegas (1988) suggests that the difficulties that students of color experience in school are far more complex than "differences between the language and culture of home and school" (p. 262). According to Villegas, culturally diverse students' school failure results from societal conflict and struggle for power. This view is consistent with the work of critical theorists like Giroux (1983) and McLaren (1989). Some African American scholars have argued that although they are in agreement with the critical theorists about schools as a battleground for the struggle for power and the exercise of authority, the failure of these theorists to adequately examine the special historical, social, economic and political role that race plays in the United States leaves their arguments lacking (Asante 1987; King & Mitchell 1990).

Some researchers have focused on the significance of teacher expectations and its effect on student achievement (Crano & Mellon 1978; Cooper 1979; Smith 1980). In her work on teacher beliefs and expectations, Winfield (1986) suggests that teachers' beliefs towards inner urban students can be categorized along the dimensions of improvement versus maintenance and assuming versus shifting responsibility. Her cross-classification yields four possibilities of teacher belief/behavior patterns—tutors, general contractors, custodians and referral agents. The tutors believe that the students can improve and they believe it is their responsibility to help them improve. The general contractors believe also that improvement is possible but they look for ancillary personnel (aides, resource teachers, etc.) to provide academic assistance. The custodians do not believe much can be done to help the students but they do not look for others to help them maintain the students at these low levels. Like the custodians, the referral agents do not believe that much can be done to help students improve. However, they shift the responsibility for maintaining low levels on to others like the school psychologist or special education personnel. It can be argued that these low levels of expectation and negative beliefs about African American learners are related to the societal invalidation of African American culture, as King discusses in chapter 2 of this volume (Ladson-Billings & King 1990; King & Wilson 1990).

An alternative conception, "culturally relevant" teaching (Ladson-Billings 1990; 1991), utilizes student culture as a way to both maintain student culture and transcend the negative effects of the dominant culture. The primary aim of culturally relevant teaching is to assist in the development of a "relevant Black personality" (Ladson-Billings & King 1990) that allows students to choose academic excellence and simultaneously identify with African and African American culture. Culturally relevant teachers are identified by the way they see themselves and others. They see teaching as an art rather than a technical task. They believe all of their students can succeed rather than believing failure is inevitable for some students. They see themselves as a part of the community and teaching as giving back to the community. They help students make connections between their community, national, ethnic and global identities. Culturally relevant teachers are also identified by the ways in which they structure classroom social interactions. Their teacher-student relationships are fluid, humanely equitable, and extend to interactions beyond the classroom. They demonstrate a connectedness with all of their students and encourage that same connectedness among the students. They encourage a community of learners and encourage their students to learn collaboratively. Finally, culturally relevant teachers are identified by their conceptions of knowledge. They believe that knowledge is continuously recreated, recycled and shared by both teachers and students. They view the content of the curriculum critically and are passionate about the content. Rather than expecting students to demonstrate prerequisite knowledge and skills, they help students develop those prerequisites by building bridges or scaffolding for learning.

The majority of the studies that examine how classroom teachers can better meet the educational needs of culturally diverse students focus on examples of practitioners who are effective and not on ways that teacher education programs can change and incorporate their methodology. Goodlad (1990b) suggests that the linkage between schooling and teacher induction guarantees that there will be little change in teaching because "tomorrow's teachers are mentored by today's" (p. 185). At the level of colleges, schools or departments of education, Goodlad (1990b) further suggests that teacher preparation programs continue to suffer from low prestige and status, unclear missions and identity, faculty disquietude, and ill-defined study body, and lack of program coherence. Unfortunately, meeting the needs of African American learners is given low priority in the face of these overwhelming systemic problems facing teacher education.

Rather than capitalize on the culture, most of the research literature on successfully teaching African American learners has focused on the "effective schools" model (Brookover 1985; Edmonds 1979). This model emphasizes strong instructional leadership by the administration, high expectations for achievement, an emphasis on basic skills, an orderly environment, increased time-on-task, and frequent, systematic evaluations of students. But there has been criticism of the effective schools approach as a practical strategy for meeting the needs of African American learners (Stedman 1987). Stedman suggests that an alternative conception of effectiveness includes ethnic and racial pluralism, parent participation, shared governance with teachers and parents, academically rich programs, skilled use and training of teachers, personal attention to students, student responsibility for school affairs, an accepting and supportive environment, and teaching aimed at preventing academic problems. (See also, Michele Foster's discussion of the significance of teacher ethnicity in chapter 12 of this volume.)

Some Reasons for Hope

There are, perhaps, three bright spots that may point the way for improving the preparation of teachers for African American learners. One is the success of the Black Independent School movement, another is the proactive response of those preparing teachers for language minority students, and the third includes a number of isolated programs and courses that have demonstrated modest but impressive results with prospective teachers of African American (and other culturally diverse) learners. Other authors in Part II address such proactive responses.

Both the Council for Independent Black Institutions (CIBI) and the Institute for Independent Education (IIE) report that there are schools and programs outside of the public arena that are successfully meeting the needs of African American learners. Programs like Chicago's Westside Preparatory School, founded by Marva Collins, post impressive academic gains among African American learners. There is documentation to suggest that African American learners in Catholic schools, even in the most economically depressed communities, outperform their peers in public schools (Steers 1990). However, it can be argued that these independent schools serve a population that is already motivated to achieve more than public schools expect and whose parents are prepared to examine educational programs carefully and critically. It is interesting to note that many of the religious and independent schools do not require teachers to have the same level of professional preparation that is necessary for public school licensure. This suggests that something other than conventional preparation is necessary for teachers who seek to be successful with African American learners. The typical sequence of foundations courses in education, followed by methods courses and a six to twelve week student teaching experience does not adequately prepare students for successful teaching of white middle-income students (Goodlad 1990c; Goodlad, Soder, & Sirotnik 1990). Thus, the added challenge of successfully teaching African American students is rarely considered.[1]

While the literature has been particularly sparse in the areas of preparing teachers for successfully teaching African American learners, there appears to be more extensive research and documentation of programs designed to prepare teachers for teaching linguistically diverse students. Cummins (1986) has provided a theoretical framework for understanding ways in which linguistic minority students can be successfully taught. Additionally, Moll (1988) has identified important aspects of successful pedagogy for Latino students. Garcia (1990) concludes that even though the production of competent teachers has lagged, the research base, instructional practices, and organizations are in place and vital for preparing these teachers. Garcia also concludes that the literature for preparing teachers to teach the linguistically diverse is rapidly expanding.

I contend that the reason for this burgeoning research is twofold. On the one hand there are growing linguistically diverse populations entering our schools. Thus, the need for instructional strategies are immediate and acute. The other reason lies in the fact that the cultures of these diverse linguistic populations are seen as legitimate—and they are. This does not mean that linguistically diverse learners do not suffer from negative treatment from schools and teachers (Hakuta 1985; Garcia 1988), but their educational needs and strengths are often seen as rooted in their culture. However, African Americans continue to suffer from a nebulous cultural status in this society. Because their academic problems continue to be associated solely with the effects of poverty, deprivation and discrimination, the needs of African American learners are defined primarily in economic and social psychological terms. However, we know that "in addition to stereotypic beliefs about poor children in general, teachers can develop lower expectations for and perceptions of the academic abilities of black students based on negative evaluations of and ethnocentric reactions to 'Africanity,' 'blackness,' or the African American expressive cultural style" (Ladson-Billings & King 1990). Although African American scholars and researchers are faced with a series of professional obstacles including individual and institutional racism and lack of mentoring and support (Frierson 1990), they bear some responsibility for addressing this literature void. More of their work must be directed at finding better ways to articulate the culture and to investigate the most successful ways to educate African American learners. Several of these issues are taken up in Part III of this volume.

On a smaller scale and less well-disseminated level are the individual teachers and teacher preparation programs that have attempted to focus their efforts towards preparing teachers for diversity. Hollins' (1990b) description of her work with white pre-service teachers centers on ways to help these teachers understand their own cultural heritage as a vehicle for developing an understanding of cultural backgrounds different from their own. Diez (1988) and Reed and Diez (1989) described a change at Alverno College (Milwaukee, WI) that emphasized the development of teaching abilities that will prepare teachers for working in multiple and diverse contexts. It is significant that this change at Alverno took almost ten years to implement. King and Ladson-Billings (1990) have described their attempts to help students consider multicultural competence and critical perspectives "as a continuum that begins with self-awareness and knowledge and extends to thinking critically about society and making a commitment to tranformative teaching" (p. 26). Both King and Ladson-Billings are African American teacher educators who work with predominantly white, upper middle class preservice teachers. Thus, some aspect of their work involves helping students to understand that the need for attention to issues of diversity extends beyond the personal and research agendas of the professors.

Conclusion

Countless discussions and studies about African American learners have fostered a tradition of viewing African American learners as deficient. This tradition that has been maintained through the language of deficiency has sought for ways to make African American learners just like whites. Very little of this literature has supported the integrity of African American culture as a way to develop and maintain academic excellence. Moreover, the literature is extremely limited in addressing the preparation of teachers for successfully teaching African American learners.

The efforts mentioned in the preceding section of this chapter suggest that there are avenues that can be explored to help expand the knowledge base for preparing teachers to educate African American learners. These efforts suggest some broad implications for the preparation of teachers.

1. *Prospective teachers need to systematically study the long history of African American education.* Even during the slavery, when teaching a slave to read was illegal, African Americans craved an education. From the midnight slave schools, to the early African American colleges, the citizenship schools of the 1950s, the freedom schools of the 1960s, and the current independent schools, this desire for learning has persisted. Teacher educators need to help pro-

spective teachers examine the current educational crisis in its full historical, socio-political and economic context. This history may help prospective teachers understand that African Americans have always taken responsibility for educating themselves and must have a significant role in combating these contemporary educational setbacks.

2. *There is a need for clearer and more plentiful explanations of African American culture as a vehicle for better understanding African American learners.* These explanations must correct the distortions that exist about Africa and African Americans. They will help situate African and African American history in their rightful places in the development of the world and the nation. They may help prospective teachers to see African American culture as legitimate and distinct yet connected to various cultures throughout the nation. Indeed, Latinos, Asians, Native Americans, and Europeans share cultural heritages with Africans and African Americans. In much the same way that educators have begun to endorse the need for systematic training for linguistically diverse students, this cultural information may make the same need apparent for African American leaders.

3. *There is a need for more and better scholarly investigations of the pedagogy of those teachers who are successful with African American learners.* These close to the classroom investigations will give researchers a better understanding of the array of teaching behaviors and beliefs that support African American learners in multiple contexts. These teachers, through their "wisdom of practice" (Shulman 1987) can help researchers begin to construct new paradigms for teacher education that may prove beneficial to all learners. Coupled with these K–12 investigations, we need to work more closely with the historically Black colleges and universities. The evidence is clear that African American collegians fare much better in historically Black colleges and universities where they have higher retention and graduation rates (Fleming 1984). This suggests that researchers should pay closer attention to what is happening at these institutions as we begin to formulate a knowledge base for teaching African American learners.

4. *There is a need to develop a more extensive network for advocacy on behalf of African American learners.* The whimsical nature of the public's interest and concerns mandates well developed, ongoing structures and organizations to keep the needs of African American learners in the forefront of educational debates. No matter what the educational issue, the question needs to be asked, "But what does this mean for African American learners?" In addition to

developing organizations and associations to support research, development and implementation of programs and designs for African American learners, we need more of a voice and a presence in existing mainstream professional and community-based organizations. Advocates for African American learners cannot exist solely as special interest groups because their "special" interest is ultimately in the interest of the maintenance of a multicultural and democratic society. Their advocacy must extend beyond professional and community organizations into educational policy making bodies and research associations. The sustained effort required to meet the educational needs of African American learners is a part of the overall commitment of the nation to educate all learners.

African American learners are in a crisis situation. There is much work to be done in the preparation of teachers for African American learners. The scope of this work is unduly broadened by the lack of a coherent and useful knowledge base. Fortunately, scholars who have been particularly interested in African American learners (e.g., Boykin 1978; Hilliard 1976; Hale-Benson 1986; Irvine 1990; Hollins 1990a; King 1991) have begun to lay a good foundation and provided a starting point. There needs to be more systematic and concentrated study to develop this research base. There is a need for a variety of studies, employing a variety of methodologies and from the perspectives of various disciplines. This challenge is so great that there need not be "turf wars" over who will participate. Indeed, the Bible says, "The harvest is plentiful but the laborers are few."

Note

1. A school administrator in a predominantly African American school remarked that many of the student teachers she received from a local state university understood their assignment to the school to be "just something they had to endure" to verify they had had an "inner city experience." They felt their "real teaching" would begin when they were placed in the suburban school.

Part II: References

Anderson, R. C., Heibert, E. H., Scott, J. A., & Wilkinson, I. A. G. (1985). *Becoming a nation of readers*. Washington, D.C.: United States Department of Education.

Anyon, J. (1980). Social class and the hidden curriculum of work. *Journal of Education, 162*:67–92

Appalachian Educational Laboratory (1988). *AEL Interim Report of the Status of Rural Education in the AEL Region.* Charleston, WV: Appalachian Educational Laboratory, (ERIC Document Reproduction Service No. ED 313 200).

Appalachian Land Ownership Task Force (1983). *Who owns Appalachia? Landownership and its impact.* Lexington: The University Press of Kentucky.

Arenas, S. (July/August 1978). Bilingual/bicultural programs for preschool children. *Children Today, 43*–48.

Asante, M. K. (February 1989). Build lessons from students' heritage. *New Jersey Educational Association Review, 21*–22.

Asante, M. K. (1987). *The Afrocentric idea.* Philadelphia: Temple University Press.

Au, K. & Jordan, C. (1981). Teaching reading to Hawaiian children: Finding a culturally appropriate solution. In H. Trueba et al. (Eds.). *Culture and the bilingual classroom: Studies in classroom ethnography,* pp. 139–152. Rowley, MA: Newbury House.

Austin, G. (1979). Exemplary schools and the search for effectiveness. *Educational Leadership, 37*:10–14.

Bagby, J. W., Carpenter, C., Crew, K., De Young, A., Eller, R., Hougland, J., Jones, J., Nash, F., & Tickamyer C. (1985). *Education and financial resources in Appalachian Kentucky,* (Appalachian Data Bank Report #2). Lexington: University of Kentucky Appalachian Center.

Baldwin, J. (Dec. 21, 1963). The Negro child—His self-image. *The Saturday Review.*

Banks, J. A. (1980). The emergence of a capitalistic labor market in eastern Kentucky. *Appalachian Journal, 3*:188–198.

Banks, J. A. (1988). Ethnicity, class, cognitive, and motivational styles: Research and teaching implications. *Journal of Negro Education, 57* (4):452–466.

Banks, J. A. (1973). Curriculum strategies for Black liberation. *School Review, 81*:404–414.

Batteau, A. (1983). Rituals of dependence in Appalachian Kentucky. In A. Batteau (Ed.). *Appalachia and America: Autonomy and regional dependence,* pp. 142–167. Lexington: University Press of Kentucky.

Beaver, P. D. (1986). *Rural community in the Appalachian South*. Lexington: University Press of Kentucky.

Bennett, K. P. (1991). Doing school in an urban Appalachian first grade. In C. E. Sleeter (Ed.). *Empowerment through multicultural education*, pp. 27–47. Albany: State University of New York Press.

Bettleheim, B. (1965). Teaching the disadvantaged. *National Educational Association Journal, 54:*8–12.

Billings, D. B., & Goldman, R. (1983). Religion and class consciousness in the Kanawha County school textbook controversy. In A. Batteau (Ed.). *Appalachia and America: Autonomy and regional dependence*, pp. 68–85. Lexington: University Press of Kentucky.

Bloom, A. (1987). *The closing of the American mind*. New York: Simon and Schuster, Inc.

Bloom, B., Davis, A., & Hess, R. (1965). *Compensatory education for cultural deprivation*. New York: Holt, Rinehart & Winston.

Borman, K. M., Mueninghoff, E., & Piazza, S. (1988). Urban Appalachian girls and young women: Bowing to no one. In L. Weis (Ed.). *Class, race, and gender in American education*, pp. 230–248. Albany: State University of New York Press.

Boyd, T. A. (1987). The manipulation of symbols in one school consolidation struggle. *Education in Appalachia: Proceedings from the 1987 Conference on Appalachia*, pp. 33–39. Lexington: University of Kentucky Appalachian Center.

Boyd, T., & De Young, A. (1986). Experts vs. amateurs: The irony of school consolidation in Jackson County, Kentucky. *Appalachian Journal, 13:*275–283.

Boykin, A. W. (1978). Psychological/behavioral verve in academic/task performance: Pretheoretical considerations. *Journal of Negro Education, 47:*343–54.

Branscome, J. (1974). The case for Appalachian studies. In M. Clark, J. Branscome, & B. Snyder (Eds.). *Miseducation in Appalachia*, pp. 14–37. Huntington, WV: Appalachian Press.

Branscome, J. (1978). Annihilating the hillbilly: The Appalachian's struggle with America's institutions. In H. M. Lewis, L. Johnson, & D. Askins (Eds.). *Colonialism in modern America: The Appalachian case*, pp. 211–227. Boone, NC: Appalachian Consortium Press.

Brizius, J. A., Foster, S. E., & Patton, H. M. (June 1988). *Education reform in rural Appalachia, 1982–1987*. Washington, DC: Appalachian Regional Commission.

Brookover, W. B. & Lezotte, L. (1979). Changes in school characteristics coincident with changes in student achievement. Unpublished paper, Michigan State University, ERIC ED 181 005.

Brookover, W. B. (1985). Can we make schools effective for minority students? *Journal of Negro Education 54:*257–268.

Brown, C. (1966). *Manchild in the promised land.* New York: Signet.

Brown, R. G. (1991). *Schools of thought: How the politics of literacy shape thinking in the classroom.* San Francisco: Jossey-Bass.

California State Department of Education. (1984). Studies on immersion education. Sacramento, CA: Author.

Carrasco, R. L. (1984). *Collective engagement in the 'segundo hogar': A microethnography of engagement in a bilingual first grade classroom.* Unpublished doctoral dissertation, Harvard University, Cambridge, MA.

Carter, T. P. & Chatfield, M. L. (1986). Effective bilingual schools: Implications for policy and practice. *American Journal of Education, 95* (1):200–234.

Caudill, H. M. (1963). *Night comes to the Cumberlands: A biography of a depressed area.* Boston: Little, Brown & Co.

Cazden, C. & Leggett, E. (1981). Culturally responsive education: Recommendations for achieving Lau remedies II. In H. Trueba et al. (Eds.). *Culture and the bilingual classroom: Studies in classroom ethnography,* pp. 69–86. Rowley, MA: Newbury House.

Center for Education Statistics (1987). *The condition of education.* Washington, DC: U.S. Government Printing Office.

Christie, F. (1985). Language and schooling. In S. N. Tchudi (Ed.). *Language, schooling, and society,* pp. 21–40. Upper Montclair, NJ: Boynton/Cook.

Clark, K. (1965). *Dark ghetto.* New York: Harper.

Clement-Brutto, S. (1987). Community response to educational policy: A case from rural Kentucky. *Education in Appalachia: Proceedings from the 1987 Conference on Appalachia,* pp. 25–32. Lexington: University of Kentucky Appalachian Center.

Cole, M. & Griffin, P. (Eds.). (1987). *Contextual factors in education. Improving mathematics and science instruction for minorities and women.* Madison, WI: Wisconsin Center for Educational Research, School of Education, University of Wisconsin.

Cooper, H. (1979). Pygmalion grows up: A model for teacher expectation communication and performance influence. *Review of Educational Research, 49* (3):389–410.

Coughlin, E. K. (1990). Despite successes, scholars express ambivalence about place of minority literature in academe. *Chronicle of Higher Education, 35* (17):A7–A13.

Crano, W. & Mellon, P. (1978). Causal influences of teachers' expectations of children's academic performance: A cross-lagged panel analysis. *Journal of Educational Psychology, 70,* (1):39–49.

Crawford, J. (1989). Language freedom and restriction: A historical approach to the official English controversy. In J. Reyhner (Ed.). *Effective language education practices and native languages survival.* Billings, MT: Eastern Montana College.

Crew, B. K. (1985). *Dropout and functional illiteracy rates in Central Appalachia,* (Appalachian Data Bank Report #1). Lexington: University of Kentucky Appalachian Center.

Cuban, L. (1990). Four stories about national goals for American education. *Phi Delta Kappan, 72* (4):264–271.

Cuban, L. (1989). The 'at-risk' label and the problem of urban school reform. *Phi Delta Kappan, 70* (10):780–784, 799–801.

Cummins, J. (1986). Empowering minority students: A framework for intervention. *Harvard Educational Review, 56* (1):18–36.

Daniels, D. (Ed.). (1972). *Education by, for, and about African-Americans.* University of Nebraska: The Nebraska Curriculum Development Center.

De Young, A. J. (1985). Economic development and educational status in Appalachian Kentucky. *Comparative Education Review, 29:*47–67.

De Young, A. J., Vaught, C., & Porter, J. D. (1981). Evaluating educational performance in Appalachian Kentucky. *Appalachian Journal, 8:*50–58.

Deloria, V. (1974). *The Indian affair.* New York: Friendship Press.

Delpit, L. D. (1988). The silenced dialogue: Power and pedagogy in educating other people's children. *Harvard Educational Review, 58:*280–298.

Diez, M. (1988). A thrust from within: Reconceptualizing teacher education at Alverno College. *Peabody Journal of Education, 65* (2):4–18.

Doll, R. & Hawkins, M. (1971). *Educating the disadvantaged.* New York: AMS Press.

Duncan, C. (1987). What do people in the Fifth District think about education? *Education in Appalachia: Proceedings from the 1987 Conference on Appalachia,* p. 139. Lexington: University of Kentucky Appalachian Center.

Dunn, R. & Dunn, K. (1979). Learning styles/teaching styles: Should they ... can they ... be matched? *Educational Leadership, 36* (4):238–244.

Edmonds, R. (1970). Effective schools for the urban poor. *Educational Leadership, 37:*15–24.

Education Week, (May 14, 1986). Special Report. Ready or not, here they come.

Eller, R. D. (1982). *Miners, millhands, and mountaineers: Industrialization of the Appalachian South, 1880–1930.* Knoxville: University of Tennessee Press.

Eller, R. G. (1989a). *Teacher resistance and educational change: Toward a critical theory of literacy in Appalachia.* Unpublished doctoral dissertation, University of Kentucky, Lexington, KY.

Eller, R. G. (1989b). Ways of meaning: Exploring cultural differences in students' writing compositions. *Linguistics and Education, 1:*341–358.

Elmore, R. F. (1989). How we teach is what we teach. *AAHE Bulletin, 41:*11–14.

Erickson, F. (1977). Some approaches to inquiry in school-community ethnography. *Anthropology and Education Quarterly, 8:*58–69.

Erickson, F. & Mohatt, G. (1982). Cultural organization and participation structures in two classrooms of Indian students. In G. Spindler (Ed.). *Doing the Ethnography of Schooling,* pp. 131–174. New York: Holt, Rinehart & Winston.

Erickson, F. & Schultz, J. (1981). When is a context? Some issues and methods in the analysis of social competence. In J. Green & C. Wallat (Eds.). *Ethnography and language in educational settings,* pp. 147–160. Norwood, NJ: Ablex Publishing.

Fleming, J. (1984). *Blacks in college.* San Francisco: Jossey-Bass.

Fortune Magazine (Spring 1990). Special issue, Saving our schools.

Ford, T. R. (1962). The passing of provincialism. In T. R. Ford (Ed.). *The southern Appalachian region: A survey,* pp. 9–34. Lexington, University of Kentucky Press.

Foxfire, Inc. (n.d.). *Hands On.* Rabun Gap, GA: Author.

Freire, P. (1978). *Pedagogy in process.* New York: Seabury Press.

Freire, P. (1970). *Pedagogy of the oppressed.* (M. Bergman Ramos, trans.) New York: Herder & Herder. (Original work published 1968).

Frierson, H. T. (1990). Black researchers: Continuation of a crisis. *Educational Researcher, 19* (2):12–17.

Frost, N. (1915). *A statistical study of the public schools in the Southern Appalachian mountains,* (Bulletin No. 11). Washington, DC: U.S. Government Printing Office.

Garcia, E. (1990). Educating teachers for language minority students. In W. R. Houston (Ed.). *Handbook of research on teacher education,* pp. 717–729. New York: Macmillan Publishing Co.

Garcia, E. (1988). Effective schooling for language minority students. In National Clearing-house for Bilingual Education (Ed.). *New Focus.* Arlington, VA.

Garcia, E. (1986). Bilingual development and the education of bilingual children during early childhood. *American Journal of Education, 95* (1):96–121.

Garcia, E. & August, D. (1988). *The education of language minority students in the United States.* Springfield, IL: Charles C. Thomas.

Garcia, E., Flores, B., Moll, L., Prieto, A. (1988). *Effective schooling for Hispanics: A final report.* Tempe AZ: Bilingual/Bicultural Education Center, Arizona State University.

Gaumnitz, W. H. (1933). Extent and nature of public education in the mountains. *Mountain Life and Work, 9* (2):20–25.

Gephart, W., Strother, D., & Duckett, W. (1980). On mixing and matching of teaching and learning styles. *Practical Applications of Research, 3* (2):1–4.

Gilmore, P. (1987). Sulking, stepping, and tracking: The effects of attitude assessment on access to literacy. In D. Bloome (Ed.). *Literacy and schooling,* pp. 98–120. Norwood, NJ: Ablex.

Giroux, H. A. (1983). *Theory and resistance in education.* South Hadley, MA: Bergin & Garvey Publishers.

Giroux, H. A. (1988). *Teachers as intellectuals: Toward a critical pedagogy of learning.* South Hadley, MA: Bergin & Garvey.

Giroux H. A. (1983). *Theory & resistance in education: A pedagogy for the opposition.* South Hadley, MA: Bergin & Garvey.

Goldenberg, C. N. (1989). Making success a more common occurrence for children at risk for failure: Lessons from Hispanic first graders learning to read. In J. Allen & J. M. Mason (Eds.). *Risk makers, risk takers, risk breakers: Reducing the risks for young literacy learners,* pp. 48–79. Portsmouth, NH: Heinemann.

Goodlad, J. (1990a). Common schools for the common weal: Reconciling self-interest with the common good. In John Goodlad and Pamela Keating (Eds.). *Access to knowledge: An agenda for our nation's schools,* pp. 3–21. New York: College Entrance Examination Board.

Goodlad, J. (1990b). Better teachers for our nation's schools. *Phi Delta Kappan, 72* (3):184–194.

Goodlad, J. (1990c). *Teachers for our nation's schools.* San Francisco, CA: Jossey-Bass.

Goodlad, J. (1984). *A place called school.* New York: McGraw-Hill.

Goodlad, J., Soder, R. & Sirotnik, K. (Eds.). (1990). *Places where teachers are taught.* San Francisco: Jossey-Bass.

Grant, C. (1990). Urban teachers: Their new colleagues and the curriculum. *Phi Delta Kappan, 70* (10):764–770.

Grant, C. & Secada, W. (1990). Preparing teachers for diversity. In W. R. Houston (Ed.). *Handbook of research on teacher education,* pp. 403–422. New York: Macmillan Publishing Co.

Grant, L. & Rothenberg, J. (1986). The social enhancement of ability differences: Teacher-student interactions in first- and second-grade reading groups. *The Elementary School Journal, 87:*29–49.

Greenberg, J. B. (1989). *Funds of knowledge: Historical constitution, social distribution and transmission.* Paper presented at the annual meeting of the Society for Applied Anthropology. Santa Fe, NM.

Gumperz, J. (1985). The speech community. In P. P. Giglioli (Ed.). *Language and social context,* pp. 219–231. New York: Viking Penguin.

Haberman, M. (1989). More minority teachers. *Phi Delta Kappan, 70* (10):771–779.

Hakuta, K. (1985). *Mirror of language: The debate on bilingualism.* New York: Basic Books.

Hakuta, K. & Gould, L. J. (1987). Synthesis of research in bilingual education. *Educational Leadership, 44* (6):39–45.

Halcon, J. (1981). Features of federal bilingual programs. *NABE Journal, 6* (1):27–39.

Hale-Benson, J. (1986). *Black children: Their roots, culture and learning styles* (revised edition). Baltimore: Johns Hopkins University Press.

Harris, V. (1990). *At risk: A world view of problems and solutions.* Paper presented at the annual meeting of the National Reading Conference. Miami, FL.

Hazi, H. M. (1989). *Teachers and the Recht decision: A West Virginia case study of school reform.* Charleston, WV: Appalachian Educational Laboratory. (ERIC Document Reproduction Service No. ED 318 597).

Heath, S. G. (1985). Literacy or literate skills? Consideration for ESL/EFL learners. In P. Larson, E. L. Judd, & Messerschmidt (Eds.). *On Tesol '84: A brave new world for TESOL*. Washington, DC: TESOL.

Heath, S. B. (1983). *Ways with words: Language, life, and work in communities and classrooms*. Cambridge: Cambridge University Press.

Hicks, G. L. (1976). *Appalachian valley*. New York: Holt, Rinehart & Winston.

Hilliard, A. (1976). *Alternatives to IQ testing: An approach to the identification of gifted minority children*. Final report to the California State Department of Education. Sacramento, CA.

Hirsch, E. D. (1988). *The dictionary of cultural literacy*. Boston: Houghton Mifflin.

Hirsch, E. D. (1987). *Cultural literacy: What every American needs to know*. Boston: Houghton Mifflin.

Hodgkinson, H. (1985). *All one system: Demographics of education—kindergarten through graduate school*. Washington, DC: Institute for Educational Leadership.

Hollins, E. R. (1990a). *A re-examination of what works for inner city Black children*. Paper presented at the annual meeting of the American Educational Research Association meeting. Boston, MA.

Hollins, E. R. (1990b). Debunking the myth of a monolithic white American culture; or, moving toward cultural inclusion. *American Behavioral Scientist, 34* (2):201–209.

Huber, T. & Pewewardy, C. D. (1990). A review of literature to determine successful programs for and approaches to maximizing learning for diverse learners. *Collected Original Resources in Education* (CORE), *14* (3). An International Journal of Educational Research in Microfiche: Birmingham, West Midlands, Great Britain.

Hyram, G. (1972). *Challenge to society: The education of the culturally disadvantaged child*. Vol. 1. New York: Pageant-Poseidon, Ltd.

Irvine, J. J. (1990). *Black students and school failure: Policies, practices and prescriptions*. Westport, CT: Greenwood Press.

Irvine, J. J. (1990). Transforming teaching for the twenty-first century. *Educational Horizons, 69* (1):16–21.

Jordan, C. (1985). Translating culture: From ethnographic information to educational program. *Anthropology and Education Quarterly, 16* (2):105–123.

Jordan, J. (1988). Nobody mean more to me than you and the future life of Willie Jordan. *Harvard Educational Review, 58:*363–374.

Karmiloff-Smith, A. & Inhelder, B. (1975). If you want to get ahead, get a theory. *Cognition, 3:*199–212.

Keefe, S. E., Reck, U. M., & Reck, G. G. (1987). *The context of education in an Appalachian county,* (NSF Grant No. BNS–8218234). Boone, NC: Appalachian State University.

Kennedy, M., Jung, R., & Orland, M. (1986). *Poverty, achievement, and the distribution of compensatory education services,* (An interim report from the National Assessment of Chapter 1). Washington, DC: U.S. Government Printing Office.

King, J. (1991). Unfinished business: Black student alienation and black teachers' emancipatory pedagogy. In M. Foster (Ed.). *Readings on equal education, 11:*245–271. New York: AMS Press.

King, J. & Ladson-Billings, G. (1990). The teacher education challenge in elite university settings: Developing critical perspectives for teaching in a democratic and multicultural society. *European Journal of Intercultural Studies, 1* (2):15–30.

King, J. & Mitchell, C. A. (1990). *Black mothers to sons: Juxtaposing African American literature with social practice.* New York: Peter Lang.

Komoski, P. K. (1990). Needed: A whole-curriculum approach. *Educational Leadership, 47* (5):72–78.

Kublawi, S. (1986). The economy of Appalachia in the national context. *The land and economy of Appalachia: Proceedings of the 1986 Conference on Appalachia,* pp. 16–24. Lexington: University of Kentucky Appalachian Center.

Kuhn, T. S. (1970). *The structure of scientific revolutions.* Chicago: The University Press.

Kunjufu, J. (1984). *Developing discipline and positive self-images in Black children.* Chicago, IL: Afro-American Images.

Ladson-Billings, G. (1991). Like lightning in a bottle: Attempting to capture the pedagogical excellence of successful teachers of Black students. *International Journal of Qualitative Studies in Education, 3* (4):335–344.

Ladson-Billings, G. (1990). Culturally relevant teaching: Effective instruction for Black students. *The College Board Review, 155:*20–25.

Ladson-Billings, G. & King, J. (1990). *Cultural identity of African-Americans: Implications for achievement.* Aurora, CO: Mid-Continental Regional Educational Laboratory (MCREL).

Lave, J. (1988). *Cognition in practice.* Cambridge: Cambridge University Press.

Lewis, H. M., & Knipe, E. E. (1978). The colonialism model: The Appalachian case. In H. M. Lewis, L. Johnson, & D. Askins (Eds.). *Colonialism in modern America: The Appalachian case*, pp. 9–31. Boone, NC: Appalachian Consortium Press.

Lewis, H. M., Kobak, S. E., & Johnson, L. (1978). Family religion and colonialism in Central Appalachia, or bury my rifle at Big Stone Gap. In H. M. Lewis, L. Johnson, & D. Askins (Ed.). *Colonialism in modern America: The Appalachian case*, pp. 113–139. Boone, NC: Appalachian Consortium Press.

Lucas, T., Henze, R., & Donato, R. (1990). Promoting the success of Latino language-minority students: An exploratory study of six high schools. *Harvard Educational Review, 60:*315–328.

Martin, L. (1987). The politics of school reform in the eighties. *Education in Appalachia: Proceedings from the 1987 Conference on Appalachia*, pp. 59–63. Lexington: University of Kentucky Appalachian Center.

Martín-Baro, I. (1989). La investigación y el cambio social. *Cuadernos de investigación, 1:*7–22. Centro de Investigaciones Educativas, Facultad de Educación, Río Piedras, Universidad de Puerto Rico.

McCarthy, C. (1988). Rethinking liberal and radical perspectives on racial inequality in schooling: Making the case for nonsynchrony. *Harvard Educational Review, 58* (3):265–279.

McDermott, R. P. (1974). Achieving school failure: An anthropological approach to illiteracy and social stratification. In G. D. Spindler (Ed.). *Education and cultural process: Toward an anthropology of education*, pp. 82–118. New York: Holt, Rinehart, & Winston.

McDermott, R. P. & Gospodinoff, K. (1981). Social contexts for ethnic borders and school failure. In H. T. Trueba, G. P. Guthrie, K. H. Au (Eds.). *Culture and the bilingual classroom: Studies in classroom ethnography*, pp. 212–230. Rowley, MA: Newbury House Publishers.

McLaren, P. (1989). *Life in schools*. White Plains, NY: Longman.

Michaels, S. (1986). Narrative presentations: An oral preparation for literacy with first graders. In J. Cook-Gumperz (Ed.). *The social construction of literacy*, pp. 94–116. Cambridge: Cambridge University Press.

Michaels, S. (1981). "Sharing time": Children's narrative styles and differential access to literacy. *Language in Society, 10:*423–442

Miller, J. W. (1977). Appalachian education: A critique and suggestions for reform. *Appalachian Journal, 5:*13–22.

Miller, J. W. (1975). A mirror for Appalachia. In R. J. Higgs & A. N. Manning (Eds.). *Voices from the Hills: Selected readings of Southern Appalachia*, pp. 447–459. New York: Frederick Ungar.

Mitchell, J. (1982). Reflections of a Black social scientist: Some struggles, some doubts, some hopes. *Harvard Educational Review, 52* (1):27–44.

Mohatt, G. & Erickson, F. (1981). Cultural differences in teaching styles in an Odawa school: A sociolinguistic approach. In H. Trueba, G. P. Guthrie, & K. H. Au (Eds.). *Culture and the bilingual classroom: Studies in classroom ethnography*, pp. 105–119. Rowley, MA: Newbury House.

Moll, L. (1988). Some key issues in teaching Latino students. *Language Arts, 65* (5):465–472.

Moll, L. C. & Diaz, S. (1987). Change as the goal of educational research. In E. Jacob & C. Jordan (Eds.). *Explaining the school performance of minority students* [Theme Issue]. *Anthropology and Education Quarterly, 18:*300–311.

National Assessment of Educational Progress (1986). *Literacy: Profiles of America's young adults.* Princeton, NJ: Educational Testing Service.

National Education Association (November 1986). The mountains are moving. *Sixth NEA national conference on human rights in education conference report: Equality of educational opportunity for children of Appalachia.* Washington, DC: NEA.

Nobles, W. W. (1974). African root and American fruit: The Black family. *Journal of Social and Behavioral Sciences, 20:*52–63.

Oakes, J. (1985). *Keeping track: How schools structure inequality.* New Haven: Yale University Press.

Ogbu, J. U. (1987). Variability in minority school performance: A problem in search of an explanation. In E. Jacob and C. Jordan (Eds.). *Explaining the school performance of minority students* [Theme Issue]. *Anthropology and Education Quarterly, 18:*312–334.

Ornstein, A. (1971). The need for research on teaching the disadvantaged. *Journal of Negro Education, 40:*133–139.

Ornstein, A. & Vairo, P. (Eds.). (1968). *How to teach disadvantaged youth.* New York: David McKay, Co.

Ovando, C. J. & Collier, V. P. (1985). *Bilingual and ESL classrooms.* New York: McGraw-Hill Book Company.

Oxendine, L. (1989). *Dick and Jane are dead: Basal reader takes a back seat to student writings.* Charleston, WV: Appalachia Educational Laboratory, Policy and Planning Center.

Page, R. (1987). Teachers' perceptions of students: A link between classrooms, school cultures, and the social order. *Anthropology and Education Quarterly, 18:*77–99.

Pearson, P. D. & Dole, J. A. (1987). Explicit comprehension instruction: A review of research and a new conceptualization. *The Elementary School Journal, 88:*151–185.

Perry, T. D. (1975). *History of the American Teachers Association.* Washington, DC: National Education Association.

Pewewardy, C. D. (1990). *The effect of school environment on the academic performance of African-American and Native American college students.* Paper presented at the Fifteenth Annual Meeting, Association for the Study of Higher Education. Portland, Oregon.

Pewewardy C. D. (1989). *A study of perceptions of American Indian high school students attending public school.* Unpublished doctoral dissertation, The Pennsylvania State University, PA.

Piaget, J. (1959). *The language and thought of the child.* London: Routledge & Kegan Paul.

Piestrup, A. (1973). *Black dialect interference and accommodation of reading instruction in first grade,* (Monograph No. 4). Berkeley, CA: Language Behavior Research Laboratory.

Popkewitz, T. S. (1987). Ideology and social formation in teacher education. In T. S. Popkewitz (Ed.). *Critical studies in teacher education: Its folklore, theory and practice,* pp. 2–33. Philadelphia, PA: The Falmer Press.

Precourt, W. (1983). The image of Appalachian poverty. In A. Batteau (Ed.). *Appalachia and America: Autonomy and regional dependence,* pp. 86–110. Lexington: University Press of Kentucky.

Purkey, S. C. & Smith, M. S. (1983). Effective schools: A review. *Elementary School Journal, 83:*52–78.

Quintero, A. H. (1989). The University of Puerto Rico's partnership project with schools: A case study for the analysis of school improvement. *Harvard Educational Review, 59:*347–361.

Ramirez, A. (1984). *Bilingualism through schooling.* Albany: State University of New York Press.

Ramirez, M. & Castaneda, A. (1974). *Cultural democracy, bicognitive development and education,* New York: Academic Press.

Ravitch, D. (1990). Multiculturalism. *American Scholar, 59:*337–354.

Reck, U. M. (March 1982). *Self-concept, school, and social setting: An in-depth view of rural Appalachian and urban non-Appalachian sixth graders.* Paper presented at the annual meeting of the American Educational Research Association, New York, NY. (ERIC Document Reproduction Service No. ED 215 849).

Reck, G. G., Keefe, S. E., & Reck, M. (1987). Ethnicity and education in Southern Appalachia: Implications for educational equity. *Education in Appalachia: Proceedings from the 1987 Conference on Appalachia,* pp. 14–24. Lexington: University of Kentucky Appalachian Center.

Reck, U. M., Reck, G. G., & Keefe, S. (April 1987). *Teachers' perceptions of Appalachian and non-Appalachian students.* Paper presented at the meeting of the American Educational Research Association. Washington, D.C.

Reed, C. & Diez, M. (1989). *Empowerment for teachers in multicultural schools: Inviting the teaching-learning exchange.* Paper presented at the 3rd National Forum on Teacher Education Association of Independent Liberal Arts Colleges for Teacher Education. Butler University, Indianapolis, Indiana.

Reyhner, J. & Eder, J. (1989). *A history of Indian education.* Billings, MT: Eastern Montana College.

Rist, R. C. (1970). Student social class and teacher expectations: The self-fulfilling prophecy in ghetto education. *Harvard Educational Review, 40:*411–451.

Rosenbaum, J. E. (1976). *Making inequality: The hidden curriculum of high school tracking.* New York: John Wiley & Sons.

Roser, M. A. (June 1, 1988). Kentuckians may pay higher taxes because of ruling in school funding suit. *Lexington Herald-Leader,* p. A–1.

Sandoval-Martinez, R. (1982). Findings from the Head Start bilingual curriculum development and evaluation report. *NABE Journal,* 7:1–12.

Santos, S. L. (1986). Promoting intercultural understanding through multicultural teacher training. *Action in Teacher Education, 8* (1):19–25.

Schwarzweller, H. K. & Brown, J. S. (1971). Education as a cultural bridge between Appalachian Kentucky and the Great Society. In J. D. Photiadis & H. K. Schwarzweller (Eds.). *Change in rural Appalachia: Implications for action programs,* pp. 129–145. Philadelphia: University of Pennsylvania Press.

Shade, B. J. (1982). Afro-American cognitive style: A variable in school success? *Review of Educational Research, 52* (2):219–244.

Shapiro, H. D. (1978). *Appalachia on our mind: The southern mountains and mountaineers in the American consciousness, 1870–1920.* Chapel Hill: University of North Carolina Press.

Sher, J. (Ed.). (1977). *Education in rural America: A reassessment of conventional wisdom. Boulder, CO: Westview Press.*

Shulman, L. S. (1989). Teaching alone, learning together: Needed agendas for the new reforms. In T. J. Segiovanni & J. H. Moore (Eds.). *Schooling for tomorrow,* pp. 166–187. Boston: Allyn and Bacon.

Shulman, L. S. (1987). Knowledge and teaching: Foundations of the new reform. *Harvard Educational Review, 57* (1)1–22.

Simonson, R. & Walker, S. (1988). *Opening the American mind. The graywolf annual five: Multicultural literacy.* Saint Paul, MN: Graywolf Press.

Sizemore, B. (1972). Is there a case for separate schools? *Phi Delta Kappan, 53:*281–285.

Sleeter, C. (1989). Multicultural education as a form of resistance to oppression. *Journal of Education, 171* (3):51–71.

Sleeter, C. E. & Grant, C. A. (1991). Mapping terrains of power: Student cultural knowledge versus classroom knowledge. In C. E. Sleeter (Ed.). *Empowerment through multicultural education,* pp. 49–67. Albany: State University of New York Press.

Sleeter, C. E. & Grant, C. A. (1987). An analysis of multicultural education in the United States. *Harvard Educational Review, 57* (4):421–444.

Smith, M. (1980). Meta analyses of research on teacher expectation. *Evaluation in Education, 4:*53–55.

Smith, D. T. (1988). *Appalachia's last one room school: A case study.* Unpublished doctoral dissertation, University of Kentucky, Lexington, KY.

Spindler, G. D. (1974). Beth-Anne: A case study of culturally defined adjustment and teacher perceptions. In G. D. Spindler (Ed.). *Education and cultural process: Toward an anthropology of education.* New York: Holt, Rinehart & Winston.

Stedman, L. (1987). It's time we changed the effective schools formula. *Phi Delta Kappan, 69* (3):215–224.

Steers, S. (Dec. 23, 1990). The Catholic schools' black students. *San Francisco Chronicle, This World,* pp. 8 ff.

Strike, K. A. (1985). Is there a conflict between equity and excellence? *Educational Evaluation and Policy Analysis, 7:*409–416.

Stumbo, C. (1989). Beyond the classroom. *Harvard Educational Review, 59:*87–97.

Taylor, D. & Dorsey-Gaines, C.(1988). *Growing up literate: Learning from inner-city families.* Portsmouth, NH: Heinemann.

Tharp, R. & Gallimore, R. (1988). *Rousing minds to life: Teaching, learning, and schooling in social contexts.* Cambridge: Cambridge University Press.

Tickamyer, A.R. & Tickamyer, C. (1987). *Poverty in Appalachia,* (Appalachian Data Bank Report #5). Lexington: University of Kentucky Appalachian Center.

Tikunoff, W. J. (September 1983). *Significant bilingual instructional features study.* San Francisco, CA: Far West Laboratory.

Torres-Guzmán, M. E. (1992). Stories of hope in the midst of despair: Culturally responsive education for Latino students in an alternative high school in New York City. In M. Saravia-Shore & S. F. Arvizu, (Eds.). *Cross-cultural literacy: Ethnographies of communication in multiethnic classrooms,* pp. 477–490. New York: Garland Publishing.

Torres-Guzmán, M. E. (1990). *Bringing it closer to home.* Paper presented at the Ethnography Forum. University of Pennsylvania, Philadelphia, PA.

U.S. Department of Education (1986). *What works: Research about teaching and learning.* Washington, DC: Author.

Vélez-Ibañez, C. G. (1988). Network of exchange among Mexicans in the U.S. and Mexico: Local level mediating responses to national and international transformations. *Urban Anthropology, 17:*27–51.

Villegas, A. (1988). School failure and cultural mismatch: Another view, *The Urban Review, 20* (4):253–265.

Vogt, L., Jordan, C. & Tharp, R. (1987). Explaining school failure, producing school success: Two cases. *Anthropology and Education Quarterly, 18* (4):276–286.

Vygotsky. L. S. (1978). *Mind in society: The development of higher psychological process.* Cambridge: Harvard University Press.

Walls, D. S. (1978). Internal colony or internal periphery? A critique of current models and an alternative formulation. In H. M. Lewis, L. Johnson, and D. Askins (Eds.). *Colonialism in modern America: The Appalachian case,* pp. 319–349. Boone, NC: Appalachian Consortium Press.

Weller, J. (1975). Education. In R. J. Higgs & A. N. Manning (Eds.). *Voices from the hills: Selected readings of Southern Appalachia,* pp. 440–446. New York: Frederick Ungar.

Wells, G. (1986). *The meaning makers.* Portsmouth, NH: Heinemann.

Whisnant, D. E. (1983). *All that is native & fine: The politics of culture in an American region.* Chapel Hill: University of North Carolina Press.

Whitaker, L. (January 1989). The disappearing black teacher. *Ebony,* pp. 122–126.

Willing, A. C. (1985). A meta-analysis of selected studies on effectiveness of bilingual education. *Review of Educational Research, 55* (33):269–318.

Willis, P. (1977). *Learning to labor.* New York: Columbia University Press.

Winfield, L. (1986). Teacher beliefs toward at risk students in inner urban schools. *The Urban Review, 18* (4):253–267.

Wolfram, W. (1984). Is there an "Appalachian English?" *Appalachian Journal, 11:*215–224.

Wolfram, W. & Christian, D. (1976). *Appalachian speech.* Arlington, VA: Center for Applied Linguistics.

Wong-Fillmore, L., Ammon, P., McLaughlin, B. & Ammon, M. S. (1985). *Final report for learning English through bilingual instruction.* Washington, DC: NIE Report.

Woodson, C. G. (1933). *The miseducation of the Negro.* Washington, DC: Associated Publishers.

PART III

Taking a Closer Look at Schooling for One
Sociocultural Group: African Americans

Introduction

The first chapter in this section, "Benchmarks. . ." by Etta Hollins, Helen Smiler and Kathleen Spencer, traces the pattern of investigation into schooling for African American and other low income students. The authors identify five benchmarks that prompted changes in the direction of the research: (1) parallel studies in sociology and linguistics that spawned specific approaches and programs for schooling, (2) the transition from studies focused on the life conditions and experiences of African American children to effective instruction, effective schools, and finally, teacher effectiveness, (3) relating school practices to the daily lives of the students (cultural congruence and cultural compatibility), (4) creative and innovative projects outside the mainstream such as Project SEED, and (5) the potential of students' voices in informing investigations into schooling practices. This chapter shows how we arrived at our present state in research on schooling for African American students and suggests two possible areas for further investigation—innovative programs developed by those in fields other than education and employing the students themselves as informants.

The second chapter in this section, "Understanding the African-American Learner" by Barbara Shade, narrows the focus to two central questions: What conditions of classroom instruction are most likely to have a positive effect on the academic performance of African American learners? What influences the learning prefer-

ences of African American students? Shade's review of the literature provides a six part response that reveals characteristics of
African American learners and the conditions of classroom instruction most likely to have a positive effect on academic performance:
(1) teacher-peer-learner interaction, (2) classroom climate, (3) African American schemata, (4) effective teaching strategies, (5) communicative style, and (6) African American learning style. Cultural
practices and values undergird the learning preferences and thinking styles found among African American students. According to
Shade, teachers who are successful with these students act upon
the hypothesis that "the modal thinking style of African Americans
appears to be holistic, intuitive, and more integrative in the processing of information."

The third chapter in Part III, ". . . Misconceptions of African
American English . . . by John Baugh, extends the discussion on African American communicative style initiated in the previous chapter. Baugh's review of the research literature is focused on
responding to the question: What is the relationship between African American English, mathematical logic, and academic learning
in school? In responding to this question Baugh provides a brief historical account of the study of African American language, identifies common stereotypes and linguistic fallacies, points out the
significance of ethnographic relevance, and recommends ethnosensitive education as an alternative to traditional approaches to
teaching students who speak a nonstandard dialect of English or
English as a second language.

Culture and ethnicity are undergirding issues in the previous
chapters of this section. The fourth chapter in this section, "Ethnic
identity as a variable in the learning equation" by Curtis Branch,
responds to the question: What is the relationship between ethnic
identity and learning in school? In reviewing the research literature Branch identifies five issues related to this question: (1) the
relationship between ethnic identity and openness to academic excellence and academic competence, (2) ethnic labels that prescribe
attitudes about learning, (3) self-attributions that govern behavior
in the classroom, (4) the relationship between children's self-
attributions and teacher attributions, and (5) self-efficacy theory as
a theoretical framework for understanding differential performances in social and academic settings. Branch concludes that "ethnic identities assumed by individuals as well as those attributed to
them by others, have implications for the learning process because
they empower the learner to self-define. In the process of creating a

definition of one's self with little or no regard for how others see the defining individual, a sense of determinism and heightened self-esteem are likely to follow." The inference that can be made is that students with heightened self-esteem are likely to feel more confident and competent as they approach academic tasks.

The previous chapters in this section dealt with issues associated with culture or ethnicity and student academic performance. The fifth chapter in this section, "Effective Black Teachers. . ." by Michele Foster, responds to the question: What are the attributes, behaviors, pedagogical practices, and philosophy characteristic of effective African American teachers? In responding to this question Foster identifies the limitations of the literature in addressing African American teachers as a group. She then provides a detailed analysis of the pertinent literature revealing five attributes of effective African American teachers (1) cultural solidarity and connectedness, (2) linking classroom content to students' experiences, (3) a focus on the whole child, (4) use of familiar cultural patterns, and (5) incorporation of culturally compatible communication patterns. Foster concludes the chapter by raising the question as to whether or not the attributes of African American teachers can be effectively incorporated into teacher preparation programs. She provides examples of preservice programs aimed at preparing teachers for culturally diverse populations, but points out that they are in the early stages of implementation and their success cannot be determined.

The final chapter, "Afrocultural Expression and Its Implications for Schooling" by A. Wade Boykin, provides an appropriate epilogue for the entire book. Boykin challenges us to examine whether our research and restructuring of schools has any substantive meaning at all if we have not taken into account the seriously negative impact of the "culture of power" on the expression and integrity of other cultures and the consequences of students who are not from the dominant culture, particularly African American students. He challenges us to move beyond the present perimeters of multiculturalism and to consider the "deep structure" of culture in determining the purpose, content, process, and social context within schools.

CHAPTER 8

Benchmarks in Meeting the Challenges of Effective Schooling for African American Youngsters

ETTA R. HOLLINS, HELEN SMILER,
AND KATHLEEN SPENCER

Questions To Think About

1. What major research studies or publications have guided theory and research on schooling for African American students?
2. What are the most significant lessons researchers and practitioners can learn from data collected in the past on schooling for African American youngsters?
3. What is the relationship between the research directions discussed by Hollins, Smiler, and Spencer and the call for culture centered research in King's chapter?

Over the past three decades scholars and practitioners have wrestled with ways to conceptualize the challenges of effective schooling for African American youngsters. The purpose of this chapter is to identify "benchmarks" in this conceptualization process. Each of the benchmarks identified represents a turning point that spawned different approaches to the study and practice of classroom instruction.

It is important to note that the benchmarks in conceptualizing the challenges of effective schooling for African American youngsters draw upon and parallel studies in other disciplines. Over the past three decades the practice and study of schooling have been visibly influenced by studies in psychology, sociology, anthropology, and linguistics. For example, in sociology there have been several models for describing African American families. In the culturally deviant or deficient model, African American families were viewed as pathological. An educational response to this characterization was the development of compensatory programs such as Title I (later called Chapter 1), Headstart, and Project Follow Through. Each of these programs aimed at preparing African American and other low income children for school learning. Their cultural and experiential backgrounds were viewed as inadequate or deficient. The cultural equivalent model for examining families assumed that the legitimacy of African American families is determined by proximity to Euro-American families. This view reduced the differences between African American and Euro-American families to social class which basically reinforced the schooling practices in the cultural deficit model. Proponents of the culturally different model recognized the adaptive functions of families. Consistent with this view is the idea that culture influences how children learn. Thus, studies of different learning styles are introduced.

Studies in linguistics had an equivalent influence on conceptualizing the challenges of schooling for African American youngsters. The deficit theory as it relates to language assumes a lack of stimulation of cognitive processes resulting in deficiencies in concept formation and the ability to reason abstractly. This type of thinking led to the development of the elementary school reading program called DISTAR (Englemann and Sterns 1972). Eleanor Orr (1987) employed another approach to instruction using the linguistic deficit theory. For a discussion of Orr's (1987) attempt to link African American language with difficulties in mathematics learning see chapter ten in this volume. Language difference theorists contend that children speaking African American language employ linguistic variations resulting from social class, ethnicity, and differences in speech; however, their language is viewed as functionally adequate. Linguists such as Charles Valentine (1971) claim that both the difference and the deficit theories are inadequate to explain African American language behavior. Valentine proposed a bicultural theory claiming that African American language draws upon its own system as well as that of the dominant culture.

The intertwining of research in sociology and linguistics concerning African American families and African American language represents a significant benchmark for studies of schooling for African American children. A classic example is the application of this research found in a volume edited by Joan Baratz and Roger Shuy entitled *Teaching Black Children to Read* published by the Center for Applied Linguistics (1969). The contributors to this volume sought to clarify the relationship between learning to read, experience with language, and culture. The focus of studies up to this point had more to do with the life conditions and experiences of African American children than with the effectiveness of instruction or the attributes of educators who were able to facilitate high academic performance for the children.

George Weber (1971) conducted a study identifying four successful programs for teaching reading to inner city children. This was a benchmark study in that it reframed the discussion to focus on identifying characteristics of *effective instruction* rather than concentrating on the life condition of the children. However, Ron Edmonds' study of characteristics of *effective schools* and school leadership for low income inner city youngsters received wider acclaim. Ron Edmonds' (1979) studies did not identify specific instructional approaches, although direct instruction was clearly implied in the research.

Barak Rosenshine (1986) reframed the discussions of effective instruction to focus on a process-product view such as that found in "direct instruction." The Chicago Mastery Learning Project described by Block and Anderson (1975) was closely tied to the process-product view of effective instruction. Mastery learning, like direct instruction, could be employed in teaching any content using a variety of approaches. An underlying assumption of direct instruction is that there are universal or generic qualities of instruction that work for all children regardless of culture or background experiences. This is tied to a universalistic view of child growth and development.

The ethnographic studies spawned by the book *Looking in Classrooms* by Tom Good and Jere Brophy (1987) helped to popularize ethnographic approaches to the study of teaching. Brophy (1981) focused on the behaviors of teachers who were effective with low income students which expanded the discussion to include teacher behaviors as important factors in understanding *teacher effectiveness* with low income children. Brophy's research on teacher effectiveness was consistent with the idea that challenges posed in educating low income children could be met through studying specific factors within the schooling process.

Following ethnographic practices, Shirley Brice Heath (1982), in an article titled "What no Bedtime Story Means," describes the use of literacy in three communities, one of which is working class African American. This examination of different literate styles brings to light the connection between schooling practices and the daily experiences of children of the dominant culture. This also highlights the discrepancy between the home culture of some children and the practices of schooling as they experience it. Heath carefully avoids a cultural deficit view by refusing to attribute value to particular cultural practices. She expands this discussion in her book *Ways with Words.*

Etta Hollins, co-author of this volume, was among the first to illustrate application of the theory of cultural congruence to instruction for African American children. In an article titled "The Marva Collins Story Revisited" (1982), she identified key aspects of African American culture employed in Marva Collins' approach to instruction at the Chicago West Side Preparatory School. Hollins contended that the inclusion of specific aspects of African American culture enhanced the effectiveness of instruction for that population of youngsters. For a more complete discussion of cultural congruence in instruction see chapter one.

These academic paradigms informing research and practice relative to schooling for African American and other low income youngsters were paralleled by creative and innovative thinking by individuals outside the mainstream. One such benchmark innovation was that designed by William Johntz in 1963 known as Project SEED (which will be discussed in depth because there is relatively little about it in the research literature). This project was developed with the hope of changing teachers' attitudes towards low income African American youngsters by demonstrating their ability to learn high level mathematics concepts while still in elementary school. The literature describing this project does not make reference to African American cultural practices; however, observations in classrooms where the project has been implemented clearly reveal use of those aspects of culture referred to in Hollins' (1982) cultural congruence model for African American students. Observable in the classroom are features common to African American culture such as audience participation, choral responses, co-operation, collective responsibility for problem solving, flexibility and strong adult leadership. Of course, these factors can be found in other cultures in varying degrees and with different perspectives.

Project SEED is a national program in which mathematicians, scientists and engineers have been successful at teaching algebra and conceptual mathematics to elementary and middle school children from diverse backgrounds since 1963. Project SEED's method, which dates back to the time of Socrates, has proven effective with students from remarkably diverse backgrounds. Student populations have included African American, Hispanic, Native American, Native Alaskan, Asian American and European American children in school districts (from Nome, Alaska and Browning, Montana to Dallas and Philadelphia). Almost all have been from low income families. Project SEED works with full size regular, classes as a supplement to the regular mathematics program. The goal of Project SEED is to increase the self-esteem and academic achievement levels of low income, minority and educationally undeserved students. Project SEED seeks to improve the preparation of these students for success in high school and college mathematics courses and, ultimately, to increase the numbers of those students who graduate from high school and college and who are prepared for jobs and careers in scientific and technical fields. Evaluations of Project SEED have documented improved mathematics achievement levels, decreased rate of repeating a grade and increased likelihood of taking advanced mathematics courses at the secondary level.

Instruction in Project SEED is based on the Socratic method. The instructors do not lecture. They ask questions which lead students to discover mathematical truths for themselves and facilitate debates and discussions about mathematics among the students in their classes. In Project SEED classes, the discovery method is used with the whole class. Students discover concepts in algebra and higher mathematics through exploring questions posed by the instructor which provide a framework for discovery. Debate and discussion are encouraged by strategically placed questions and continual positive reinforcement of students who respond thoughtfully to each other's insights and take intellectual risks. The evaluations show that the longer students remain in Project SEED, the more their mathematical knowledge and understanding increase and the more intellectual confidence they demonstrate.

Project SEED instructors use a variety of techniques to gain feedback from the students and to keep the entire class involved. The intellectual vigor of a Project SEED class finds physical expression through a set of hand signals that students use to express their opinions. Hands waved rapidly back and forth in front of the chest indicate disagreement with an answer or point being made; arms in the air indicate agreement; other signals communicate partial agreement, indecision and questions. Students may be asked to show answers on their fingers, to chorus answers as a group or to respond on paper. These techniques serve several purposes. First, they provide continuous opportunities for students to stay involved and to participate. They eliminate the letdown that students experience when they want to answer a question but are not chosen to respond. Second, the instructor is able to monitor the level of understanding of the entire class and to modify the flow of content accordingly. Third, the techniques are classroom management tools. They allow students to respond frequently while maintaining an atmosphere of decorum and respect. Finally, many students begin their participation in class with choral or nonverbal responses, gaining confidence to articulate their answers at a later date. This is particularly true of students whose language skills are limited or who have come to think of themselves as "slow."

Project SEED curriculum consists of topics from algebra and higher mathematics chosen to reinforce the regular curriculum and to prepare students for success at the high school level. It also boosts their self-confidence by providing them with success in a subject widely recognized as difficult and important in the larger society. Emphasis is placed on conceptual understanding, problem solving methods and critical thinking, not rote memorization or how to find the right answer. At each grade level, the sequence of curriculum is carefully designed to involve students in an in-depth mathematical inquiry of a unified body of material. The math specialists' questions lead students to discover mathematical methods and principles. Curriculum is presented in a spiral manner. Repeat investigation of previous topics is woven into the study of new material. This reinforces and deepens students' understanding and gives them a sense of mathematical power and accomplishment.

In the elementary grades, SEED students learn algebraic structure through the study of integers and rational numbers, exponentiation and logarithms, summations and limits. In the seventh and eighth grades, this is extended through the study of the complex number system. Topics from analytic geometry, number theory, combinatorics, probability and other branches of mathematics may also be explored.

Project SEED instructors, called math specialists, are mathematicians, scientists and engineers who hold a minimum of a bachelor's degree in mathematics or a related subject. Many have advanced degrees. Over the years a number of corporations and universities have also released their technical staff to be trained to teach in Project SEED classes, to the mutual benefit of both organizations.

The choice of instructors is a basic element of the program. In order to encourage conceptual understanding of advanced mathematics, Project SEED instructors need in-depth understanding in mathematics. This will enable them to identify the correct thinking underlying technically incorrect answers and to reward students for their efforts while encouraging them to continue their mathematical exploration. It also allows instructors to continually modify their questioning strategy based on student feedback. When students are having difficulty, the math specialist presents an alternate approach. When students master a new topic with ease, the Project SEED instructor is able to bring in advanced applications or examples to keep the lesson challenging.

Training for Project SEED instructors is rigorous and ongoing. Before being hired to teach in the program, applicants must complete a two-week training/selection process to determine their aptitude for discovery teaching. During this period, they observe model lessons, participate in discussions of curriculum and methodology, and teach short lessons to the other applicants and experienced staff. Selection is based on a variety of factors, such as their presence in front of the group, how rapidly they begin to use the methods, their ability to respond to unexpected responses and their insights during discussion and analysis.

Once hired, training is continuous based on observation, supervised teaching, critique and analysis, workshops and discussions. New instructors are carefully supervised and their classes monitored on a daily basis by experienced specialists. New specialists begin with one class and are assigned new classes only when their existing classes are running smoothly. All specialists attend weekly workshops on curriculum, methodology and mathematics. In addition to workshops, peer evaluation and coaching continues throughout a specialist's tenure with Project SEED. Project SEED instructors observe and critique their peers on a regular basis, gaining new ideas for their own classes and providing valuable professional feedback to their colleagues at the same time.

What began as a successful approach for low income African American students has been expanded to include a variety of culturally diverse populations. For example, Project SEED methods have proven particularly effective with limited-English speaking children, such as Hispanic and Southeast Asian students. Limited-English speaking students are frequently able to participate in Project SEED classes by reading problems from the chalkboard and providing numerical answers. The nonverbal responses along with written answers give these students the opportunity to demonstrate their knowledge and receive recognition from their teachers and classmates long before they are able to verbalize their answers. Project SEED instructors continually weave new mathematical and non-mathematical vocabulary into their lessons. Students are encouraged to use advanced mathematical vocabulary which helps build their confidence and ability to learn new words in general. Most importantly, Project SEED helps students develop their oral language skills by encouraging them to explain their answers to the class and to visitors. Students who are shy or have language difficulties gradually gain the confidence to venture their own opinions.

Project SEED provides a broad spectrum of inservice activities for classroom teachers including observation, seminars and workshops. While the specific curriculum taught in Project SEED classes requires substantial preparation in mathematics and methodology, there are many aspects of the program that can be incorporated by classroom teachers to improve their regular program.

The regular classroom teacher remains in the room as a participant and observer during the Project SEED lesson. Teachers are encouraged to incorporate Project SEED techniques into their own teaching of mathematics and other subjects. Teachers' expectations for their students are increased as a result of seeing them succeeding in advanced mathematics. Many teachers report understanding certain concepts in mathematics for the first time after seeing them presented during SEED classes. The Project SEED math specialist meets regularly with the classroom teacher to discuss the progress of the class and coordination with the regular mathematics program as well as to answer questions about teaching the regular mathematics curriculum. Project SEED staff also offers workshops and seminars on mathematics and methodology for other teachers in the school. Intensive training in the discovery method is also available for teachers who have Project SEED in their classrooms. In several districts, teachers with a degree in mathematics or the equivalent have received extended training as Project SEED specialists.

Project SEED methods and staff training have implications for the preparation of teachers who will work with diverse populations. Like most people, the mathematicians and scientists who teach in Project SEED often have little experience with cultural diversity when they join the program. They observe experienced specialists at work, teach sample lessons to their peers, participate in workshops, and practice extensively in other specialists' classes before they begin classes on their own. Once they begin teaching their own classes, they receive ongoing support and feedback from other members of the Project SEED team. In this way, the methods and insights that have worked successfully are transmitted to a new generation of instructors.

Observation, dry runs, workshops, discussions, supervised teaching, and peer critiquing/coaching can all be incorporated into preservice training programs. In particular, candidates for teaching should have extensive experience observing and working with master teachers in classrooms with diverse populations. They should also have a system of ongoing support and peer interaction once they begin teaching.

Preparation for teaching should include extensive introduction to successful methods and practices. In particular, the discovery method can be an important part of the arsenal provided to preservice teachers. They should experience discovery teaching in their own courses and have opportunities to observe it in action as well as practice it with supervision and feedback.

The benchmarks presented so far, including Project SEED, represent different perspectives on classroom instruction that do not include that of the learner. Although there is a dearth of literature on students' voice as a salient factor in the study of schooling for African American youngsters, what does exist suggests that it is a powerful resource that has potential for becoming one of the most important benchmarks. Traditionally, students are silenced in the schooling process and their voices are conspicuously absent in the research and examination of what goes on in schools. Michelle Fine (1989), in a study conducted in a New York public high school, defines silencing as a practice that suppresses the experiences, concerns, and interests of youngsters resulting in negative attitudes and behaviors. Silencing maintains the privilege of power for teachers and other adults in the school setting.

Students' voices are important from two perspectives: First, students' voices provide insights important for effective teaching and learning. Second, as Giroux (1988) points out, developing a radical pedagogy is "an important starting point for enabling those who have been silenced or marginalized by the schools . . . to reclaim the authorship of their own lives" (p. 63). In this instance Giroux is suggesting that critical educators "must develop pedagogical conditions in their classrooms that allow different student voices to be heard and legitimated," and that critical pedagogy "takes the problems and the needs of the students as its starting point" (p. 71).

These two perspectives are supported in a pilot study conducted by co-authors Hollins and Spencer (1990) in which a group of African American students at the elementary and secondary levels were interviewed to solicit their views about school. The questions the students were asked provided insights into teaching and learning as well as the social context within the schools they attended. The concerns and experiences the students shared reflected life conditions outside the school as well.

In the interviews students were asked the following questions:

1. Tell me about your school. What do you like most? What do you like least or what do you dislike?
2. Tell me about your favorite subject in school. Tell me about your best work in this subject.
3. Tell me about your favorite teacher. What is he or she like? What is being in class with them like? How do you interact with them?
4. Tell me about your friends. Do they attend this school? Where and how did you meet them? How do they feel about the school?
5. Tell me about the most difficult experience you have had in school. Who was involved? How was it resolved?

An analysis of the data from this pilot study revealed evidence that the relationship between the teacher and the student affected the quality of academic performance as well as the value students placed on the content. For example, the favorite teacher in all cases showed concern for the students' problems and needs as referenced by Giroux (1988). The teacher's responsiveness to students in personal ways seemed to generate positive feelings that supported persistence in completing even the most difficult assignments. The fact that the students' favorite subjects correlated with their favorite teachers is one indicator of the powerful influence of the teacher in determining the value placed on specific content. One attribute of the favorite teacher was that of empowering the students to actualize their own ideas in completing assignments and engaging in class discussions.

Project SEED provides another example of the benefit of empowering students to actualize their own ideas in the learning process. Although Project SEED math specialists were not part of the pilot study discussed here, observations of their performance conducted by co-author Hollins reveals that they systematically engage the students in expressing their own ideas in solving math problems. The students' ideas form the basis for discovering basic principles of mathematics.

The data from this pilot study revealed evidence that teachers can also make school life very difficult for students. In response to the question of difficult school experiences, most students related incidents between themselves and teachers or other staff. The students frequently expressed the belief that they received negative responses from some teachers because of their ethnicity. Some students expressed feelings of abandonment in the school environment. That is, some teachers failed to intervene or provide support in situations involving name calling related to race. At the secondary level some students even felt singled out and harassed by teachers and administrators.

These experiences are real for the students. They raise issues about the impact of the social context within schools on learning as well as those related to pedagogical practices. Students who experience emotional turmoil and social conflict in the school environment are certainly not in the best frame of mind for learning. Clearly the African American students in this pilot study identified interpersonal relationships with teachers as significant in diffusing some of the dissonance and isolation felt in the school environment. Positive relationships with teachers seem to validate the curriculum content and provide support for academic achievement among African American students.

The significance of this pilot study is that it points out the potential for empirical research to involve students' voices in conceptualizing the challenges to effective schooling in ways that reveal more precisely the direction of needed changes. This type of research uses students' voices as primary sources of information which reduces significantly the degree of speculation about students' responses to specific aspects of schooling. There are, of course, some cautions here relative to the reliability of students' voice as informant. There are many factors that affect what students are willing to share with a researcher. Included among these factors are certainly trust, confidence, and ethnicity. Students reveal more and are more honest in situations where they trust the interviewer. Students who feel confident about their abilities are more likely to be reliable sources than students who are less confident. There is some evidence to indicate that the ethnicity of the interviewer plays a significant role in the quality and quantity of information provided by the interviewee. These factors are to be taken into consideration by those who would use students' voices as primary sources.

In conclusion, we have identified what we believe are important benchmarks in conceptualizing the challenges to effective schooling for African American students. Each benchmark seems to have opened a window to understanding how to provide more effective schooling for this population of youngsters. We have shown how the conceptualization of schooling for African American youngsters parallels studies in other disciplines such as psychology, sociology, anthropology and linguistics. We noted the shift from research focusing on the life condition of the student to that focusing on the quality of instruction (see, for example Weber 1971; Edmonds 1979; Rosenshine 1986; Good and Brophy 1987). A major breakthrough was the shift to examining culture as a primary source of information about how children learn (see, for example Heath 1982 and Hollins 1982). Project SEED has been presented as a model of effective instruction in mathematics for African American youngsters that parallels some cultural practices. Finally, we have introduced the students' voices as the most promising benchmark of this decade.

CHAPTER 9

Understanding the African American Learner

BARBARA J. SHADE

Questions to Think About

1. What factors external to the schooling process influence the learning preferences of African American students?
2. What conditions of classroom instruction are most likely to have a positive effect on African American learners' academic performance?
3. What is the relationship between Shade's characterization of how African American students learn, Au and Kawakami's conceptualization of cultural congruence in instruction, and Hollins, et al.'s description of Project SEED?
4. Shade claims the DISTAR program is effective with African American children. Hollins, Smiler, and Spencer depict DISTAR as representative of the cultural deficit perspective. Can an effective program derived from a cultural deficit perspective serve King's purpose of liberatory education? Should purpose be valued over outcome?

Learning is a process which leads to the restructuring and expansion of an individuals' perception and knowledge base. However, this process is approached from different orientations. There are cultural, ethnic, social and individual differences in learning modes, information processing approaches and attitudes toward learning. Successful teachers are able to adapt both their classroom environment and their teaching strategies to accommodate these differences. Research suggests that African American students learn best in a classroom which is designed to mitigate social alienation and establish a sense of efficacy; with supportive teachers who have high expectations and standards; and through teaching strategies which accommodate information processing differences. This chapter provides a critical synthesis of each of these dimensions.

Entering the classroom as a teacher for the first time is a frightening experience, regardless of the setting. When teachers are confronted with even a small number of African American students, the experience can be traumatic for both the students and the teacher. Many teachers immediately expect African American children to exhibit certain behaviors which are perceived as incongruent with an orderly classroom. The expected behaviors include:

- Having a short attention span and being easily distractable.
- Failing to complete tasks on time.
- Speaking without raising their hands and waiting to be called upon.
- Being impulsive in their responses rather than reflective.
- Needing a great deal of physical contact.
- Interrupting the class by talking to their neighbors (Shade 1990a).
- Experiencing difficulty with the learning material.

Of some surprise to these teachers is the fact that the students do not see themselves as acting inappropriately. From the student's perspective, their behavior is perfectly natural in that they are:

- Seeking relief from monotonous tasks by moving around.
- Working at their own speed and being thorough, but perceive the teacher as not allowing sufficient time to complete the task.
- Being inclusive of all details or materials involved in an idea rather than disorganized.
- Interjecting their opinions or ideas at the point at which the information is relevant, rather than waiting until the conversation has moved to another point. Being creative and spontaneous, rather than being impulsive.
- Being cooperative, supportive and seeking assistance from others as they are able to do when they learn outside of the school setting, rather than disrupting the class (Hanna 1988).
- Experiencing difficulty with the material because the teacher does not know how to teach.

This difference in perception creates frustration for both teachers and students. McDermott (1977) and Hall (1989) suggest that this conflict results from teachers and students coming to the classroom from two different cultural contexts. The concept of a *cultural context* denotes a setting in which there are patterns of expectations, specific behavioral norms and accepted activities deemed appropriate for that particular milieu (Salamon 1981). The context of the school is one which epitomizes a cultural orientation which has been accepted as a part of proper school behavior since the establishment of the first school in this society. Individuals who function well in this particular setting are those who value and expect passive receptivity by the learner, authoritative transmission of information by the teacher, individual effort aimed at completing an assigned task, performance for recognition, avoidance of confrontation, and minimal antagonisms (Dreeben 1968).

The majority of African American youth entering school today have a different cultural orientation than the one rewarded in schools. For the most part, the African American child is more likely to have been socialized within an urban context which has its own patterns of behavior and expectations. Of the twenty-six million African Americans, eighty-two percent of them live in cities, largely metropolitan areas. More importantly over sixty percent of these urban dwellers live in central cities with physical and social decay. The cultural capital with which most African American children come to school includes a set of behaviors and mental habits which help them cope with: crime and interpersonal conflict; urban noise such as honking horns, loud engines, and general traffic; lack of adequate space in the residences and more people in the residence, the block, or the neighborhood; highly prescribed geographical boundaries which reduce contact with the larger society; and exposure to a disproportionate amount of industrial pollutants such as smoke, soot, dust, flyash, fumes and carbon monoxide which have been found to have a serious effect upon brain functioning (Shade 1990c).

In addition, African American children are more likely to participate in high levels of differentiated social interaction, are exposed to greater heterogeneity and segmentation of human relationships, and are likely to be involved with superficial and transient interpersonal interactions. Coping with these factors requires specific ways for learning to handle social interactions and different methods of acquiring information (Heath 1983, Hanna 1988). If teachers are to be successful with African American children, it is important for them to understand the view of teaching and learning from the children's perspective. Their view of the world sets the stage for their classroom responses in particular areas.

Teacher-Peer-Learner Interaction

African American students tend to be extroverts and are more likely to concentrate on the people in the teaching-learning process rather than on task requirements (Shade 1983). Another way of identifying this idea is to suggest that African American children have a high level of what Gardner (1983) calls *interpersonal intelligence*. Young (1974) suggests that African American children are socialized to concentrate on the people or social aspects of knowledge. This occurs largely through behavioral management techniques used by the parents as noted in Young's study and through the types of visual images to which children are exposed throughout the homes (Shade and Edwards, 1987).

Evidence of the importance of interpersonal dimensions is found in several studies. Damico (1983) examined the issue by permitting black and white sixth grade children to choose aspects of the school environment they wished to photograph. African American children most often selected teachers or classmates as their subjects while European American children chose physical settings or objects for subjects. Damico concluded that people in the school were more important to African American children than the concept of school. In another study, Eato and Lerner (1981) asked one hundred and eighty-three African American sixth grade youths to indicate which aspects of the school environment are most influential on their behavior or perception of school. The children placed more emphasis on the people in the environment, particularly teachers, than they did on the importance of the physical aspects of the school.

Other indications of this focus on the interpersonal aspects of the environment can be found in the literature on social cognition. Research indicates that African Americans are better able to recognize faces and emotions than other groups and are extremely sensitive to social nuances (Shade, 1983; Levy, Murphy, and Carlson 1972). These preferences tend to influence decisions about the desired level of interaction with people or ideas in the environment. Sherif (1973) pointed out that African Americans are more likely to make judgments about their level of involvement in an activity based on the interpersonal or informal demands of the task and the possible social effects of the situation; European American students make their determination based on the formal demands or rules which govern the setting.

The implications of this preference are important. African American students rely on their perception of the teacher and the affective aspects of the environment to determine their involvement with learning. Thus, as St. John (1971) and other scholars point out, African American learners' achievement is highly correlated with warm and supportive teachers, a socially interactive environment (Lipsitz 1984), and the use of affective materials to stimulate their learning (Rychlak 1975). Material which has social connotations or utilizes students' ability to work cooperatively can improve African American's school performance. As Morgan (1981) points out in his examination of the learning style of African American children, the social interaction model of teaching seems to provide an atmosphere in which African American children can do well.

Classroom Climate

African American children require an active, stimulating, and highly arousing learning environment rather than a quiet, passive, receptive setting. Boykin (1982) refers to this as the need for psychological or behavioral verve. He found that African American children prefer and need a large variety of information at a constantly changing pace and have little tolerance for monotonous or low-level passive activity. Farley (1981) suggests that this is a need or preference for high stimulation or arousal. Morgan (1990) tested this hypothesis in an observational study of five different eighth-grade classes. He found that African American students, particularly males, were five times more active than European American children. In another study Della Valla (1984) found that only twenty-five percent of African American children studied remain seated and passively involved, as consistent with school practices.

What does this mean for teachers? Perhaps the most important implication is that teachers should *not* perceive this preference for constant movement as a classroom management problem. Instead, it suggests that the pace and type of the presentations and work assignments should vary, that frequent breaks may be important, and that the classroom rules and procedures should allow for some type of variation in approach to performing tasks. The primary objective should be the completion of the task, rather than control of movement and social interaction.

This need for movement does mitigate against the use of activities which require quiet, thoughtful, reflective behavior such as writing papers and essays or completing seat work. Teachers are faced with the task of teaching students to handle quietness and reflectivity on the one hand, while acknowledging and accommodating students' need for movement or cognitive diversion on the other hand. Lipsitz (1984) found that in a school filled with energy, movement, and activity both teachers and students were able to adjust. As one teacher pointed out, it is like going into a restaurant: "You sit down at your table and focus on the few people you are dining with" Lipsitz (pg. 109).

African American Schemata

African American learners are more likely to learn material and knowledge which has meaning for them and can be related to their prior knowledge. As Simmons (1979) points out, African American children are more analytical about concepts and ideas when the information they are asked to examine comes from their particular environmental orientation. This suggests that knowledge represents a type of cultural communication. Interacting with the information is highly dependent upon whether or not students can relate, perceive, and associate the ideas with other ideas and concepts they have acquired from past experiences.

African American children have a particularly difficult time with material which is presented in school because, as Gordan et al. (1990) point out, the ideas, concepts and facts presented:

1) Have not been produced in their community, their culture or their political or economic milieu;
2) Often ignore their existence and may even demean their personal characteristics; and
3) Often distort conditions and seem to ignore their particular perspective.

When one considers these factors, it is not surprising that African American children prefer to interact with information which seems to relate to them and their identity. Rychlak and his associates (1973, 1975) point out that African American students are more likely to learn and recall information when the words represent concepts they liked rather than concepts they disliked. As Schmeck and Meier (1984) point out, individuals are more efficient at learning when they can use "self" as an organizing schema. Smith and Lewis (1985) found race to be an important schema around which the African American children organized information and, in fact, influenced their ability to recall.

Without this organizational framework, African American children are likely to handle concept development differently than other children. They develop some type of meaning for themselves which is different from the meaning developed by European American children (Shade 1983; Heath 1983; Orasanu, Lee, and Scribner 1979). The result is that they often arrive at answers on tests which differ significantly from those desired by the test constructors. As a result, their abilities are incorrectly assessed (Cohen 1969). We must conclude, therefore, that the idea of multicultural education is not merely a request for cosmetic changes as Reagan (1985) would suggest. Texts, materials, examples, and projects that are directly related to the African American child are more likely to ensure processing and acquisition of the information because it facilitates the accommodation and assimilation process.

Effective Teaching Strategies

African American children appear to learn better through observation than through passive receptivity and direct instruction. Perhaps the best indication of this is found in a statement made to Shirley Brice Heath (1983) by an African American woman when describing the differences she observed in her teaching technique and those of European American parents:

> "He got learn to know 'bout dis world, can't nobody tell im. White folks uh hear dey kids say sump/n, dey say it back to 'em, dey ask em gain and gain bout things, like they posed to be born knowin. You thing I kin tell Teegie all he goot know to get along? He just gotta be keen, keep his eyes open, . . . Gotta watch hisself by watchin other folks." (Heath, 1983, pg. 84).

This observation appears to be true throughout the community, suggesting that Bandura's social learning theory may be the primary approach to be used with African American children rather than the usually direct tell-and-do or behavioral approach to instruction. Modeling is an effective instructional strategy employed by teachers to demonstrate a new or unfamiliar process for students (Good 1983; Rosenshine 1986). It minimizes students' misinterpretation by providing explicit information. In short, it minimizes cultural conflict and takes the guess work out of learning. Two instructional programs which demonstrate this approach are the DISTAR program of Bereiter and Engleman, Duffy and associates' cognitive modeling in reading (Shade 1989); and problem solving (Whimbey 1985). An accompanying strategy is the active, questioning inquiry approach as found in reciprocal teaching used by Brown and Palinscar (1986) in the use of concept mapping (Johnson, Pittelman & Heimlich 1986) or the techniques used by Feuerstein (1980).

Communicative Style

One of the most prevalent examples of cultural behavior hindering teaching and learning in the traditional classroom is the African American practice of "breaking in and talking over people" in the midst of a discussion. Although this approach is accepted and understood within the African American community, when students interrupt others or speak out of turn in school, teachers view this behavior as disruptive and inappropriate (Hanna 1988). From the African American perspective, this is a valued method of providing a response to indicate that the individual is listening, comprehending and has anticipated the point being made. In conversations and discussions within their cultural settings, there is little need to finish explaining an idea if the listener has already assessed the intent, meaning, and outcome.

Perhaps the greatest difference in communication centers around the fact that African American children are socialized to engage in oral performance. They use verbal and nonverbal language, are more theatrical, show less restrained emotion, and demonstrate faster responses in communicating with others (Heath 1983; Hanna 1988). Kochman (1972) found that African American verbal communication patterns possessed a preponderance of words which denote action and unrestricted movement and had a kinetic quality. In addition, African Americans are more likely to further interpret meaning of communicative efforts through voice tone and quality and use of facial gestures (Pasteur and Toldson 1982). As a result,

African American children learn a variety of meanings for single utterances and learn to respond or obtain a reaction based upon variations in intonations not just the precise words.

A third area in which this difference in communication is most prevalent is in storytelling and the development of oral and written narratives. A good example of this is found in Michael's (1981) research on African American children in California. She found that European American children were more likely to tell topic-centered narrations while African American children presented episodic narratives. Topic-centered narratives focus on one event at a time while episodic narratives meander around taking episodic journeys. In the classroom, teachers often observe that African American children can never "tell a story straight." What appears to occur is that the African American children start down one path and stop to make repairs for the listener to ensure that the listener has the amount of information necessary to understand what is being said (Cazden 1988). Because this lack of linearity frustrates teachers they are very likely to intervene and attempt to structure the discussion by asking questions which require focused answers.

Inasmuch as communicative style is a highly socialized system, it is difficult to suggest methods of adaptation other than the development of an awareness or appreciation for the particular style and ensuring that attempts are not made to shortcircuit the presentations of students because their oral or written style is nonlinear.

African American Learning Style

One of the last differences to be observed is one which has yet to be researched in depth. It is closely tied to the new dimension of research relative to how African Americans process information and acquire knowledge. There is reason to believe that African American children approach the processing of information differently because of their cultural background. This difference is found in two major dimensions; (1) perceptual preference which dictates the preferred ways individuals select and transmit information to the brain for processing and (2) their approach to thinking about the material.

Perceptual Style. Perception depends upon the efficient use of individual modalities to gather and send messages to the brain so that the brain can search for prior experiences and information

that can be used for interpretation and meaning. Mangan (1978)
points out that individuals learn to perceive within the framework
of their culture. Therefore, individuals are taught to pay attention to different parts of the environment and the culture adds differential meaning to these perceptions. It is often found that visual
images such as photographs, line drawings and geometric forms
have cultural interpretations. The result is that images do not convey the same information to all individuals. Individuals prefer to
use different types of sensory mechanisms to gather information.
Barsch (1971) points out that individuals develop a prioritized use
of mediation channels to assist them in processing information
efficiently.

Studies conducted over the last thirty years which examined
African American perception using figural, visual, and spatial
tasks, present conclusions suggesting that a difference in perceptual style exists (Shade 1990c). A previous review on perceptual
preferences suggests that African Americans tend to use visual, au-
ditory and kinesthetic channels best in their acquisition of information (Shade 1983). To ascertain the validity of this hypothesis, this
author examined two groups of African American students in
grades seven through nine. The first group responded to a videotape
in which an African American announcer pronounced fifty words
from the Edmonds Learning Style Identification Exercise (ELSIE).
The students indicated whether the word generated (1) a mental
picture of the object or activity; (2) a mental picture of the word
spelled out; (3) no mental picture only the sound of the word carried
meaning; or (4) created some type of physical or emotional feeling.
The results of this survey revealed that the sensory mechanism
most often involved in processing for African American students includes (1) visual images; (2) print and aural presentation, and (3)
kinesthetic information. Of interest is the fact that students indicated a preference for visual images over all other information on a
2:1 ratio.

In the second sample, 48 students indicated the types of strategies they preferred in the teaching-learning process on the James
and Galbraith (1985) Perceptual Style Inventory. These strategies
were divided according to the modality which they best served. Visual images included photographs, tables, charts, and graphs; the
aural mode involved records or audiotapes; the social interactive
mode consisted of such strategies as discussions, and debates; the
haptic mode included drawing, sculpturing, and painting; and

the print mode was represented by reading assignments. The presentation modes most selected by this group in rank order were: kinesthetic (writing and physical games), visual, aural and social interactive with a tie for haptic and print activities.

Although there are a number of theorists who suggest that teaching to selected modalities has little effect on academic achievement, there is reason to believe that greater rapport with the material can be achieved if individuals receive information through their preferred mode (Eicher 1987). Teachers who wish to ensure African American children are engaged in tasks may find it beneficial to include visual and kinesthetic materials as an important part of the learning process that supplements the traditional aural and print related activities.

Thinking Style. Thinking represents the activities of the mind where ideas, concepts, and information are perceived, conceptualized and evaluated. The processes most often associated with thinking include reasoning, elaboration, problem solving, decision making and critical analysis. For some theorists, thinking is the equivalent of rational, linear, and sequential thinking with little attention given to the mental activities which might be defined as intuitive or creative. Arnheim (1985), however, points out that thinking represents two ways of knowing: use of intuition and intellect. The first type represents methods by which individuals produce and conceive ideas while the other presents an approach for solving a problem.

There are very few studies which examine the thinking style of African American individuals using adequate empirical methods which provide a definitive portrait of exactly how African American learners proceed in their thinking. However, some researchers have drawn conclusions based upon their own perceptions. Jensen (1969) contended that African American learners are not good reasoners or problem solvers using the analytical definition of the process. He drew his conclusions from studies which used the Ravens Progressive Matrices Test as a measure of problem solving and high level thinking. One must note, however, that comparing lower socioeconomic African Americans to middle socioeconomic European Americans suggests that the experiential and cultural backgrounds of the two groups were not comparable, thus making a comparison impossible. More importantly, the measure of problem solving used is a visual-spatial test which requires individuals to visually analyze figures or forms and, as discussed earlier, visual perception has a solid cultural base with particular environments, groups, and communities (Shade 1990; Gibson 1950). If the particular measure had been administered in another modality, other results might have occurred.

Borkowski and Krause (1983) examined the performance of African American learners using tasks similar to those used by Jensen including the Ravens Progressive Matrices and a perceptual efficiency measure. Borkowski and Krause interpreted the results as indicating that African American learners lacked sufficient metacognitive strategies or comprehension monitoring skills. Their results were based upon the fact that again, the logical-mathematical approach to thinking did not appear strongly evident.

Other studies on thinking style have focused on the conclusion that African Americans are field-dependent thinkers. The concept of being field-dependent or field-independent is determined by an individual's ability to discern figure-ground differences on the Embedded Figures Test (another visual-spatial measure). Individuals are required to recognize patterns, analyze and organize visual information, search or focus their visual attention; and demonstrate speed in detecting and organizing material. Those who can perform these tasks are labeled field-independent while those who have difficulty with this type of visual discrimination are considered field-dependent. Field independent thinking styles are equated with highly analytical and sequential type thinkers whereas field-dependent persons are perceived as holistic, simultaneous or relational thinkers. Field-independent thinkers are strongly represented in fields or subjects which require chaining of hierarchial ideas to produce a product. Field-dependent thinkers are found to be highly represented in more social-oriented fields which need concepts and ideas assessed in totality or interrelationally rather than as discrete details (Shade 1983, 1990).

Although the same caution can be raised relative to cultural influence on visual perception with these measuring instruments, variation in the African American approach to this task is consistently found to be toward field dependency (Shade 1983; Kelly 1984; Perney, 1976). One might conclude that a unique thinking style does exist within the African American community.

There are several other studies which provide some insight into the African American thinking style which also should be considered. First, Smith and Drumming (1989) suggest that African American reasoning style is the same as that of other groups. This conclusion resulted from testing a group of African American college students using a problem solving task which was designed for a European American population. No difference was found in the group's processing approach to the problem. It should, however, be noted that (1) this was an older group of students who may have already adapted their thinking style to the school context or that (2) Smith and Drumming modified the presentation of the task somewhat which may have made the task more compatible with the group's thinking style.

In a second study, Cooper (1981) used written essays to examine African American thinking style and concluded that there is a difference in style which tends toward a more holistic or integrated approach rather than the hierarchial orientation she observes in other cultural group's essays. She noted that the writing of African American students tended to examine information and ideas based upon relationships and the interdependence of the concepts.

Although there is some controversy and skepticism about this idea, TenHouton (1971) suggested that African American thinking style differs because they begin within or favor the use of the right hemisphere. Although both hemispheres are important for the thinking process, evidence suggests that individuals may favor the processes which are dominated by one hemisphere over the other. When coupled with Torrance's (1982) thesis that African American learners are highly creative and other findings relative to the holistic, integrative approach, one might conclude that there is a tendency for African Americans to respond to and approach thinking from the intuitive dimension rather than through the logical-mathematical approach honored by the texts and the schools.

Norman (1982) suggests that the thinking process incorporates three functions: (1) acquisition of new information through chunking, elaboration, and connection to existing knowledge; (2) restructuring of new information which involves the reformulation of old concepts and relationships; and (3) the adaptation of knowledge to particular uses. Although this process may be true for all individuals, there is little doubt that culture affects the use of memory, that existing knowledge may differ because of prior experiences, and the adaptation of knowledge will depend upon perceptions of the individuals. While much more empirical data is needed to clearly define this difference, the intuitive hypothesis which is generated within the community indicates that the modal thinking style of African Americans appears to be holistic, intuitive, and more integrative in the processing of information (Hilliard 1973; Hale 1982; Shade 1990a).

Teachers who are successful with African American learners have used this hypothesis as a base and developed curricular materials and teaching strategies which seem to accommodate this style. These teachers:

1. Use the concept of Bruner's (1960) spiral curriculum and his thesis that learners need to understand the underlying structure of the material they are asked to learn (Lipsitz 1984);
2. Develop a discipline integrated approach rather than attempting to address content areas as separate, discrete entities which have little relationship to each other (Hanna 1988);
3. Teach in units rather than separate discrete lessons which seemed to have little connection from one day to the next (Heath 1983);
4. Develop and facilitate directed inquiry and project oriented lessons which allowed students to, not only learn information, but also seek to apply it in real situations (Lipsitz 1984);
5. Use more case study approaches which facilitate analysis of real-life situations (Ruggierol 1988); and
6. Spend time teaching and modeling issue analysis and thinking skills which assisted African American learners in developing the logical reasoning process thus producing a well-rounded thinker who can approach any situation (Whimbey 1985).

Conclusions

Teaching African American and other children from culturally diverse backgrounds is neither difficult nor impossible. It does require a restructuring of teaching attitudes, approaches and strategies. Teachers must become facilitators and directors of the learning process, rather than information givers. Classrooms must become more group-oriented and cooperative rather than individualized and competitive and more inviting than repressive. Peers and other students must be included as teachers in the learning process along with the community and parents of the children while the materials used in the classroom must be a reflection of the experiences of the children, not just in character image, but in settings and contexts. Perhaps the greatest change needed is that talking and telling of the facts must be replaced with demonstrations, modeling and involvement in activities with the use of multiple media presentations in order for the information to be perceived and processed more easily.

Along with these changes will come a change in assessment and evaluation. No longer will the paper and pencil approaches which were oriented toward the analytical, sequential approach to learning be relevant. Instead, the authentic assessment approach advocated by Archibald and Newman (1988) will be seen as more appropriate. Students will be asked to perform, to show, and to explain what they know, not to guess the answer the teacher expects.

Ronald Edmonds (1979) pointed out that educators have the information and techniques necessary to effect a change in the academic achievement of all learners. If we are to perform the task, it requires a change in perceptions, a change in teaching strategies, and a change in expectations. Most importantly, however, it requires a professional dedicated to the task of teaching all children.

CHAPTER 10

New and Prevailing Misconceptions of African American English for Logic and Mathematics

JOHN BAUGH

Questions to Think About

1. What is the relationship between African American English, mathematical logic, and academic learning in school?
2. How should teachers approach the issue of linguistic diversity in planning classroom instruction?
3. Is there a relationship between the ethnosensitive education proposed by Baugh, cultural congruence in instruction described by Au and Kawakami, and the culture centered approach advocated by King?

The past decade has been an active one among scholars who study African American English (AAE). Ten years ago we witnessed the "black English trial" in Ann Arbor (Smitherman 1981; Labov 1982; Chambers 1983), and four years ago new linguistic evidence emerged to suggest that vernacular AAE is diverging from standard English (Bailey and Maynor 1985; Labov and Harris 1986; Myhill and Harris 1986). The diligent work of many scholars has produced a more complex and more complete linguistic profile of African American speech and ongoing changes in linguistic behavior.

This chapter focuses on two well intended exceptions to this trend, regarding linguistic and cognition, intellectual ability, and the suggestion that speakers of AAE have diminished capacities for logical thought or analytical abstraction. Specifically, the views es-

poused by Farrell (1983) regarding I.Q. and standard English, and
the more recent writings of Orr (1987) pertaining to limited performance among African American students in mathematics and science are wrong headed and constitute retrograde steps in our quest
to overcome the history of educational disparity based on race, language, or ethnicity.

The inherent racial bias in the research of Farrell (1983, 1984)
and Orr (1987) is benign in the sense that both authors are sincere
in their attempt to help African American students. Their compassion and concern are commendable, but as they endeavor to offer
positive contributions to the welfare of African American students
they inadvertently produced biased research which perpetuates
racist misconceptions regarding the general relationship between
language and thought, and consequently misrepresents the intellectual potential of African American students. This chapter identifies sources of bias in Farrell (1983) and Orr (1987), and presents
linguistic evidence that contradicts their linguistic conclusions,
thereby challenging the intellectual foundation upon which their
pedagogical suggestions are based. Alternative educational strategies are provided which emphasize the ethnographic background of
individual students (Heath 1983; Baugh 1983; Labov 1982; Smitherman 1987; Moll 1988).

A Decade of Linguistic Discovery

Ten years ago African American language received a great deal
of attention when, in 1979, several minority students brought liti-
gation against the Ann Arbor school district because they had been
mislabeled as linguistically handicapped. As a result of this misdi-
agnosis they were placed in special education classes that failed to
meet their educational needs. They were not being taught standard
English, what Smitherman (1987) and Fishman (1972) refer to as
the public dialect of wider communication. The student plaintiffs
eventually won their case on the grounds that the school district
had failed to teach them to read and write standard English. The
curriculum failed to acknowledge the special linguistic differences
between standard and nonstandard English, which are a legitimate
source of many educational problems that interfere with academic
success of nontraditional students (Baugh 1988a).

The trial also led to some concrete programs that are not central to the discussion at hand. Interested readers should consult
Smitherman (1981), Labov (1982) and Chambers (1983) for a de-

tailed survey of the trial and its educational implications. The African American English trial represented one of the first occasions, since the Supreme Court decided Brown vs. Topeka Board of Education in 1954, where scholars, educators, and the national press focused simultaneous attention on the special educational needs of African American students who do not already speak the dialect of wider communication when they enter school.

Labov (1982) remarked that the African American English trial was the first demonstration of a unified view among linguists regarding the history of AAE. The Africans who were taken as slaves have a unique linguistic history when compared to every other group that has migrated to the United States. Whereas European immigrants were able to preserve their native tongue, in ethnic ghettos in major urban centers, Africans were immediately isolated upon capture based on language, in order to restrict communication and prevent uprisings. This practice did much more than isolate the slaves linguistically. This forced slaves to be linguistically creative and to use a combination of African and English words and grammaticalizations in their intimate communication. Educators confront the linguistic vestiges of slavery every day when they serve students who are native speakers of AAE.

Expanded historical and community based research began after the Ann Arbor trial in different regions of the country. The historical evidence was based largely on Botkin's slave narratives, a series of recordings that were made with former slaves from Mississippi and Texas during the post-depression era. These tapes, which are available through the Library of Congress, have been extremely valuable to linguists as they strive to reconstruct AAE (Brewer 1986; Pitts 1981, 1986; Schneider 1983). The community based studies reveal dynamic language usage as well. For example, Baugh (1983) observed that African American adults tend to shift linguistic styles depending upon the social situation. Standard English is broached during more formal occasions, while vernacular AAE is used in the community and for intimate or personal conversations. Beyond the adult behavior that I observed, Labov and Harris (1986), Myhill and Harris (1986), and Bailey and Maynor (1985) made independent linguistic discoveries which suggested that adolescent speakers of AAE were beginning to diverge from standard English usage. Although these results have been highly controversial among linguists (Vaughn-Cooke 1987; Wolfram 1987; Dillard 1988), there appears to be agreement that linguistic changes among younger African Americans are volatile and still in a state of flux.

The linguistic research of the past decade has also demonstrated the growing complexity of our educational task, because
many African American students take pride in their speech and
prefer it instead of a variety of standard English. As a boy growing
up in Los Angeles I shared the opinion with most of my African
American peers that our speech was "hip" and it was not "cool" to
speak standard English. In fact, the boys who were willing to adopt
standard English were openly chastised, or worse; peer pressure
rewarded and reinforced the immediate social value of the street
vernacular, not standard English. The recent discoveries of independent linguistic divergence among African American adolescents
seem to reflect a rejection of standard English in favor of greater
nonstandard usage. Those who are skeptical of these results were
quick to point out that African American adolescents have always
been at the forefront of vernacular usage, and that with maturity
we may eventually expect greater linguistic conformity toward
standard English (Dillard 1972, 1988; Myhill 1988).

This decade began with a national call for linguistic sensitivity
on the part of educators, in order to appreciate that students who do
not already speak the dialect of wider communication will face special educational problems. From language usage studies of African
American speech communities we observe a more complex pattern
of linguistic behavior, where economic isolation and linguistic divergence travel hand in glove. Motivation to adopt the dialect of wider
communication is low among many African American students, and
may continue to parallel the diminished occupational prospects of
those who have not had sufficient educational opportunities.

The causes of linguistic divergence—to the extent that it exists—are intricate, and in order to meet the educational needs of
nontraditional students we must isolate plausible linguistic observations from false claims that could be harmful to the educational
welfare of minority students.

Some Common Stereotypes and Other Linguistic Fallacies

Every advanced industrial society is socially stratified, with
wealthy individuals at the top of the socioeconomic ladder while
poor people occupy the lower strata. Language usage parallels the
socioeconomic and geographic distribution of dialects for languages
in technologically developed societies. Those with wealth and power
are often considered to be "good" speakers of the language, whereas
those with less wealth and education tend to use nonstandard dia-

lects that are highly marked, serving to reinforce prevailing linguistic stereotypes. This is a global problem that plagues every urban center where speakers with diverse linguistic backgrounds strive to coexist.

The immigrant history of the United States accentuates linguistic diversity in the melting pot, because white immigrants have always melted into the pot at a significantly faster rate than have members of nonwhite minority groups, and lingering linguistic differences found in minority speech communities reflect that the United States still strives to attain the status of the color blind society it has yet to become.

Until such time that race no longer stands as a potential barrier to educational opportunities, professional prospects, or residential preference, we will continue to observe unique linguistic properties among minority populations, because their speakers are socially disenfranchised from regular and frequent contact with members of the majority culture. This type of social isolation will merely serve to accentuate existing dialect differences, because linguistic boundaries are maintained by the social boundaries that perpetuate racial isolation.

Farrell (1983, 1984) and Orr (1987) do not fully comprehend the preceding linguistic legacy and consequently revive some unfounded stereotypes about black language that could be detrimental to minority students if not corrected. Before turning to the technical foundations of these biased studies we should recognize that nonstandard dialects tend to be the object of ridicule in every advanced industrial society, depending on which group or groups of speakers compose the lower socioeconomic populations. Teachers, as members of their respective literate cultures, also recognize those dialects which are held in high esteem versus those that are readily associated with lower socioeconomic groups. Educators are expected to develop mastery of the dialect of wider communication, and to the extent that students do not already speak the standard dialect, teachers must continue to do all that they can to ensure that minority students eventually compete effectively with their peers who, by accident of birth, reside in homes where standard middle class language is the norm.

For educational purposes in the United States society can be divided into three groups:

1) those who learn standard English natively, with tolerance for variation between regional standards and the national standard (which is similar to broadcast speech);

2) those who learn nonstandard English natively, including many poor whites and minorities; and

3) those who have learned or are learning English as a second language (ESL).

Again, these linguistic divisions are a natural artifact of the immigrant history of the United States, and the dominant role that English plays for official purposes. Since educational parity is our ultimate goal we must recognize that students in all three groups require different pedagogical strategies.

One of the primary reasons that average citizens assume that nonstandard English is inferior to standard English lies in the correspondence between speech and social class. We inherit language and wealth (or poverty) from the same source, and most observant individuals find cause-and-effect relationships that often distort linguistic reality. As long as minority dialects are devalued socially it is difficult to convince the typical speaker that nonstandard dialects are just as complex and logical as the standard dialect of the language. This fact becomes clearer upon reflection, because nonstandard dialects have thrived in every advanced industrial society, despite stringent efforts on the part of educated speakers to eradicate them. Nonstandard dialects meet the communicative needs of those who use them; if they were grammatically inadequate or logically incomplete they would either change or vanish, as Latin did. Few ordinary speakers are familiar with the history of Latin or their own language, and under these conditions stereotypes that diminish the value of lower socioeconomic dialects will prevail.

The socioeconomic wealth in the United States also parallels the preceding linguistic divisions. Monolingual speakers of standard English control most of the wealth. Nonstandard dialects, by striking socioeconomic contrast, do not reflect significant economic influence; speakers in groups 2 and 3 tend to be among the poorer citizens, including newly arrived immigrants who seek to gain citizenship.

This history of linguistic diversity was born on the lips of ancestors who came from all parts of the globe, but, again, it was only the descendants of the Africans taken as slaves who were denied the preservation of their native language, and the linguistic consequences of this fact are still with us today, and still misunderstood. Indeed, when the typical American hears AAE it is equated with limited intelligence. A twenty-six year old African American male from Los Angeles addressed this point directly during an interview about race relations:

J: Do you think the racial situation has improved, y'know after civil rights and all that?

R: No, I think it's worse, cause I'm still not comfortable around a majority of white folks and I'm sure they ain't comfortable around me. And . . . another thing . . . most whites don't figure blacks think too well . . . they think they smarter, and that don't make for no equal conversation.

In other words, R is convinced that many whites harbor negative stereotypes about African Americans.

This negative characterization of nonstandard speech has been identified as the "deficit hypothesis" by scholars (Dittmar 1976), and it came to our attention twenty years ago when Jensen (1969) claimed that African Americans performed poorly on standardized I.Q. tests based on genetic differences. Bereiter and Engelmann (1966) also confused linguistic distinctions between standard and nonstandard English with false cognitive conclusions. Labov (1969) not only refuted the misleading claims of Bereiter and Engelmann, but also demonstrated that logical foundations of nonstandard English have a highly rule governed mode of linguistic behavior. From Labov (1969, 1972) we learned two important facts: (1) Language and race should not be associated with claims regarding intelligence and (2) Nonstandard English is a systematic dialect capable of logical abstraction.

Despite these observations Labov did not predict the shrouded resurgence of the deficit hypothesis in the writings of Farrell (1983) and Orr (1987).

Reviving the Deficit Hypothesis

Farrell (1983) rejects the racial foundation of Jensen's (1969) original hypothesis in favor of literacy. That is, rather than argue that African Americans do not perform well on standardized I.Q. tests on the basis of race, Farrell (1983, 1984) claims that the acquisition of literacy is a more reliable measure of intelligence. African Americans who are literate do well on these tests, while those who have not mastered standard English and related literacy skills continue to receive low scores that parallel other poor academic performance. Farrell's tenuous thesis is predicated on the assumption that the post-Socratic Greeks were the first humans capable of abstract thought, because their alphabet was the first to develop symbols that correspond to vowels in speech. Other alphabets, including Hebrew, Arabic, and the pictographic alphabets from Asia, do not contain symbols that correspond to vowels. Nevertheless, one is hard pressed to claim that those who read these languages to the exclusion of the Romance and Germanic languages are incapable of abstract thought, yet a strict interpretation of Farrell's thesis would lead one to such a false conclusion.

Farrell also claims that omission of present tense forms of the verb *to be* has the result of reducing the logical capacity of AAE. I.Q. test scores are offered as further validation of this new deficit hypothesis. The deficit, in this case, would occur when speakers of AAE omit either "is/'s" or "are/'re" from their speech or writing (i.e., "He coming" versus "He is/'s coming"). Orr (1987) makes similar pronouncements about the structure of AAE that are inconsistent with linguistic research (see Baugh 1988b). One such claim is that black English does not include comparatives, such as "X is as big as Y" or "Q is the same as R"; this observation is wrong. AAE speakers engage in comparisons frequently, although the language is quite different from that employed in mathematics.

Farrell (1983) and Orr (1987) have independently and inadvertently revived the deficit hypothesis, because they assume AAE lacks some vital linguistic content that is essential to educational success, and this just ain't so. As illustrated, with tongue firmly in cheek, "ain't" has significant grammatical functions, and despite the fact that we rarely use "ain't" in print or during formal speech, most of us recognize how and when to use "ain't" if we choose to do so. Indeed, "ain't" creeps into the formal speech of many executives, as they use it to accentuate strategic points.

Far from being the deficient dialect that Farrell (1983) and Orr (1987) imply, AAE contains unique grammatical properties that defy simplistic explanation, to say nothing of the educational consequences of many dialect differences. We have known for many years, however, that linguistic differences do not correspond to diminished intellectual potential on the part of minority students; such an interpretation of linguistic diversity is not only wrong, it places additional barriers in the path of educational development for students who are the object of misleading stereotypes and other forms of linguistic ridicule or coercion.

Some Critical Linguists Considerations

It is wrong to assume that English must use present tense forms of to be in order to maintain the logical foundations of the language. "Is" and "are" represent the present tense in utterances where they are used, either fully (usually for writing) or in contracted form (as with most of our conversation). To suggest, as Farrell has, that omission of the copula somehow reduces the logical power of English attributes more to these verbs than is necessary or justified. The following table contrasts standard auxiliary verbs with their nonstandard equivalents: Table 1 illustrates an important fact about logic and linguistic efficiency. Because nonstandard English does not require overt specification of the present tense, it can remain unmarked as long as the logical distinction between future and past tense is preserved. This greater linguistic efficiency does not imply that speakers of AAE should now spurn standard English, nothing could be further from their urgent educational needs. Rather, the efficiency of nonstandard English, which in this case, has eliminated a redundant linguistic element (i.e., either "is" or "are"), creates special problems for both teachers and students who recognize the importance of mastering the dialect of wider communication, despite the archaic and redundant nature of prescribed standard English.

Recalling the three linguistic divisions that include all American students, we must examine educational policies based on language judiciously in order to eliminate those that are based on erroneous assumptions. In this way we will be better equipped to take full advantage of linguistic expertise as we strive to identify alternative educational strategies to meet diverse pedagogical needs. The child who learns standard English at his mother's knee has no guarantee of literacy, but does possess a solid linguistic foundation upon which to begin the tasks of reading and writing. The student who speaks nonstandard English natively will be required to master standard English as a second dialect. Learning a second dialect of one's language is not the same as learning an entirely different language. Dialects differ in subtle ways, and complete mastery of a second dialect is extremely difficult. Meryl Streep is a highly regarded actress because of her ability to manipulate

Table 1

Comparison of tense marking to be *for*
American (non) standard English

	Past	Present	Future
standard	was/were	is='s/are='re	will (be)
nonstandard	was/were	unmarked=0	gon/gonna

different English dialects, but we demand this type of linguistic dexterity from our minority student as if the task were somehow quite simple.

Those who must learn English as a second language also strive for socioeconomic parity, and seek educational opportunities that will provide them and their children with prompt access to English and corresponding literacy skills. American educators have always faced linguistic diversity in their classrooms, and as demographics continue to change the racial and ethnic distribution of those who seek to melt into the larger society, the cycle of multilingual linguistic diversity will continue.

Orr (1987) draws other dangerous conclusions about the intellectual virtues of standard English and its history that are dramatically false. "I believe that in the case of these three modes of expressing comparisons (that is, multiplicative, additive and indefinite), the grammar of standard English has been shaped by what is true mathematically" (p. 158). In other words, Orr claims that the evolution of standard English has been endowed with linguistic properties that are not available to nonstandard English dialects, and speculation alone is provided in support of this highly significant contention, which she concludes is essential to logical thought and successful analytic abstraction in mathematics and science.

Standard English, as a highly prescribed dialect with a long standing literary tradition, is more archaic than nonstandard English, but it is certainly not more logical, and the history of English has not been shaped by mathematical principles. There is no reputable linguistic evidence of any kind to support this opinion. Yet it is upon this speculative hypothesis that Orr builds her arguments against African American language, revealing significant misunderstanding of AAE. While it is undoubtedly true that students must have a full literate command of mathematical jargon in order to complete a broad range of algebraic problems, one should not conclude that a lack of linguistic exposure to technical jargon is tantamount to diminished capacities for analytic abstraction.

Because of Orr's misconception regarding the logical foundations of English, she fails to appreciate that many logical and mathematical conceptions can be handled more easily by AAE. For example, standard English does not employ habitual forms of to be as does African American English, which allows one to distinguish between permanent and momentary states (e.g., *He is crazy* and *He be crazy,* convey different meanings; the latter refers to habitual events while the former represents a momentary state). Such a semantic distinction in the verb to be, could prove to be useful in distinguishing between permanent and fluctuating mathematical phenomena (Baugh 1988b). A similar grammatical distinction is found in the Spanish verbs ser and estar.

I am not suggesting that we should somehow try to incorporate nonstandard English into our basic mathematical curriculum; rather, it is vital to recognize that artificial linguistic elevation of standard usage over nonstandard dialects, without a full appreciation of the relevant linguistic facts, can yield misleading results and faulty educational policies that could unnecessarily retard the academic development of minority students.

To further illustrate the educational consequences of linguistic diversity, let us assume that a secondary school math teacher plans to discuss the concept of "zero" and other vacuous mathematical concepts. "Zero," or nothing can be expressed quite differently in purely linguistic terms, and it is helpful to know which dialect or language students are most familiar with before we attempt to teach this kind of abstract concept, particularly in mathematics and the sciences where technical jargon is essential and therefore prolific. The following sentences are semantically equivalent, and quite similar grammatically, but the educational consequences for students who are familiar with different norms will have significant educational consequences:

Table 2

Semantically equivalent examples of standard and nonstandard English (including Spanish)

1. He does not have any.
2. He doesn't have any.
_____ Standard English
3. He don't have any.
4. He don't have none.
5. He don't got any.
6. He don't got none.
7. He ain't got any.
8. He ain't got none.
_____ Nonstandard English
9. El muchacho no tengo nada.
_____ Spanish

Students who are most familiar with examples 1 and 2 should be prepared to evaluate "zero" through traditional instructional methods and maintain existing levels of academic success. Students who

are familiar with examples 3 through 9 will require linguistic enrichment and academic acceleration in order to eventually compete
with students who are already familiar with the dominant linguistic norm.

By failing to fully appreciate the significance of linguistic diversity among students, particularly for less fortunate students,
Farrell (1983) and Orr (1987) fault African American language as
the cause of African American academic failure. AAE is, more properly, symptomatic of the racial and socioeconomic isolation that
poverty perpetuates, but language is certainly not the cause of educational inequality. Attributing minority educational failure to
language alone ignores the socioeconomic and ethnographic foundations of the problem.

In a 1981 study of successful minorities it was discovered that
educational persistence was central to the economic advancement
of minorities who had somehow overcome racism, including physi-
cians, attorneys, judges, professors and entrepreneurs. In the vast
majority of cases someone outside of the school took direct inter-
ventive action to ensure that their education reflected the highest
possible standards. Some were successful in suburban white communities, where they were among the first to integrate "better
schools" while others fared well despite the poverty of racially segregated inner-city or rural African American schools. In many such
cases the adults who were educated in segregated schools felt they
were able to escape racial discrimination, while those who achieved
success in predominantly white schools regularly commented on the
need to work even harder than their white peers in order to overcome racial discrimination and negative stereotypes.

Stated another way, direct extracurricular intervention helped
to ensure academic success regardless of the racial composition of
the corresponding school. Parents who were unable to provide educational tutoring directly for their children would often seek the assistance of other family members, friends, or clergy in order to
guarantee that their children were learning to the best of their ability. Church leaders in African American communities continue to
play important roles in soliciting the assistance of volunteers to tu-
tor youth with their schooling and religious training.

The Significance of Ethnographic Relevance

There is a long standing tradition in social science that has devoted vast sums of print to the sources, causes, and consequences of

minority failure in several social domains, including education. By shifting emphasis toward excellence we now seek to identify strategies that can be successful, since they will be developed based upon successful experiences of individuals who have overcome many of the same social and linguistic obstacles that confront so many minority students in school today. Those educational programs which have been most successful with minority students are *ethnosensitive*; they acknowledge the importance of the student's culture and linguistic experience, and this information is then utilized to meet the special educational needs of that student (Heath 1983; Hakuta 1986; Baugh 1983).

Those who are native speakers of standard English have inherent, and significant, linguistic advantages over students who do not already speak the dialect of wider communication. Such nontraditional students will, of course, face the same demands in the job market as their standard English speaking peers. We must have the clarity of vision to fully recognize the relevance of linguistic diversity and how it corresponds to relative rates of educational success or failure among all students.

Smitherman (1981, 1987); Moll (1988); Baugh (1981, 1987); and Labov (1972) present alternative strategies for educating nontraditional students that first require a thorough appreciation of the language and culture that is native to the student. Those who fail to account for this background are forced to approach the education of nontraditional students in highly speculative ways.

In order to accommodate ethnosensitive instruction, teachers may wish to use alternative texts that hold high interest for students. Local newspapers are a valuable educational tool in this regard, not the least of which being that stories of local interest tend to capture student's attention. Various assignments covering diverse subjects from history, economics, math, and geography are routinely presented as part of every major newspaper. The American Newspaper Publishers Association Foundation has been active in work with educators and literacy volunteers. Interested parents, teachers, and civic leaders may wish to consult with managing editors of their regional newspapers in order to develop or strengthen educational ties between schools and the news media.

Some successful programs have used newspapers combined with teams of students who work on selected topics of shared interests. Students with keen interests in sports were grouped together and presented with math assignments that maintained statistics for their favorite teams and players. Other students showed greater interest in fashion, and, based on prices that appeared in advertisements, fashion teams were formed and assigned tasks of compiling alternative budgets for clothing and different combinations of seasonal ensembles. Still others with an interest in science, history or anthropology may develop teams of aspiring meterologists, young historians, or anthropologists. These efforts work well when combined with comprehensive programs such as those that offer writing across the curriculum, or journal writing, among other highly cooperative educational programs.

The team orientation of these suggestions are offered to emphasize cooperation, because most occupations require some form of interpersonal working relationships, and team projects allow students to exchange ideas rather than harbor knowledge as a self-fulfilling entity. The suggestions provided here are more representative of a philosophy of cooperative education, rather than a precise recipe that should be administered in some strictly regimented procedure.

Elsewhere (Baugh 1981, 1987) the value of culturally relevant educational procedures is stressed, with the provision that every effort should be made to determine individualized educational requirements. Public schools have not regularly had the luxury of sufficient resources to ensure that each student, and especially nontraditional students, are afforded this kind of personalized attention. It is at this critical juncture, where students must reinforce and supplement classroom instruction, that so many minority students escape adequate educational attention. While newspapers and corporate sponsorship of special extracurricular programs are not the only innovative strategies that may offer additional, albeit voluntary, assistance to minority students, my own fieldwork has revealed a strong commitment within minority communities from parents, church leaders, local librarians, and other concerned citizens who are willing to work closely with educators to ensure that minority children obtain the finest education, bounded only by the limits of each student's abilities.

Conclusion

Greater linguistic sensitivity on the part of educators and others who are concerned with the academic development of culturally diverse students is essential. As our appreciation of linguistic diversity matures, so too must the relative sophistication of the policies that we adopt to overcome the history of educational failure that has plagued nontraditional students. Language has all too often been a misdiagnosed component of various educational strategies which, often inadvertently, attribute minority failure to linguistic causes.

Existing linguistic stereotypes lend popular credence to many misconceptions about language, and therefore require careful evaluation by trained scholars who can distinguish linguistic fact from fiction. These educational requirements are more pronounced in the present social climate, which often attribute such efforts to "affirmative action" now regarded by many whites as preferential treatment for minorities. Such an interpretation is not only racially divisive, it fails to acknowledge the legacy of discrimination that has been perpetuated by the exclusion of minorities and women from the majority of influential professions.

Despite changing public opinion, the linguistic legacy of African Americans is unique when compared to any other group that has migrated to the United States. Until adequate resources are allocated to overcome the history of racial isolation, we will continue to observe substantial gaps in the educational achievement of those who learn standard English natively, versus those students who did not learn English in their homes.

My effort grows from the egalitarian principles upon which true democratic societies are based, because educational parity is essential to the continued growth and economic development of the United States or any other nation where linguistic diversity thrives. Greater linguistic understanding and tolerance may lead to better educational programs that will be more effective than those that have failed us in the past. The adoption of ethnosensitive educational programs is advocated because they have demonstrated the highest prospects for academic achievement among nontraditional minority students. The value of extracurricular community based programs is also endorsed as a supplement to the educational training offered by teachers and other public school officials.

CHAPTER 11

Ethnic Identity as a Variable in the Learning Equation

CURTIS W. BRANCH

Questions to Think About

1. How do African American students respond psychologically to academic failure derived from inappropriate instruction? Does this academic failure influence students' ethnic identity, racial attitudes, self-esteem, or self-concept? Or, is academic performance influenced by the students' ethnic identity, racial attitudes, self-esteem, or self-concept?
2. To what extent is the ethnic identity of African American students influenced by acculturation? Does acculturation account for part of the variation in school success experienced by African American students? Are there psychological consequences for African American students who lose their ethnic identity in the process of acculturation?
3. How does Branch's discussion of self-efficacy theory in explaining differential performance in social and academic settings compare with King's discussion of John Ogbu's analysis of variation in academic performance among African American students?

Ethnic identity has often been discussed as a significant contributor to the social development process. It is also frequently cited as a dimension of racial attitude which has implications for adjustment in the social spheres. The exact relationship between ethnic identity and other dimensions of racial attitudes, however, is never clearly established or articulated. This has led to a frequent interchange of concepts such as self-esteem, racial identity, and racial attitude. H. McAdoo (1971) and Teplin (1976) showed that the aforementioned variables, plus others, collectively formulate the construct racial attitude. Despite their contribution to the same construct they are not necessarily correlated. Similar findings have been reported more recently by Branch and Newcombe (1986, 1988).

The relationship of ethnic identity to self-esteem and racial attitudes has often been blurred for several reasons. Some of them are related to theoretical difficulties and others are rooted in methodological deficits. First, there has been a consistent failure on the part of researchers to operationalize the constructs without cross-referencing them. This has led to tautological arguments which attempt to define a variable by referring to concepts assumed to be related. The exact nature of the relationships is never verified empirically but is accepted as being real. For example, the literature on racial attitudes among young black children is filled with historic studies which suggest, without statistical verification, that young black children's expression of a white preference is evidence of self-hatred and negative self-concept. Aboud and Skerry (1984) and others (Baldwin 1979; Banks & Rompf 1973; Branch & Newcombe 1988) have provided another set of analyses which cast considerable doubts on the older position.

Secondly, ethnic identity has frequently been defined as a unidimensional construct. Cross (1987) has shown that there are at least two types, personal and group. He proposes that the two often operate quite distinctly of each other and are inextricably linked to the context in which they are measured as well as the instrumentation used to sample them.

Another problem with the assumed interrelatedness of ethnic identity, self-esteem, and racial attitudes is that the context within which measurements have occurred have rarely considered the impact of the environment in any way that can be subjected to statistical scrutiny. There has, however, been attention devoted to the effect of the race of the examiner (Sattler 1970). In light of the significant shifts in the area of racial self attributions and the ensuing interracial climate in America since the early 1970s a systematic reexamination of this variable appears to be overdue.

Lastly, the issue of ethnic identity and all of its related constructs (self-esteem, self-concept, racial awareness, racial attitude) are always discussed in a social context with precious little attention given to the academic prowess as being incongruent with a sense of blackness? Do teachers subliminally suggest to young African Americans that particular fields of study/work are off limits because for them to enter therein would be politically incorrect? If the answer to either of these is yes, how do we change the pattern?

This chapter will discuss the concept of ethnic identities and show how they are critical variables in facilitating children's openness to academic excellence and fostering a sense of academic competence. Specifically, the use of ethnic labels as a way of making self attributions which implicitly prescribe attitudes about learning will be discussed. Before that, however, a brief redefinition of concepts used throughout this chapter will be presented. It will be followed by a review of the literature on personal and group identities. Their importance in shaping attributions which govern behavior in the classroom will be discussed. Self attributions made by young African American children will be examined as well as teacher attributions. The classic situation of identities in conflict will be discussed at length. Self-efficacy theory will be presented as a theoretical framework for understanding differential performances in social and academic settings.

Conceptual Foundation

Racial attitudes, ethnic identity, and self-esteem collectively influence the learning and development process of the African American child in an interactive manner which is missed when the concepts are examined individually. The importance of each of these issues is also reinforced when learning is defined more broadly than simply acquiring new knowledge in a classroom setting. Instead, learning should be thought of as encompassing "school learning" and "social learning" (i.e., political development, social cognition, etc.). Each has implications for how work can be done in the other area. It is proposed that the learning process be conceptualized as an equation. Variables to be considered in the equation include the teacher, the student, the environment, and the curriculum. For the purpose of this chapter, emphasis is placed primarily on the teacher and the student. Specifically, their racial identities and the behaviors and attitudes spawned by them will be the focal point. Let's begin our analysis of the variables in the equation by defining basic concepts which can be applied to the teacher and the student.

Basic Concepts

Racial Attitudes. The understanding of the human developmental process is enhanced when there is a clear conceptual framework against which to explore the behavior. Within the last ten years there has been a measurable shift among African American scholars, away from Eurocentric ideologies toward an Afrocentric perspective or some variation thereof. Despite that quantum leap from old ideas/behaviors there has not been a similar shift toward redefining, perhaps even eliminating antiquated concepts and theoretical lore. The result is old baggage in new garments. This collage of old and new is nowhere more apparent than in the areas of racial attitudes, ethnic identity, and social cognition. Concepts are often used interchangeably, despite there being no empirical evidence to justify such behavior.

Racial Attitudes are Multifaceted. Historically they have been inferred from tasks of racial preference. That is to say, subjects are asked to indicate a preference for one race of individuals. Typically the choices have been in forced choice formats (i.e., dolls, pictures, etc.). From the results of choices researchers have deduced that the subject's preferences are reflective of their racial attitude and implicitly a statement about themselves, especially if they state a preference for someone of a race other than their own. One major problem with this line of logic is that when preference has been measured, rarely has it been shown to reflect preference in real-life situations (Branch and Newcombe 1988). The same can be said of racial attitudes as a global construct. They seem to be related to the context in which they are exhibited/expressed and the global or specific nature of the tests being used to measure them. Additionally, racial attitudes have been shown to be multifaceted, including elements of awareness, preference, identification and esteem. Methodologically it has been difficult to tap into all of the facets simultaneously, without contaminating the measurement process. A critical issue it seems then is whether attitudes toward one's own racial group can/should be measured in the same way as attitudes toward other groups. Likewise, psychometrically it is appropriate to assume that one attitude (e.g., in-group oriented) is the antithesis of another attitude (e.g., out-group oriented).

Patterns of apparent White preference have been reported in the inter-cultural literature on racial attitude development. A study of racial identification and racial preference among Black pre-schoolers in New York and Trinidad (Gopaul-McNicol 1988) found that the children preferred the white doll. However, in attempting to explain the variance in performance she points to the media, parental attitudes and favoritism in school as explanatory variables. Not clear in her discussion, however, is the impact of cultural variables which defy accurate measurement. That is to say, how novel is the testing situation for the Trinidadian children and how much does that show in the results, if at all.

One central question concerning racial attitudes is their fluidity over time. Branch and Newcombe (1986) and McAdoo (1970) have shown that children's racial attitudes do change over time, as a function of social development and a variety of environmental contingencies. For the purpose of the present discussion racial attitudes will be seen as representing a conglomeration of many dimensions. Those dimensions are not necessarily correlated. Finally, racial attitudes towards one's own group are seen as being essentially of the same structural variety as attitudes about other groups. Closely associated with the concept of racial attitude(s) is the idea of self-esteem.

Conventional research wisdom and lore have suggested that racial attitudes, particularly statements of preference, and self-esteem are highly correlated. The system of logic that has been used in this instance is that if a child expresses a preference for someone other than a stimulus resembling him or her self they are evidencing self-hatred and logically they have a low level of self-esteem. Such linear thinking ignores the novelty of the stimuli as a source of variance (Baldwin 1979) and the possibility that the preference is a statement of an external reality which has little if anything to do with the respondent's inner psychological life. A vivid reminder of this point occurred while the author was collecting data for a racial attitude study. The respondent, a five year old African American girl remarked (after choosing white dolls over black dolls in a multiple choice task) ". . . I really like these white dolls best. . . . Black people do bad things to people . . . like rob them and shoot them . . . I'm black . . . but I still like myself." After some reflection on the scenario it was concluded by the researcher that indeed the respondent's public attitude about some African Americans did not necessarily reflect her self appraisal.

Evidence from the racial attitudes studies seems to point in the direction of too much importance having been placed on a doll choice (i.e., Do doll choices approximate real life statements of preference?); racial attitudes are multidimensional; racial attitudes are functions of a variety of causal agents; and racial attitudes change dramatically over time.

Self-esteem. In this section I want to show how self-esteem is highly contextualized. That is to say that different people base their sense of self worth/self love on different dimensions. Likewise how learning is effected by self-esteem is rather idiosyncratic.

The literature on self-esteem is difficult to interpret because of problems with terminology and measurement issues. Frequently self-esteem is used interchangeably with self-concept and without a clear operational definition of the word or its evidences. Marsh and Shavelson (1985) have raised the problems of definition and measurement as being very closely related. They have suggested that self-concept is multi-faceted and hierarchical in nature. Self-esteem is seen as one dimension of self-concept. They also suggest that self-concept becomes more distinct with increases in age. Late adolescence is, they suggest, the point at which self-concept is crystallized and the varied dimensions of it are distinct. Similarly, measurement issues have been highlighted in the writings of Benson and Rentsch (1988); Coates (1985); Enggaard (1983); and Williams, Apenahier, and Haynes (1987).

Benson and Rentsch examined the dimensionality of the Piers-Harris Self-Concept Scale, one of the most widely used instruments of its type. Black, White, and Hispanic students in grades 3–6 were included in their study. It was discovered that the construct validity of the test is a function not only of its content but also of the manner phrasing of questions. Enggaard reports a similar general concern about interviews based research on children's self-perceptions and self-esteem. She also suggests the possibility that interview data may provide information on the child's social character, thought processes, and perception. It is further hypothesized in the Enggaard work that the behavior of the child during the interview (i.e., perseverance, initiative, value judgment) potentially interact paradigmatically with the child's individuality, intentions, and scale of values. Greater levels of interaction are seen as being reflective of a more developed and adjusted personality.

The works of Coates and Williams et al. specifically address African American children and adolescents. Both studies uncover measurement issues which seem to attenuate the merits of traditional theory in its application to people of color. The Piers-Harris Children's Self-Concept Scale was the focal point in the Williams et al. study. Over four hundred, predominantly African American, children in gifted educational programs in grades 1–9 were tested. The result was that the authors identified six othorgonal factors.

Deborah Coates used the twenty-five item Coopersmith Self-Esteem Inventory (factor scores); nonverbal identification-with-others tasks; and four semantic differential scales designed to assess the adolescent's perception of how parents, male friends, and female friends see them. In her sample of three hundred and forty-three middle-income African American adolescents, it was found that "while network structure measures are more related to 'how others see me' self-judgments and to a measure of social affiliation, the support scales are more related to overall self-esteem."

It appears that the difference in dimensionality of the Piers-Harris Children's Self-Concept Test as well as Coates' work with social networks as a determinant of self-esteem raises the question of validity of techniques of measurement when the subjects are African Americans. Another related issue which is not culture specific is the idea of dimensions of self-esteem and constructs which collectively compose it. Marsh and Shavelson (1985) have suggested that there seems to be "a clear separation of the verbal and mathematical self-concepts; they are distinct and cannot be incorporated into a general academic self-concept." What then are the dimensions and contributors to self-concept in academic settings? How closely related are general self-concept and self-concept in the classroom? Preliminary answers to parts of these questions are discernible from the recent literature on self-esteem and African American children.

Factors which have been identified as contributors to self attributions of elementary school children include: teacher assessments and expectations (Harris, Rosenthal & Snodgrass 1986; Haynes, Comer, Hamilton-Lee, Boger, et al. 1987); social variables such as race, social class, and social structure (Entwistle, Alexander, Pallas & Cadigan 1987; Kohr, Coldiron, Skiffington, Masters, et al. 1988); television viewing (Stroman 1986; Wiggins 1987); and attitudes of parents and teachers (Alawiye, Alawiye & Thomas 1989).

The role of the teacher in monitoring the progress of students is undenied. Likewise the role of the teacher in influencing the motivation of students, even with their nonverbal behaviors, is also critical. The importance of teachers' impressions of students and how those impressions get conveyed and internalized was the focal point of a study by Haynes et al. (1987). The one hundred and forty-two children in grades 3, 4, and 5 who were included in their study were rated by teachers on classroom behavior, group participation and

attitude toward authority. Results of teacher ratings were correlated with student self appraisals as revealed by the Piers-Harris
Children's Self-Concept Scale. Seventy-two percent of the variance
in school related self-concept was explained by teacher assessments.
In a somewhat related study by Harris et al. (1986) significant differences in teaching behaviors were noted between peer and adult
teachers. That is to say "seven female and three male professional
teachers and five female and five male peer teachers (4th, 5th, and
6th graders) were videotaped while teaching a short lesson to a total of eighty students, some of whom the teachers had been told had
exceptional ability. Detailed codings and ratings of the videotapes
allowed an examination of the interrelationships among teacher expectations, gender, teaching behaviors, and student outcome measures of cognitive performance and academic self-concept." The peer
and adult teachers were significantly different in their approach to
the students.

Reliable sex differences in teaching behaviors were found for
the peer teachers only. However, no significant effects were found for
teachers' manipulated expectations for students' performance. It
was also found that better student outcomes were positively associated with such variables as task orientation, explanation, nonverbal warmth, and no interruption of lesson to give feedback.

The work of Entwistle et al. (1987) has also explored self-image
and its contribution to academic performance. Because of its focus
on the developmental aspect of self-image this work is of critical importance. Also, the use of multiple data sources (i.e., parents, students, teachers) gives this study a global perspective which is often
missing in other works. The subject pool was an interracial sam-
pling of first graders (three hundred forty-one girls, three hundred
thirty-two boys). No racial differences were found in the subject's academic self-image according to race or parent background. The two
sexes do, however, define their images differently. Images held by
the girls strongly reflect stereotypic sex-role notions. Boys on the
other hand reflect instrumental role concerns. Self-evaluations
were a greater component of the profile of boys in contrast to girls
who depended more on external valuations (i.e., parental evaluations). Stroman's (1986) study of television and self-concept among
Black children came to a similar conclusion (i.e., girls depended
more on others for a sense of self than did boys). Another study by
Kohr et al. (1988) found striking sex differences and self-esteem.
The relationship, however, turned out to be non-linear and to shift
with SES and grade in school. Students in grades 5, 8, and 11 were

included in the study. The sample was racially heterogeneous. It was observed that self-esteem scores significantly paralleled students' SES level at all grade levels, in both low- and high-SES schools. Significant differences were found for self-esteem by race only among the low-SES schools at the elementary level. This pattern disappeared at grades 8 and 11. Girls showed significantly higher self-esteem than boys at all grade levels in low-SES schools and for grades 8 and 11 in high-SES schools.

In addition to SES, teacher evaluations of student environmental factors, especially television watching, have been suspected of being a prime contributor to children's self-esteem and sense of social worth. Wiggins (1987) investigated the relationship between self-esteem, earned grades, and television viewing habits. Among the four hundred and eighty-three students from grades 4, 6, 8, 10, and 12, it was found that earned grades, self-esteem scores, and locus of control scores were not significantly correlated with television viewing. The single most important finding was a positive correlation between self-esteem scores and earned grades. Operating under the same premise of television watching being a causative factor in self-esteem Stroman (1986) studied the association between amount of time spent watching television and perceptions of self-concept as measured by the Piers-Harris Self-Concept Scale. The research sample consisted of one hundred and two Black children, ages seven to thirteen. Global patterns of causation were not found. Instead it was found that self-concepts of girls were more related to television watching than those of boys. The relationship between self-concept and academic achievement found by Wiggins has been challenged slightly by a more recent study from the cross-cultural literature (Alawiye, Alawiye & Thomas 1989). Participants in their study, fifty parents and teachers in Ghana and Gambia, felt that there is a positive relationship between self-concept and academic achievement. They also viewed enrichment of academic achievement as a desirable academic goal.

Surprisingly, there was no consensus that poor academic achievement was related to negative self-concept. They seem to suggest that the relationship between the two constructs is not linear. Additionally, the fact that the positive relationship between self-concept and academic achievement was found outside of the Americas is interesting. It raises the possibility of the universality of this finding. Perhaps universal is a bit strong but it does raise the idea that self-concept and academic achievement links are not an Americanism.

Self-esteem is a multi-faceted construct. It is perhaps too multidimensional to be reduced to simple cause and effect statements answerable by pencil and paper. The literature to date has not done a good job in determining whether self-concept in academic settings is the same as self-concept in familial and other social contexts. Assuming that there are different variations of self-concept we must continue to explore how they are the same and dissimilar. More specifically, how closely related are general self-concept and self-concept in the classroom?

Racial Attitudes and Self-concept. Despite conventional wisdom's frequent linking of racial attitudes and self-concept (esteem) the literature has not supported such a relationship. The works of Hernandez (1984), McAdoo (1985) and Spencer (1984) focus on different dimensions of racial attitudes but all agree on the finding that racial attitudes and self-concept are not directly linked.

Hernandez studied a racially mixed sample of six to nine year old children. He found that attributions relative to racial designations and preferences were not in any way interactive with self-esteem statements. The nature of their relationship to each other was so weak that he concluded that racial attitudes and self-esteem are not significantly related at all. A similar study by Clark (1979), using third to sixth graders, suggests a different but non-linear relationship between the two constructs. Clark found age differences in the relationships. Younger children tended to value racial group concepts more in their overall self-evaluations than did their older counterparts. The sample used in the Clark study was all black.

More compelling evidence for the absence of a positive self-esteem and racial attitude relationship is found in the longitudinal study of McAdoo (1985). The study focused on four aspects of Black child development, "the development of self-esteem and racial attitudes in Black children from preschool age and over a period of time; the relationship between those variables; the impact of demographic factors upon these developments; and the occupational and educational aspirations of the children." Three studies were completed with data being collected over a five year period, in Michigan and Mississippi. Instruments utilized included the Thomas Self-Concept Values Test, Engle Self-Concept Procedures, Preschool Racial Attitude Measure II (PRAM II), and direct questions.

In Study I (Mississippi and Michigan Preschool data) the race attitude and self-concept relationship was mixed, at best. Among children of northern one-parent families no relationship was found. Likewise there was no relationship when the samples were divided

on the basis of gender. The groups were found to feel positive about
their own self-worth independent of what racial group orientation
they held.

"A relationship was found with the southern boys, $r = .534$,
$p < .01$, and the combined two-parent family groups, $r = .404$,
$p < .01$. In these groups, those with positive self-concepts had more
out-group orientation. The southern relationship was attributed to
the divergent scores obtained by the southern boys, the group with
the highest self-concept scores." (McAdoo 1985).

Similar patterns of mixed results and non linearity when self-
esteem was assessed for a relationship with self identification, a
narrowly defined dimension of racial attitudes. "Self-concept was
positively correlated with the accuracy of racial identification for
the southern boys, $r = .712$, $p < .01$, and southern girls, $r = .712$,
$p < .05$. The children in the south who were more accurate in des-
ignating the race of the picture also scored higher in self-esteem.
Different relationships were found in the northern sample. The
northern girls, with the lowest self-concept scores, had a significantly negative relationship; those who had positive self-esteem
tended to make inaccurate identifications. No relationships were
found among these boys" (McAdoo 1985).

Overall the results of the first study in the McAdoo trilogy suggested that the children (all black), had positive self-esteem but
were moderately out-group oriented, as measured by the PRAM II.
Most of the children were able to identify pictures by their racial
labels. McAdoo concluded that the children tended to compartmen-
talize their feelings about themselves and their status attitude toward their racial group, a finding also echoed in the work of Cross
(1987) and Spencer (1982a, 1982b, 1984).

The second study in the McAdoo series was a one year follow-up
study conducted in Washington, D.C. The same instruments used in
Study I were employed as was the same set of research questions.
"No support for the self-hatred hypothesis was found. No relationship was found between Thomas self-concept and racial attitude, or
between self-concept and dolls self-identity. Relationships were
found on doll race preference questions for three subgroups: the
girls ($r = -.556$), two-parent ($r = -.596$), and middle-class ($r = -.588$) groups when they were high on self-concept, they were also
outgroup oriented. No relationships were evident in the other
groups. Again, the children's self-concept was intact, regardless
of how they felt about the status differential of racial groups"
(McAdoo 1985).

Upon follow-up testing the self-hatred hypothesis was not rejected for three groups of children. "Those with high self-concept scores were out-group oriented. Significant relationships on Thomas self-concept were found the second year in the boys, one-parent and working-class homes, $r = .501$, $p < .01$, $r = .391$, $p < .008$ and $r = .343$, $p < .05$, respectively. These two groups could be considered the most vulnerable within the sample. For the children from the three most "secure" groups—girls, two-parent and middle-income families—no such relationship was found, rejecting the view of Black self-hatred. Self-concept and self-race identity were not related for any of the groups" (McAdoo 1985).

Study III was a five year follow-up study of the children tested in Study I. Despite significant changes in both self-concept and race attitudes no relationship was found between the two constructs. McAdoo interpreted that finding as supporting the compartmentalization notion. That is, children were able to feel good about themselves, independent of their feelings about their racial group.

Research of the same genre has been completed by Spencer (1982a, 1982b, 1984). Her focus has been a bit more in the direction of cognitive development serving as mediational factor which tempers children's racial attitudes and attributions to self." In each of her studies Spencer has used a variety of instruments, each measuring a different construct (e.g., racial attitudes, racial preference, race awareness, self-concept, and verbal ability). She assesses and examines the relationship between aspects of personal identity and group identity while simultaneously considering the role of race awareness. Results from her works show that the quality and level of children's personal and group identity vary. They are not simple linear relationships, as has often been theorized" (Branch & Newcombe 1988).

Self-efficacy Theory: The Synthesizing Point?   Bandura (1986) has suggested that beliefs which individuals hold about their ability to affect significant outcomes in their lives play a central role in mediating behavior. This postulation is most often called self-efficacy theory. Its relevance to the area of learning and mastery of academic subject matter is quite high. According to Bandura the beliefs individuals hold about themselves determine choice of behavioral activities, including motivational level, thought patterns, and reactions to new situations. Self-efficacy theory has been invoked as an explanatory variable in many types of treatment and learning situations.

Data presented in this review suggests that how children think about themselves racially and globally conceptually is important. Also apparent from the studies reviewed is the idea that social variables such as gender and economic class contribute partially to the attitudes that students develop about themselves and their ability to master their life space.

Much has been said about role models and their influence on children. Unfortunately many of those suggestions are reductionistic and simple minded in approach. That is to say, the presence of role models is not likely to significantly impact a child's view of self and his/her ability to accomplish new goals if children don't see themselves as being competent and capable of aspiring to what the role model has attained. Put another way, if children don't have a healthy sense and mastery of one's space they won't be able to even fantasize about high levels of achievement.

Self-efficacy appears to be a good conceptual framework for starting to think about how young African American learners develop a cognitive set about themselves as learners. In some stratas of the African American community learning is stereotyped as "acting white." Fordham and Ogbu (1986) have discussed this syndrome at length from the perspective of strategies that African American students have developed to counteract accusations of "acting white." The empirical support for their conclusions was obtained in a 1982 study completed in a historically black section of Washington, D.C., in a relatively low-income area.

Fictive kinship was found to be extensive among the students at the school. It showed up, according to Fordham and Ogbu (1985), "not only in conflicts between blacks and whites and between black students and black teachers, who are often perceived to be 'functionaries' of the dominant society, but also in the students' constant need to reassure one another of black loyalty and identity. They appear to achieve this group loyalty by defining certain attitudes and behaviors as 'white' and therefore unacceptable, and then employing numerous devices to discourage one another from engaging in those behaviors and attitudes, i.e., from 'acting white' " (pp. 185–186). Through an analysis of ethnographic data, a subset of thirty-three students are selected for intensive follow-up. From that sample Fordham and Ogbu identified several strategies which partially counteract the ridicule that high achieving adolescents experienced at the hands of their friends. They contend that, "the strategies of the academically successful students include engaging in activities which mute perceptions of their being preoccupied with academic excellence leading eventually to individual success outside the group, i.e., eventual upward mobility. Among them are athletic activities (which are regarded as 'black activities') and other 'team'-oriented activities, for male students." Fordham and Ogbu further conclude that ". . . The black community has an important part to play in changing the situation. The community should develop programs to teach black children that academic pursuit is not synonymous with one-way acculturation into a white cultural frame of reference or acting white. To do this effectively, however, the black community must reexamine its own perceptions and interpretations of school learning. Apparently, black children's general perception that academic pursuit is 'acting white' is learned in the black community" (Fordham & Ogbu 1986, pp. 202–203).

There is much evidence to support the idea that the student interpretation of "acting white" is a reflection of societal stereotypes of black and white capabilities.

The findings and observations reported by Fordham and Ogbu are cause for much concern. The literature is saturated with other examples of the black community not being able to rise above the burden of a great potential. What is missing, unfortunately, is an equivalent discourse on the youngsters who learned and achieved despite the odds. How is this perseverance and strength of character to be explained? Despite being ostracized as "brainiacs" the high achieving students in the Fordham and Ogbu study continued to achieve, even at the risk of attenuating the fictive kinship bonds implicitly present in Capital High.

It is clear that a high sense of self-efficacy is pronounced in the behavior of the high achievers who continue to achieve even in the face of negative reinforcers. The value of Bandura's notions to further examine achievement and exemplary behavior among African American learners is clear, at least to this writer. Comparatively speaking, we know so little about the success stories. Why? Following the lead of cultural anthropologist, studying single cases potentially can provide educators and psychologists many insights into the success motives and strategies of high achievers.

Learning Equation

Personal and individual identity are two dimensions along which many individuals identify themselves. According to the work of Cross and Spencer, most African American children have very clear compartmentalizations of their attitude about identity. That is to say, a sense of ethnicity can be very personalized or it can be more diffused and related to some sense of connectedness to a larger group. The research writings in this area have consistently shown that while the two types of identity are usually born out of the same cognitive set about the world, they may in fact be quite distinct in their presentation in daily life activities. Individuals may have very narrowly defined senses of individual ethnic identity, but may be more global when they think about themselves as belonging to a communal group. The research in this area strongly suggests that physical characteristics have a different value in the importance attributed to it by children. As they grow older, physical characteristics are more defined by group standards than an individual's idiosyncratic assessment. The matter of ethnic identity as a function of group relatedness can be seen in the various ethnic group titles or labels that are assumed by members of the African American community. The recent widespread acceptance of the designation of African American to replace the more historic designation of Black is a prime example. It has been suggested by many writers that a movement in this direction is more a political statement borne out of a sense of group belonging and also an attempt to connect with the African diaspora. Fordham and Ogbu (1985) have described this type of group affiliation as fictive relationships.

The importance of group and individual identities in the learning equation seems to be related to how invested children are in learning and how much of that investment may be attributed to a group norm. Again, the work of Fordham and Ogbu identify the stressors of children succeeding academically in an environment in which academic excellence is not valued or even encouraged. It is my opinion that the identity that an individual assumes for her or himself and what that means personally will have many implications for the extent of involvement in achieving some level of academic success.

Racial attitudes as discussed in this Chapter include concepts of ethnicity, one's own as well as that of others. It is apparent that again the racial attitudes that children have, as it relates to the issue of ethnic identity, will foster or interfere with their belief in the need for acquiring new knowledge. Assuming this to be true, coupled with what we know about the changing nature of racial attitudes, it appears that educators and parents need to be concerned about the dynamics between their children and the environment.

Branch and Newcombe (1986) have suggested that children become more in-group oriented with the passage of time. A similar pattern was highlighted in the work of McAdoo (1985). These two pieces of research then raise the question of whether racial attitudes including ethnic identity are subject to dynamic fluctuations over time; are children's attributions to racial identity subject to change over time also? The big question that arose from this concern is, whether children become more or less interested in learning and things that are superficially defined as academic as they grow older. Racial attitudes then seem to play a critical dimension in the learning equation in that those attitudes may create or discourage the development of a sense of academic growth and development through expansion of one's knowledge base.

Racial attitudes and self-concept have been shown in this Chapter to be constructs that are very vital but not correlated in a linear fashion as has been often discussed in various theoretical and empirical writings. It has been shown that the self-concept that African American children express also is a function of their developmental stage. That is to say, as children grow older they find dimensions in their environment which validate them as individuals. Those dimensions come to have increasing importance for children, and those dimensions on which the children do not perform very successfully, or distinguish themselves, become less central to generating statements of self-esteem. This problem of whether or not the dimensions used by individuals to define themselves are also used by the constructors of the tests is a very common one.

Ethnic identities assumed by individuals as well as those attributed to them by others, have implications for the learning process because they empower the learner to self-define. In the process of creating a definition of one's self with little or no regard for how others see the defining individual, a sense of determinism and heightened self-esteem are likely to follow. Additionally, given the definition of learning that is often used in professional literature, ethnic identities are important because they are ways by which the learners can exercise some control over their life space. That is to say, they can determine what is and what is not important. It is striking that in most of the current literature on learning, social cognition and a sense of the political realities of life are rarely, if ever, included in those definitions. Instead the focus is exclusively on learning in the academic sense of the word. It is strongly suggested that in order to be more facilitative of global and intense growth and development on the part of the African American child, teachers, parents, and children themselves will have to redefine the definition of learning and give greater value to the life skills and awarenesses of the world around them and how they have implications for our preparedness to master the task of the classroom.

CHAPTER 12

Effective Black Teachers: A Literature Review

MICHELE FOSTER

Questions to Think About

1. Is it possible for pre-service teachers to be taught the characteristics, skills and dispositions found in effective Black teachers?
2. In which settings, under which circumstances and in which kinds of programs can these characteristics, skills and dispositions be taught to pre-service teachers?
3. Is it possible on the basis of well-developed interviews to determine which individuals are best suited for teaching cuturally diverse students?

This chapter reviews the literature on effective Black teachers written since the mid-1960s. My choice of this particular time period has been influenced by two factors. First, prior to the mid-1960s, the majority of Black teachers were concentrated in segregated, de facto or de jure Black schools. Therefore most of the literature written about Blacks prior to this time concerns desegregation, with a particular focus on Black students not teachers. The second reason influencing my decision to focus on this twenty-five year period is because 1966 is the first year that the ERIC database became available.

The review draws on several bodies of literature, but concentrates primarily on the work of a small number of scholars, many but not all African American, whose work employs the qualitative methodology of sociology, anthropology, sociolinguistics and ethnography of speaking, and whose work uses the cultural and social aspects of the Black community and its integrity as a starting point. For the most part, this research rejects the dominant psychological paradigm in educational research because of its over reliance on normative characteristics—individually valued personality, behavioral and cognitive traits—and its failure to consider the collective meaning systems that characterize different cultural groups.

In so doing, it seeks to counter the excessively negative portrayal of Black teachers by researchers, who with few exceptions (Lerner 1972; Sterling 1972; Lightfoot 1973, 1978) have characterized Black teachers in decidedly negative ways, a point discussed in greater detail later in this chapter.

Before undertaking this review, let me consider a number of limitations and problems evident in the database itself that limit the review. When one examines the database on Black teachers, it becomes clear that most of the research concerns their relationship to the larger social order. Indeed, while the research literature prior to the 1960s focuses on the need to desegregate the schools, the 1980s research literature deals almost entirely with the declining numbers of Black teachers and offers various analyses of the causes of this decline, a point made by Ladson-Billings in chapter 7. Some of the more recent literature stresses the need to increase the number of Black teachers. The justification advanced most often is a role model argument, rather than an analysis of any unique characteristics, pedagogy or philosophy of education believed to be possessed by Black teachers who work primarily with Black students.

Another limitation of the research base on teachers has been that, except for issues of access, it does not adequately consider the influence of ethnic background in its analyses. Research on teachers though extensive has generally failed to highlight the practice of Black teachers. This is true for the various bodies of literature including the research on effective teachers, as well as the anthropological, sociological and first person literature on teaching.

Research on Effective Teaching

A substantial body of literature on effective and successful teachers exists in the ERIC database. Nonetheless, despite more than 4500 entries and 7000 entries respectively in the 1983–1991

ERIC database, as well as 5887 on Black teachers, there are no records in the database that include both the descriptors effective or successful and Black teachers. Neither does the literature on effective teaching contained in the ERIC database link the descriptors effective teachers with teacher characteristics. Although the literature on effective teachers is quite large, it does not differentiate between Anglo teachers and teachers of color particularly Black teachers, making it difficult to focus a literature review exclusively on effective Black teachers. This review, however, concentrates on those studies, which explicitly link teachers' racial and ethnic identity and background with effective practice.

Research on Teacher Thinking

Studies of teacher thinking, including the more recent "wisdom of practice" studies (Shulman 1987), for the most part do not consider the racial identity of teachers or their belief systems even though previous life experience of teachers, their background, identities, culture and the critical incidents in their lives help shape their view of teaching as well as essential elements of their practice (Goodson 1988). Though limited, research comparing the views of Black teachers and majority group teachers has concluded that these groups differ in their job satisfaction patterns; their perception of the status of the profession and the school environment; and the changes required in order to educate Black students effectively (Provenzo 1988; Metropolitan Life 1988). Some of the literature on teacher thinking has also found differences between the beliefs of pre-service Anglo teachers and preservice teachers of color (Murrell 1991).

Socialogical, Anthropological and First Person Literature

There is substantial sociological, anthropological and first person literature on teaching. In large measure, however, this literature, like the literature on teacher thinking and the wisdom of practice studies, has failed to include Black teachers. It must be noted that of sixty-five first person narratives written in this century reviewed by this author, only seven were written by Black teachers (Foster 1991a). Black teachers do not fare much better in the sociological and anthropological literature. As mentioned earlier, except for the few balanced portrayals of Black teachers (Lightfoot 1973,1978; Sterling 1972; Lerner 1972), this literature has characterized Black teachers as insensitive, authoritarian individuals, who are upholders of the status quo and ill-suited to teach Black students effectively (Rist 1970, 1973; Conroy 1972; Spencer 1986). Positive portrayals of Black teachers are infrequent especially when compared to those of White teachers. As a result, researchers have, perhaps unwittingly through omission, distortion and excessively negative portrayals, conveyed the idea that Black teachers are indifferent, uncaring and unsympathetic. These negative characterizations diverge from other portrayals of Black teachers found in the essays, sociological studies, and autobiographies written by and from the point of view of Black people. Though largely anecdotal, these accounts portray Black teachers as individuals who not only forged productive relationships with their Black students, but by encouraging many of them to succeed, challenged the status quo (Cohen 1991; Reed 1990; Blauner 1989; Monroe & Goldman 1988; Anson 1987; Baker 1987; Fields 1985; Kluger 1979; Murray 1970; Clark 1962).

Another limitation can be found in the different criteria which are used to determine effective practice. A few of the studies analyzed herein specifically target Black teachers whose students have shown significant gains in achievement as measured by test scores. However, the scholarship of other researchers on effective Black teachers is included because they argue rather convincingly that such narrow criteria obscures the search for effective Black teachers, especially since their practice is often concerned with aspects of education broader than achievement. Most of these researchers have used some version of "community nomination" (Foster 1989a, 1990, 1991a, 1991b, 1991c, 1991d, 1991e, 1991f). Community nomination is a method of selection and a term coined specifically to capture what anthropologists call an "emic," an insider's perspective. In this case, the Black community's perspective on an effective teacher means that informants were secured through direct contact with African American communities. African American periodicals, churches, organizations and individuals—parents, students, and principals provided the names of the teachers.

These limitations notwithstanding, there is a small body of literature on effective Black teachers that will be discussed in detail and will then be used as a conceptual framework to derive key factors. The critical and overriding factor that characterizes effective Black teachers is their reliance on the cultural and social underpinnings of the Black community.

Attributes of Effective Black Teachers

Cultural solidarity. Similar background does not guarantee productive, fluid or uncomplicated relationships between teacher and student. Teachers of similar background will sometimes judge students more harshly because they remind them of their younger selves. Cazden (1976, 1988), however, drawing on the pioneering sociolinguistic research on power and solidarity (Brown & Gillman 1972), on the more focused ethnographic approach of question asking (Goody 1975) and building on research which proposes that the high rate of school failure among Black students results from the politics enacted between pariah and host group teachers (McDermott 1974, 1977), as well as a rejection by Black students of the mainstream values of the larger society (Ogbu 1987)[1], has argued conversely that some of the most effective schooling occurs in settings—Amish schools, Black Muslim schools, Catholic schools, and Jewish shtetels—where cultural solidarity and power are combined.[2] Where students and teachers share a common cultural background and when they are able to engage in productive interactions, it is possible that they might develop attachments to education that they otherwise might not. This sense of cultural solidarity can be implicit, unspoken, and accepted as given because teachers are recognized members of the particular reference group. Or the cultural solidarity may be explicit and continuously reinforced in classroom interactions, a point taken up later in this chapter. Researchers who have examined the beliefs and practices of effective Black teachers have found that such teachers have strong attachments to the Black community and consider themselves a part of it (Foster 1990, 1991a, 1991e; Ladson-Billings 1991a, 1991b; Ladson-Billings & Henry 1990). Often, but not always, these attachments are expressed in the teachers' use of kin terms as well as in their use of metaphors to express a particular kind of alliance between themselves and their students (Foster 1991a, 1991e; Casey 1990). From her study of eighteen effective Black teachers, Foster (1991e) has noted that, irrespective of gender and grade level, unprompted, over half of them used kin terms or metaphors to describe their relationship with students. The following quotes illustrate the metaphorical references to this conception of solidarity and connectedness.

> I mean this is what my teaching job consists of, not just the physical education program, but an *extended family* program because I feel as though this is a part of what I'm about. (emphasis added)

> Black people have to convince Blacks of how important it [education] is. And how they are all part of that Black *umbilical cord* because a lot of [Black] teachers, they don't do it consciously, but we are forgetting about our roots, about how we're *connected to this cord,* and about everyone we've left behind. We have it now, and we don't have time for the so-called underclass. But we have to educate ourselves as a group because otherwise what's going to happen to us all? You see what I mean? If I can't see that kid out there in the biggest project, if I can't see how he and I or she and I are of the same *umbilical cord* and do not strive to make us more *connected to that cord,* with a common destiny, then we're lost. (emphasis added)

These attachments in many cases are further strengthened by intergenerational employment and long-term community residence patterns of Black teachers. The evidence suggests, further, that often these interactions extend beyond school into the larger community (Foster 1990, 1991a, 1991e; Casey 1990; Ladson-Billings 1991a, 1991b).

Connectedness is a prominent theme in the work of scholars who have examined historical and contemporary Black family life. These studies describe the strong kinship bonds and the sense of mutual obligation that have existed in Black communities that are reflected in fictive kin relationships and the use of kin terms, as well as the tendency of non-kin to take on parental social roles. These extensive kin-networks have historically contributed significantly to the well-being of children (Guttman 1976; Jones 1985).

Contemporary anthropological studies of both urban and rural Black communities also demonstrate the continuing significance of these extended kin-networks to the well-being of Black children (Hill 1972; Stack 1974). Rarely have scholars of Black life extended this analysis to relationships among non intimates in particular to those occupying institutional roles like teachers. Nonetheless, almost without exception, connectedness to Black communities seems to be a recurring theme characterizing the practice of effective Black teachers.

Scholars who have applied the concepts of connectedness and care to schooling argue that the ability to relate to others is a critical component of responsible teachers (Noddings 1984; Lyons 1983). Other researchers have noted that increased motivation and engagement exist in schools where students, especially those labelled "at risk," are able to develop personal bonds with adults (McLaughlin & Talbert 1990). Finally, a personalized style and a close and caring relationship between Hispanic teachers and pupils, characterized as cariño (kind) has been noted as one of several influential factors in classrooms that exhibit high degrees of co-membership (Cazden 1988). Complementing these findings are those of Gallo (1969), Meltzer and Levy (1970), cited in Massey, Scott and Dornbusch (1975), Woods (1979), and Payne (1984), who in separate studies found that students differentiate among teachers, form their perceptions of them, and respond to their behaviors based on their ability to interact with them on a more personal level.

This does not suggest that effective Black teachers are overly permissive, nor does it suggest as some scholars have contended that Black teachers, like Black mothers, are unnecessarily authoritarian and controlling (Conroy 1972; Rist 1970, 1973; Spencer 1986).[3] Neither do Black teachers display excessive warmth without communicating correspondingly high expectations for effort and achievement, as has been noted in some school settings (Massey, Scott and Dornbusch 1975). On the contrary, the modal description of effective Black teachers found in the scholarly as well as the more popular literature is of concerned adults, who command respect, are respectful of pupils, and who though caring require all students to meet high academic and behavioral standards (Cohen 1991; Foster 1989a, 1990, 1991e, 1991d, 1991f; Ladson-Billings 1991a, 1991b; Casey 1990; Reed 1990; Blauner 1989; Monroe & Goldman 1988; Wyatt cited in Cazden 1988; Anson 1987; Baker 1987; Fields 1985; Kluger 1979; Murray 1970; Clark 1962).

This style of teaching closely resembles the authoritative parenting style which integrates acceptance and involvement and firm control and psychological autonomy (Baumarind 1971, 1972, 1978; Dornbusch, Ritter, Liederman, Roberts & Fraleigh 1987; Lanborn & Mounts 1990; Steinberg 1990). Quoting a Black woman, Casey's (1990) research provides an example of what she calls a teacher's "sensitive and benevolent assertion of her authority," which illustrates how an authoritative style, one that integrates acceptance and involvement, and firm control and psychological autonomy, is enacted in a teacher pupil relationship:

> There were times when I said, "If you skip my class, I'm coming down to the mall to get you. So sometimes, I would go down to the mall, and it would be a big scene because the class would be waiting there, anticipating my coming back with these six feet, you know, men. And I would go down to the mall, and I would say, "Hi John!" "Uh, Hi !" You know. They were always really surprised. I said, "Well, we come to get you." And they looked, "We?"
>
> Those kind of confrontations could really get to be sticky, because you had to measure how you were going to approach that, and you had to know who you were talking to and what kind of child this was, and how they gonna react to you. The students, of course, thought I was just walking into it, and not thinking each step of the way as to how I was going to do it, because some of the these students were very, very belligerent about coming to class, and some of the classes they didn't go to. And it was just kind of, they'd like pass the word, "Don't skip_____ 's class, I mean, she'll come and get you and that's embarrassing you know.
>
> . . . We would start up the stairs together, and then I would notice that they were walking ahead of me. And that was my signal, to not go in the door at the same time with them, because that would be really embarrassing, and the objective was not to embarrass somebody once you get them to class.

Research on Black mother-daughter relationships has also concluded that Black mothers are admired, respected and feared precisely because of their ability to balance the toughness required for discipline with the tenderness required for emotional support (Joseph & Lewis 1981). When effective Black teachers take on the role of kin, they embrace a complex set of behaviors that demand appropriate doses of firmness and nurturance.

Linking Classroom Content to Students' Experiences

Linking classroom content to student experiences characterizes the practice of effective Black teachers. Students are encouraged to bring community experiences into the classroom (Foster 1987, 1989; Ladson-Billings 1991a, 1991b; Henry 1990; Ladson-Billings & Henry 1990). Teachers deliberately structure classroom activities to make this possible and the literature provides evidence that some of the classroom speech events reflect these community classroom linkages (Hollins 1982; Foster 1987, 1989). Finally, these teachers do not silence student voices (Fine 1987) by avoiding controversial topics (Foster 1987; Ladson-Billings 1990; Henry 1990; Ladson-Billings & Henry 1991).

Focus on the whole child. Effective Black teachers concern themselves with the development of children not just with their cognitive growth. The effective Black teachers described in the literature conceive of their role more broadly than that assigned them by the narrow, utilitarian purposes of schooling. Thus, while they accept the institutional goal of promoting cognitive growth, their personal definition of the teachers' role is not only confined to developing academic skills but includes the social and emotional growth of students.

Their practice reflects this fact. Effective Black teachers accept responsibility for nurturing their students' prerequisite skills and knowledge needed for success in school. They explicitly teach and model personal values—patience, persistence, responsibility to self and others—that can serve as a foundation to current as well as future learning. They foster the development of student attitudes and interests motivation—aspiration, self-confidence and leadership skills. They are also aware of the structural inequalities in society and their practice evidences a "hidden curriculum" of self-determination designed to help students cope with the exigencies of living in a society which perpetuates institutional racism while professing a rhetoric of equal opportunity (Foster 1987; King 1991; Ladson-Billings & Henry 1990; Hollins 1982; Casey 1990).

Interviews with several of the teachers in Foster's study provide evidence of a "hidden curriculum" that encourages students to understand the personal value, the collective power and the political consequences of choosing academic achievement. The interviews of several Black teachers in Foster's study illustrate this "hidden curriculum." Observing that Black students no longer "hunger and thirst" for education, one Black male teacher, with forty-three years experience in both segregated and desegregated southern schools, described some of the means he used to convey the importance of academic achievement to Black students. In the following excerpt, he reconstructs the critical dialogue he engaged in with his Black students, a dialogue he believes is necessary to engage students in their own learning, but one which has been compromised in desegregated settings:

> The big difference was that I can see we were able to do more with the Black students. In other words, if I wanted to come in this morning, have my kids put their books under the desk or on top of

the desk and I'd get up on top of my desk and sit down and just talk
to them. "Why are you here? Are you here just to make out another
day? Or are you here because the law says you must go to school?
Are you here to try to better yourself?" This kind of thing I could
talk to them about. "Well, now I'm here to better myself. Well what
must you do? What are the requirements? Do you know where your
competition is?" And I could talk to them about things like that.
"Your competition is not your little cousin that's sittin' over there.
Your competition is that White person over there in that other
school. He's your competition. He's the one you've got to compete
with for a job. And the only way that you're going to be able to get
that job is that you can't be as good as he is, you got to be better."
And I could drill that into their heads. But once you integrated, I
mean you didn't feel, I didn't—I don't feel comfortable really in a
mixed setting to really get into the things that the Whites did to us
as Black people. I don't really feel too comfortable doing that in a
mixed group because I think I know how I felt when they talked
about me. And surely they have feelings even though sometimes I
didn't think they had any, but that kind of thing we, I mean I,
couldn't do. I didn't want to pull them aside because then they
would feel that they had been moved out of the mainstream because then you were just talking to just Blacks. But, this is the big
difference that I saw, that you couldn't do. Well, I guess another
thing, I got disillusioned with integration because of that type
thing, because I could not get to my people and tell them all the
things that they needed to know. I could not beat into their minds
that they had to be better—that to compete with that White kid on
an equal basis was not enough. I couldn't tell them that. I couldn't
stop my class and tell him that so that he would understand.
I think this is one of the things that they miss, Black kids, in
general.

Use of familiar cultural patterns. Anthropological research
indicates that the Black community has maintained the cultural
values of equality, collective responsibility in the domain of work, as
well as the many other tasks, including literacy activities, which
are generally performed within a group context, not by individuals
alone (Stack 1974; Szwed & Abrahams 1979; Heath 1983). Most of
what occurs in traditional classrooms, however, encourages competitive behavior and individual achievement. As Shade points out in
chapter 9, some research has shown that tremendous gains have
been achieved in schools and classrooms for Black students where
learning is organized as a social event, not as a competitive or individual endeavor (Triesman 1988; Bishop 1985).

Effective Black teachers embrace cultural patterns of collectivity, incorporating them into classroom activities. Students are encouraged to support each other, work together, and study collaboratively (Foster 1987, 1989; Ladson-Billings 1991a, 1991b). Ladson-Billings (1991a, 1991b) reports that the teachers she interviewed continually stressed the need to build "a community or family" and that both they and their students were more at ease working in cooperative, collaborative classrooms. Rituals and routines reinforce this sense of collectivity and there are negative sanctions for belittling, humiliating and embarrassing others (Foster 1987; Noblit 1991).

Incorporation of culturally compatible communication patterns. Several researchers have noted the significance of interactional style, especially the ways teachers handle the interactions between themselves and their students, as Au and Kawakami indicate in chapter 1 (Cazden & Leggett 1981). Philips' (1972, 1983) study of the Warm Springs Indian Reservation addresses the cultural discontinuities in instructional style between Anglo teachers and Native American students. Less well known, but equally compelling is Dumont's (1972) study of two Cherokee classrooms in which students would actively participate or remain silent depending on whether the teachers' interactional strategies were compatible with their own. With reference to this research literature, it should be noted that studies documenting congruent interactional styles between Black teacher and Black students are rare. In fact, as noted earlier, most studies that examine the interaction between Black teachers and their students document the failures rather than the successes (Rist 1970, 1973).

The Piestrup (1973) study is a notable exception. Trying to determine whether certain teaching styles were more successful than others in teaching Black dialect speaking students to read, Piestrup studied fourteen first grade classrooms in the Oakland area. She identified four distinct teaching styles, but determined that one style, which she labelled the *Black Artful Style* was the most successful. She found that students taught with this style not only demonstrated greater achievement on standardized reading tests than children taught using another style, but that pupils of Black Artful teachers used dialect more appropriately depending on the context. Piestrup concluded that this style may have been the most effective because it resembled many of the expressive art forms of Black culture.

Heath's (1983) decade long research in North Carolina, which examined language learning and use in Trackton, a Black community in North Carolina, and then incorporated some interactional features into the classroom, is another study that demonstrates that reducing the sociolinguistic discontinuity between students' home and school environments can positively influence Black students' participation in school lessons. Each of these studies, as well as the more theoretically oriented literature, highlights the fact that individual growth always occurs within particular social and cultural groups. This suggests that learning is facilitated and enhanced when it occurs in settings that are socioculturally familiar and linguistically meaningful to students (Vygotsky 1962, 1978; Scribner & Cole 1985).

Effective Black teachers incorporate aspects of Black communicative patterns into classroom events (Hollins 1982; Ladson-Billings & Henry 1990; Foster 1987, 1989). In one of the few analyses of the pedagogy of Marva Collins, founder of Westside Prep, a school well-known for its students' high rate of achievement on standardized tests, Hollins (1982) found evidence of cultural congruence between aspects of Black communicative behavior and Collins' teaching style. According to Hollins, familiar participation patterns—call and response, use of analogies and rhythm—were all important characteristics of Collins' teaching style.

In their studies of effective Black teachers, both African American and Canadian researchers have alluded to the incorporation of familiar communicative patterns into classroom activities. Henry (1990) and Ladson-Billings & Henry (1990) suggest that the rhythms, call and response and use of proverbs extant in the vocal expressive communication patterns of the African diaspora characterize the pedagogy of the effective Black teachers they studied. Finally, in a systematic sociolinguistic analysis of a successful Black teacher, Foster (1987, 1989) found evidence of code-switching between the teacher's more standard English used for regulatory purposes and the Black expressive speech found in raps, sermons, and events labelled performances in this study, used almost exclusively during academic tasks (cf Cazden 1988). This study also documents a highly systematic use of metaphors around which the teachers structured classroom activities (cf Heath 1983). In many cases, the use of Black expressive language, manipulation of metaphors, and code-switching into familiar Black English patterns are conscious and deliberate choices made by teachers (Foster 1987, 1989; Ladson-Billings & Henry 1990).

To summarize, this literature review, though based on a limited empirical research base, suggests that several factors characterize the pedagogy of effective Black teachers. First, these teachers express cultural solidarity, affiliation and connectedness with the Black community. Often reinforced in long term residence and employment patterns, this solidarity is manifested in the way teachers characterize their relationship to students; the responsibility they take for educating the whole child by teaching values, skills and knowledge that enable school success and participation in the larger society; and their demonstrated competence in the norms of the Black community. Effective Black teachers draw on community patterns and norms in structuring interaction in their classrooms. They link classroom activities to students' out-of-school experiences and incorporate familiar cultural and communicative patterns into their classroom practices, routines, and activities.

Certain critical features of effective Black teachers can be found in curricular projects which have been successful in raising the achievement of Black students. The Algebra Project (Moses et. al. 1989) is a comprehensive curriculum that acknowledges the significance and interdependence of community, social, pedagogical and psychological environments of its students. Incorporating students' out of school experiences into the math curriculum, encouraging academic success in math by linking personal and community empowerment, and developing habits of concentration, patience and perseverance in approaching schoolwork are all critical elements of the Algebra Project of the King Open Middle School. These elements are consistent with theorists who argue that power relationships between communities and schools explain the failure of disadvantaged students better than theories of cultural discontinuity alone (Cummins 1986).[4]

Cultural Diversity and Teacher Preparation

The extent to which these behaviors of effective Black teachers can be learned by other teachers remains unclear. Although national organizations concerned with teacher preparation and assessment have begun to include issues of cultural diversity in their documents, (Shulman 1989; Villegas 1990) for the most part these competencies have not been included in many teacher preparation programs in the United States.

There are of course, a few exceptions. Burstein and Cabello (1989) report on one such effort underway in a large urban area. Designed for teachers seeking a master's degree in Special Education and a Specialist Learning Handicapped Credential, this federally funded program has infused its curriculum with content on cultural diversity and provided field experiences in culturally diverse settings for students enrolled in the program. Though students enrolled in this program have shown changes in attitudes and knowledge of cultural diversity as measured by pre- and post- tests, examinations, students logs, and projects, the authors note that it is unclear whether these outcomes reflect real changes in attitude or whether they are the result of having learned the socially appropriate answer. Nor is it clear whether a change in attitude will influence teacher student interaction and improve student achievement.

Another teacher education program, the Urban Teacher Education Program at Milwaukee Area Technical College (MATC) has also made cultural diversity the central focus of its curriculum and students' field experiences. Unlike the program discussed earlier, however, all of the students enrolled in MATC's program are ethnic minorities, since one of the Program's primary purposes is to increase the number of ethnic minorities eligible to teach. Funded by a Title VII Grant, the Urban Teachers Program also has a bilingual teachers component.

In order to address issues of cultural diversity, two new one-semester courses, entitled Issues in Urban Education Modules I and II, have been developed. These modules include issues of equity and diversity. Topics dealing with language and culture, child-rearing and socialization in non-mainstream families, testing and tracking, power in the classroom (discipline) are also included in the curriculum. Court cases—Brown vs. Board, Ann Arbor—that affect schools and schooling are covered in the courses. Not only do students read the work of minority scholars, but they are encouraged to compare their personal family and community experiences with the findings in the research literature.

Field experiences form an important part of the modules. During their first semester, students observe an effective urban teacher; in their second semester, they do fifteen hours of field placement, which is applied to the seventy hours of field placement required at the University. Second year students are paid to work up to fifteen hours a week as teacher interns in community literacy centers or in public schools. As part of their internship, students attend mini-workshops on how to teach someone to read, or on other related topics.

Not only are students in this program exposed to minority perspectives through course readings, but their field experiences take place in effective schools with large populations of minority students and in the classrooms of successful teachers of color. Finally, in an effort to insure cross-pollination of ideas and more contact between diverse groups of teacher education students, the Urban Teachers Program Coordinator co-teaches an introductory teaching course at the University in Milwaukee, one of four Wisconsin university campuses, with which MATC has developed articulation agreements. The introductory teaching course is attended by students from the community college as well as students from the university (Foster 1989b).

Since the first cohort of students has not yet begun to teach, it is too early to assess the results of this program, either the number of ethnic minority students who actually enter the teaching profession or the extent to which they join the ranks of effective teachers of color for culturally diverse pupils.

Conclusion

The increasing number of ethnic minority students currently enrolled and expected to populate public schools in the next decade has been widely documented. Given these changing demographics, it is critical not only that researchers continue to identify teaching strategies that are effective with children from different cultural backgrounds, but that teacher preparation programs insure that the content, dispositions and strategies become part of the knowledge base of teaching and are included in the repertoire of skills of all teachers preparing to teach in the nation's schools.

Notes

[1] Ogbu contends that in response to historical oppression and limited employment opportunities, a "job ceiling" for involuntary minority groups—African Americans, Mexican Americans and Native Americans—have spawned collective oppositional strategies, including the rejection of mainstream cultural values such as school success.

[2] Cummins (1986) lays out a conceptual framework for intervention that combines cultural solidarity and power that will empower minority students to achieve academically.

[3] See Delpit (1988) for a discussion of the claim by White teachers that Black teachers are authoritarian. Lubeck (1988) discusses her impressions of the authoritarian nature of Black teachers who worked in a Headstart Center. Talbert (1973) describes the authoritarian stance of Black teachers whose teaching style, she contends, resembles that characteristic of Black mothers. Finally in an extended discussion of the social factors that affect the intellectual development of Black and White children, Blau (1981) argues that Black mothers who are excessive religiosity, hold fundamental religious beliefs, and are authoritarian in their child rearing behaviors, tend to be anti-intellectual. Blau found that religious background and authoritarian behavior are associated to lowered intellectual functioning of children as measured by IQ scores and school achievement scores.

[4] There are a number of other math projects and other educational interventions that incorporate some or all of these features into their programs. Ganas, the watchword of students who study calculus in Escalante's classroom in preparation for the Advanced Placement Exam, loosely translates as the desire or the urge to succeed. In Escalante's classroom, it is not ability but rather determination, discipline and hard work that equal success in mathematics (Mathews 1988). A second instance is a research project currently underway at Learning Research and Development Center (Pittsburgh, PA) which aims to improve the mathematics achievement of elementary students attending a predominantly Black Catholic school. The teacher, in consultation with researchers, has developed a number of classroom activities, one in particular that encourages children to come up with creative ways to solve math problems and describe them in front of classmates (Resnick, personal communication). Finally, with respect to math projects, Triesman's work with Black students studying calculus at Berkeley also incorporates elements discussed in this chapter—specificifically peer group learning, and an academically challenging curriculum. Cooperative learning groups, widely advocated and currently used with students in various settings with favorable results, is another educational intervention that incorporates some of the features discussed in this review. Several researchers have noted the preference of certain cultural and low-income groups for group over individual activities, a preference reflected in their social organization, work activity and literacy events. Cooperative learning groups may actually be more compatible with the values and cultural norms of certain groups of disadvantaged children and their use may actually confer an advantage by providing them with a familiar social context. (Ramirez & Castaneda 1974; Au 1980; Philips 1982; Erickson & Mohatt 1982; Heath 1983; Foster 1989a). Though not designed to be culturally compatible, many of these approaches may in fact be instances of culturally responsive and empowering pedagogy. Perhaps without intending to and

despite an explicit framework, both the research underway at LRDC and the use of co-operative leaning groups may be tapping into specific cultural norms. While it could be argued that these innovations are simply instances of sound pedagogy, as Delpit (1988) argues, it can not be assumed that all instances of good pedagogy will also be culturally responsive or promote high achievement among disadvantaged students.

CHAPTER 13

Afrocultural Expression and Its Implications for Schooling

A. WADE BOYKIN

Questions to Think About

1. Why might Afrocultural expression and the maintenance of cultural integrity be indispensable aspects of appropriate and effective schooling for African American students?
2. How might classroom teachers go about acquiring an understanding of the "deep structure" of African American culture?
3. How can Afrocultural expression be incorporated into classroom instruction?

Advocates for taking aspects of Afrocultural expression into account in the schooling of African American children are growing in numbers. While this stance has gained increasing adherents, we should hasten to admit that such Afrocultural incorporation poses several challenges, and raises several issues. It is one thing to call for such infusion. It is another to discern how such should be done or for that matter, could be done. What roadblocks might arise? What insights, information and skills must teachers possess to carry out this responsibility? I submit that the expertise that is to be required of classroom teachers can not be simply reduced to a list of specific teaching strategies. This knowledge base should not be in the form of the possession of specific teaching techniques or the do's and don'ts of "appropriate" teaching activities per se. There is a more fundamental knowledge base that takes precedence that must be acquired—one that acknowledges that the issues of relevance are complex, profound and deeply woven into the very marrow of American pedagogy. Since teaching is properly viewed as an artform, it is more crucial for a given teacher to get a feel for the landscape, texture, contours, and conditions of the relevant educational responsibility in order to create the pedagogy, rather than acquire a new set of procedures that are to be adhered to.

Therefore, it becomes more crucial to provide for the acquisition of penetrating, critical insights into the attendant challenges, issues, elements and contexts. Given space limitations, this chapter will focus on the most indispensable aspects of the knowledge base for teachers. Such aspects include developing a functional awareness and a sufficiently analytical posture and orientation toward the permeating, saturating cultural character of traditional schooling practices. It is also essential that teachers understand the character and manifestations of Afrocultural integrity and the processes which undergird incorporating aspects of African American culture. It is essential to discern the educational benefits that may accrue, as well as the forces and predicaments which stymie such Afrocultural incorporation. It is also crucial to discern the consequences that can manifest when such incorporation is not meaningfully done. This chapter will be principally devoted to these ends. This chapter will also include a brief compendium of recent research that examines the proactive infusion of Afrocultural expression into learning and problem solving contexts. Implications of the conceptual analysis for teacher training will also be considered, as will some discussion of issues in need of further clarification and suggestions for future research directions.

The Mainstream Cultural Character of Traditional Schooling

We must be mindful that issues of culture have been persistently played out, even if not always acknowledged, in our nation's schools. We must recognize that there has always been a profound and inescapable cultural fabric to the schooling process in America. To be sure, this fabric was quite blatantly promoted during the initial implementation of public education (Vallance 1974). But the overtness has receded and now the avowed acculturation function has become fully institutionalized into the very texture of how schooling is done (Carnoy 1974; Apple 1979). It is now manifested without fanfare. It is simply how schools are. The institutionalized practices, behavioral expectations and values paid homage to are construed as universal phenomena whenever their existence is acknowledged. They are seen to represent simply the "correct" procedures for education, "civilized" values, and merely how any normal person should be expected to operate. Yet, this putative universalistic posture only occludes the fact that a certain cultural fabric continues to form the deep structure of the schooling process. It is a major "point" of the socialization function that schools so profoundly, even if now more tacitly, serve.

To more fully appreciate the role that culture plays, and in turn the kinds of transformations needed, it will require accessing the presence of culture in schooling at the level of *deep structure* (Apple 1979). This should be contrasted with culture manifested at the surface structure level. Much of the recent call for incorporating multiculturalism has been for changes at the level of surface structure. At the surface structure level, such cultural infusion would entail concerns such as including presentations on the history of distinct cultural, ethnic or racial groups into the curriculum rather than the "standard" European American fare. It would require that the "heroes and sheroes" highlighted are drawn from people of color as well. It would entail bringing in direct or explicit information on the practices, traditions and customs of racially or culturally distinct people that heretofore have been omitted. These no doubt would be worthwhile changes. They are not unimportant. They would not be sufficient changes in and of themselves precisely because they are not penetrating enough to the fundamental core of the schooling process. At the deep structure level we should recognize and acknowledge that culture inheres in the schooling process per se. It is inherent in the very fabric and texture of how schooling is done. At the deep structure level of culture, this entails appreciation of culture in its most profound forms.

In its most fundamental form, culture entails the way a particular group codifies reality. As Giroux and Mclaren (1986) postulate, "it embodies a set of practices and ideologies from which different groups draw to make sense of the world." Culture implies cosmological, epistemological and axiological considerations. In other words, it embodies belief systems, ways of knowing and values, respectively (Boykin 1983). In light of the cultural texture of the schooling process, it can be posited that formal education is not simply about learning to read, write or think. Instead it is about learning how to read, write and think about certain prescribed things that certain people deem important. Learning how to read, write and think in certain prescribed ways consistent with certain beliefs, prescribed vantage points, value-laden conditions and value-laden formats (Hall 1989). These prescribed ways of educating, these certain vantage points, conditions, proper practices and inherent values are the materials and texture of a profound cultural socialization process that forms the very fabric of the medium through which schooling is done.

These issues have been brought into very sharp focus recently by Lisa Delpit (1988). Delpit has argued that there exists a "culture of power" extant in American classrooms. Undeniably this culture of power reflects the practices of those in power and consequently reflects mainstream Anglo-European American ideals. Delpit further posits that the rules of this culture of power often go unarticulated. Some kids come to school with the rules already understood, even if only implicitly. They come to school inclined to be receptive to the culture of power, because of their prior contact with and prior exposure to its positive valuation. They come to school possessing the rudiments of expected behaviors and are thus in a position to more readily behave accordingly. Other kids who for whatever reason do not have or have not had ready access to the "rules" are penalized for not knowing them. Some children possess the requisite "cultural capital" (Bourdieux & Passeron 1977) as a matter of course. Others do not. But I would argue that those who do not possess the requisite cultural capital do indeed possess some cultural capital that they bring with them to the school setting. Unfortunately, the possession of this alternative capital often leads to detrimental consequences. One such consequence is the disempowerment of these students. Yet if this alternative capital is capitalized upon through better appreciation and acknowledgement, it can become the basis of talent development. Surely these arguments require further, more concrete elaboration.

First, we should get a better handle on the character and function of the prevailing cultural fabric which predominates the American schooling process. Silverstein and Krate (1975) quite cogently illuminate manifestations of the culture of power and their academic implications. They note that schools are more favorably inclined toward students who readily display certain mainstream cultural characteristics. These include strongly controlling students' impulses; elevating rational thinking over emotionality; and exerting autonomous, dispassionate and considerable effort to achieve on tasks that can be unconnected to personal interest and needs. Silverstein and Krate argue further that students who most ably display such cultural capital are viewed favorably precisely because such characteristics are seen as most virtuous in a corporate-industrial-bureaucratic-technocratic system. Geneva Gay (1975) has highlighted additional attributes especially treasured in mainstream academic settings. She cites a proclivity for individualistic competition, low levels of physical movement and stimulation and impersonal task orientation rather than social orientation. Other relevant factors have been identified by Judith Katz (1985). These include receptiveness to delayed gratification emphasis, adherence to rigid time schedules with time construed as a commodity, and individual status being bound up in possessions— material, physical or intellectual. These characteristics are fundamental elements of European American cultural ethos which constitute the cultural currency that schools were historically conceived to implicitly if not explicitly demand.

Schools reward individual possession of specific intellectual and social attributes. By emphasizing doing better than others and devising a reward system to honor such accomplishment, schools reinforce individual competition. Discouraging talking to other students while "on task" encourages elevating impersonal task orientation over social orientation. Dictating that children sit still for extended periods of time reinforces movement compression over movement expression. Advocating that noise be kept at a minimum during work time underscores a premium placed on low physical stimulation. Working on "abstract" tasks, or tasks consistently disconnected from children's daily lives during work time reinforces the notion that the content of the learning activity per se is unimportant. Through the promotion of the classroom as a place of "sobriety and seriousness" (Gay 1975), where gaiety and emotional "outbursts" are suppressed, schools reinforce emotional containment and the elevation of the cognitive over the emotional. Consistently confining learning to inflexible time boundaries results in binding children to a commodity orientation towards time.

Indeed, the cultural character of such activities goes largely unexamined. They are approached as simply proven, time-honored, correct classroom procedures that create the proper learning atmosphere and get children to behave appropriately. And why should this not be the case? Such characteristics have in recent years been all too often passed off as universally embraced attributes that any civilized human being should possess and display (Khan 1982). They are often taken for granted as appropriate to such an extent that educators may not even realize that they are promoting, advocating and imposing their centrality and indispensability on the students.

Educators all too often act as though context for education is unimportant—students either get it or they don't, regardless of the situational fabric. Yet presenting educational material as though its context is unimportant to the learning process rewards those who do well come hell or high water. A premium is placed on rugged, acontextual individualism, a mainstream culturally valued trait. Much of the functioning that transpires at the cultural deep structure level is especially effective because it is done in an unarticulated, matter of fact way without explicit reference to the cultural power issues at play. These dynamics often are effective, but not for the officially intended goal of educating children. They are effective for children who have different cultural capital in the process of uneducating them, alienating them, and disempowering them (Cummins 1986). Herein lies the tragedy of our failure to genuinely embrace multiculturalism in education.

Afrocultural Expression and Its Implications for Schooling

There are some rather clear implications for the schooling of African American children which follow from the line of reasoning proffered in this chapter. Current arguments contend that if we (1) acknowledge the cultural fabric of the schooling process and the issues of power contained therein; (2) acknowledge the social cultural integrity of the African American experience; (3) create greater home-school cultural continuity; and (4) predicate the mainstream socialization function on these preceding considerations, then we can make significant progress in more effectively schooling African American children.

The cultural integrity of certain domestic cultural groups is increasingly being acknowledged in school settings, for example that of American Indians, Native Hawaiians, and Hispanics (Tharp 1989). However, as other authors in this volume have pointed out, Afrocultural expression has proven to be quite difficult to accept. This lack of acceptance is perhaps in part because of the belief that vestiges of such expression have been eliminated for all intents and purposes by slavery and geographical dislocation. But perhaps even more crucially, many of the characteristics ascribed to Afrocultural expression simply violate the cultural sensibilities of those, be they Black or White, who have bought into or internalized mainstream cultural ideologies and values. The amassing of compelling documentation from such scholars as Lawrence Levine (1977), Sterling Stuckey (1987), Robert Farris Thompson (1983), Wade Nobles (1991) and Lorenzo Turner (1949), among others, points to a cultural integrity among African Americans. Although it is not shared by all African Americans to the same degree, and does not encompass all of their experiences, it is currently present and represents the continuation of the traditional African ethos. Boykin (1983, 1986) has delineated nine dimensions of Afrocultural expression that find manifestation in the lives of African Americans. These dimensions are (1) Spirituality—which connotes an acknowledgement of a nonmaterial life force that permeates all human affairs, (2) Harmony—which implies that one's functioning is fundamentally linked to events in nature and the elements of the universe, (3) Movement—implying a premium placed on the interwoven mosaic of movement, dance, percussiveness and rhythm personified by the musical beat, (4) Verve—which connotes an especial receptiveness to relatively high levels of sensate (i.e., variability and intensity of) stimulation, (5) Affect—which implies the centrality of affective information and emotional expressiveness linked to the co-importance of feelings and thoughts, (6) Expressive Individualism—which connotes the gleaning of uniqueness of personal expression, of style and of sincerity of self expression, (7) Communalism—which denotes a commitment to the fundamental interdependence of people and to social bonds and relationships. (8) Orality—which denotes the centrality of oral/aural modes of communication for conveying true meaning and to cultivating speaking as a performance, (9) Social Time Perspective—which connotes a commitment to time as a social construction such that there is an event orientation towards time.

As mentioned earlier, there is surely diversity in expression of these dimensions in the lives of African American people. This means that they are not all expressed or manifested to the same degree by any given person, or that they are expressed in like manner across the population of African Americans in America. There is also the case that many African Americans would deny the existence of these cultural realities, or dismiss or dishonor them. This is because factors like a rhythmic movement orientation, an affective emphasis and communalism go against the grain of the mainstream thrust towards movement compression, emotional containment and possessive self-contained individualism (Boykin 1986). Movement orientation would even be construed by mainstream oriented persons as evidence of hyperactivity, affect as being too emotional and

250 A. Wade Boykin

communalism as being insecurely dependent. Moreover, many African Americans are even unaware that in expressing such attributes they are expressing things cultural, representing an ethos of coherence and integrity. It must be reemphasized that not every African American expresses or possesses all of these attributes to the same degree, but their presence still is substantial. It must also be acknowledged that such cultural experiences do not exhaust the realm of the African American experience; there is a minority component bred by the legacy of oppression African American people have faced in America, and there is also the mainstream experience that comes through living and participating in mainstream institutions, and being exposed to mainstream channels of information transmission (Boykin 1983, 1986; Boykin & Toms 1985). Yet these Afrocultural attributes exist. And we would be making a serious error if we presume we are dealing in school settings with children whose out of school experiences lack cultural integrity. African American children are not tabula rasas and they certainly are not simply inadequate dark skinned White children.

Perhaps all of these Afrocultural factors may not be able to be proactively incorporated into the classroom, but their existence should be acknowledged. Where appropriate, their incorporation should be attempted. Their interface with the culture of power must be better understood to exact better negotiation. It is crucial to directly address the processes, pitfalls and promises involved in creating a more proactive cultural climate in the classroom for African American children.

Let us first examine the issue of cultural integrity. When we fail to acknowledge the integrity of the cultural capital many African American children bring with them, we foster greater negative teacher expectations for these children. We alienate these children. We disempower them by demeaning their integrity (Cummins 1986). We create power struggles that result in more control and behavior management time being necessary than pedagogy time. By genuinely acknowledging that such cultural integrity exists, it can lead to greater positive perceptions of academic potential, and it can mitigate power struggles and lead to educational partnerships in the process of empowering African American children in the classroom setting (Irvine 1990). By acknowledging the legitimacy of their cultural expressions, we give the children their own "voice" in the classroom (Giroux & McLaren 1986). Indeed, one upshot of multicultural education should be student empowerment per se. When I refer to empowerment, I mean that providing a climate of cultural integrity should lead to the dignification of the individual student whereby a student acquires "social-cultural" leverage, and in turn comes to believe that through becoming educated, he/she can become an impactful person. Empowerment is a powerful psychological motive. Children who don't acquire empowerment from education will surely acquire it in other arenas.

A second cultural implication is to provide for greater cultural continuity for African American children in the classroom setting by proactively building on their cultural capital. Of course this is predicated on a genuine acknowledgement of the cultural integrity of Afrocultural expression. This issue of cultural continuity suggests providing culturally compatible learning and performance contexts in order to create a better fit with the prevailing cultural repertoires of many African American children. The reasons this makes good pedagogical sense can be gleaned from recent work in the arena of culture and cognition referred to earlier in this chapter. By providing culturally compatible or culturally appropriate contexts we (1) provide outlets for, and further develop, already or potentially existing competencies that have been fundamentally linked to such contexts out of school, (2) discern intellectually valued skills in groups for whom such skills were thought to be absent, (3) create more intrinsically motivating learning environments that can lead to increased academic time on task (Boykin 1983), and (4) insure that the cultural values implicit in the "personal epistemologies" (Greeno 1989) of the students would not be so apt to contradict those inherent in the fabric of the schooling process. This reduces alienation and defensiveness and contributes to increased academic motivation. Yet if such cultural incompatibility is allowed to persist, then the vehicles and outlets for intellectual competencies will continue to be denied; existing or potentially existing skills will be overlooked; children's boredom and motivational stifling will persist; and impenetrable cultural borders between African American children and the school will continue to be constructed (Erickson 1987).

None of this analysis thus far should be taken to mean that no effort should be made to provide "training" in mainstream cultural mores, or that such mores should be cast away in the schooling process. On the contrary, in the foreseeable future, cultural fluency in mainstream cultural expression will continue to be a requirement for successful functioning in American society. The key here is fluency, not inculcation or internalization of the mores. African American children have not sufficiently accessed the prevailing culture of power primarily because they have been denied access to it in the schooling process. (Delpit 1988). But as Delpit (1988) persuades us, we should make the mainstream cultural socialization process more explicit to these students. We should not penalize them for not knowing the culture of power but instead explicitly teach them what the rules of the culture of power are and that indeed this is presently the culture of power. By demystifying the culture of power for them we make its acquisition a functional exercise that can be successfully negotiated and not a cryptic code of ethics, rules and practices whose lack of mastery condemns ones humanity. It must be emphasized that because many African American children *don't* display certain attributes, this in no way indicates that they *can't* do so. Just because these children don't show receptiveness to certain culturally informed learning contexts in no way implies that they are unable to become receptive. This needs to be stated because some writers on African American culture have mistakenly drawn such erroneous conclusions (e.g., Chimezie 1988).

The path to acquiring such fluency should be predicated on the realization that educators are not dealing with tabula rasas, "uncultured" children, children who lack civility. Acquiring this mainstream fluency should be predicated on acknowledging these children's own cultural integrity and done in the frame of efforts to provide greater cultural continuity. Handling the introduction of mainstream ethos in this way actually makes acquiring mainstream cultural fluency an empowering process (Cummins 1986). Indeed, continuity and integrity issues should perhaps be more greatly emphasized in the early school years while the explicit efforts at providing mainstream fluency should be subsequently focused on in later years, perhaps late elementary school (Boykin 1983).

Over the last several years, I, along with my graduate student colleagues, have launched a basic research program aimed at discerning the potential value of proactively infusing Afrocultural expression into formal educational contexts. In our work, we have provided learning and performance contexts which afford the opportunity for rhythmic movement expression (Boykin & Allen 1988; Allen & Boykin 1991); responsiveness to stimulation variability Boykin 1982; Tuck & Boykin 1989;), and co-operative/communal expression (Jagers 1988; Ellison & Boykin 1992; Albury 1991). We have examined the impact of such contexts, relative to more traditional ones on learning and performance outcomes and processes, and on motivation.

More specifically, in one line of work we have found that providing rhythmic music and the opportunity for movement expression significantly enhanced learning for low-income African American children but proved detrimental to low income White children's learning (Allen & Boykin 1991). Using a task which required these first and second grade students to learn to pair certain pictures together, it was revealed that the music and movement opportunities positively affected both the initial encoding of information and the subsequent recall of that learned information. African American children's performance was significantly superior to that of European American children when both music and movement opportunities are available but significantly lower than that of their European American counterparts when music and movement were not allowed for. African American children also expressed overwhelming preference for learning under a music and rhythmic movement condition as opposed to a more sedentary one (Boykin & Allen 1988).

Elsewhere, Tuck and Boykin (1989) presented low income fourth and sixth grade African American and European American children with four different types of tasks to perform in an experimental session. There were five exemplars of each type and therefore twenty tasks in all. The set of twenty tasks was presented to the children under two different format conditions. In one condition, all five of one type were first presented, followed by all five of a second, followed by all five of a third, followed by the five of the fourth type. This was considered to be a relatively unvaried format, and therefore one relatively low in "verve." In the second condition, the twenty tasks, representing the four types, were presented in essentially a random sequential order. This was considered to be a relatively more varied format. As such, it was deemed higher in "verve." It was found that the White children performed overall better than the African American children under the unvaried format. However, while both African American and European American children's performance increment was substantially greater. Consequently, there was no difference between the performance of African American and European American children with this varied format. Moreover, for the African American children only, performance under the varied format was directly related to the perceived level of physical stimulation present in a child's home environment. That is, the greater the perceived home stimulation, the greater the African American child's performance under the varied format condition. This is an important finding. It suggests that being more responsive to varied stimulation may be cultivated in the home environment. What is culture if it is not what is cultivated? Yet for the African American children, the level of home stimulation was inversely related to teacher perceptions of a child's academic performance and motivation levels.

In an investigation by Aretha Albury (1991), the vocabulary knowledge of low income fourth and fifth trade African American and European American children was compared under four different learning conditions. These conditions were sandwiched between a twenty-five word vocabulary pre-test and post-test. They were: (1) individual criterion—where three children at a time studied the words alone and were rewarded on an individual basis if their post-test score reached eighteen correct responses; (2) interpersonal competition—where three children studied the words in the same setting and the one who performed best on the post-test received a reward; (3) group competition—where three children studied together and were informed that if their group was among the highest scoring on the posttest, each member would receive a reward; and (4) communal—where three children studied together and were urged to work together simply for the good of the group, because it is important to help each other out. No reward was given. It should be noted that all of the study conditions were conducted in race homogeneous groupings. It was revealed that White children's learning gains were at their highest and low income African American children's gains were at their lowest under the individual criterion learning condition. However, learning gains were at their highest for African American children and their lowest for European American children who were placed in the communal learning condition. In this study, it was further revealed that in the communal condition, African American children reported utilizing more sophisticated group process learning strategies than did their European counterparts. It was also revealed that African American children indicated a strong preference for group study conditions, while the European American children displayed a tendency to favor individual study conditions.

Results from our work seem to support the cultural process arguments of this chapter. Failure to acknowledge the integrity of Afrocultural expression can have detrimental consequences for many African American children. Yet, when contexts offer opportunity for Afrocultural expression, competencies are revealed and performance and motivation are enhanced. It must again be underscored that African American children can and perhaps should be responsive to performance under more mainstream contexts. By the same token, in spite of their performance deficiencies, European American children also can and, given the increasingly pluralistic landscape of American society, perhaps should become more fluent in contexts marked by African American culture.

Further Questions and Issues The analyses and findings offered in this chapter are surely not exhaustive. There are issues in need of further understanding, and they hopefully will be addressed in subsequent conceptualizations and empirical research. For example, we need to know how issues of Afrocultural incorporation and mainstream cultural inculcation play themselves out across different age levels and for children from different economic status backgrounds. Do the cultural dynamics and processes discussed in this chapter manifest differently in racially heterogeneous versus more homogeneous settings? How do different learning and performance outcomes, and different subject matters interact with the cultural contexts of pedagogy? We also need to know more about the perceptions of the various cultural attributes in learning environments from the vantage points of both students and teachers. Of course, the findings from our research program need to be replicated in actual classroom settings.

Implications for Teacher Training

It seems clear that if the remarks presented in this chapter have merit, then some very definite implications for teacher training would follow. For one, teachers in their training experiences must come to understand the cultural fabric which inheres in the schooling process and how this fabric manifests itself in ordinary daily school activities. They should learn to confront their own biases honestly and work to overcome them. They should come to grips with their own cultural ideologies and values, and how these become actualized in their approach to teaching. Yet, such analyses should not be approached as exercises in unveiling the evils of Western civilization or the shortcomings of European American culture. Teachers must also gain genuine appreciation for cultural diversity. They must discern the integrity of differing cultural orientations. They must learn to distinguish between expressions of cultural integrity and expressions which are simply unacceptable. They must appreciate that certain expressions of cultural integrity may at times be inappropriate or maladaptive for a certain school activity but the expressions nonetheless have integrity. They must also learn how to separate legitimate cultural distinctiveness from individual variation. Then too, teachers must receive practical experience in how to effectively infuse the cultural manifestations into pedagogical contexts that are appropriate for their student clientele. They must also learn how to produce mainstream fluency without undermining existing alternative cultural integrity.

Part III: References

Aboud, F. E. & Skerry, S. (1984). The development of ethnic attitudes. *Journal of Cross-Cultural, 15:* 3–34.

Alawiye, O., Alawiye, C. & Thomas J. (1989). Attitudes of English-speaking West African parents and teachers: Implications for elementary school counselors. *Elementary School Guidance and Counseling, 23* (4): 260–265.

Albury, A. (1991). *Social orientations, learning conditions and learning outcomes among low-income Black and White grade school children.* Unpublished doctoral dissertation. Howard University, Washington, D.C.

Allen, B. & Boykin, A. W. (1991). The influence of contextual factors on Afro-American and Euro-American children's performance: Effects of movement opportunity and music. *International Journal of Psychology, 26:* 373–387.

Anderson, J. (1988). Cognitive styles and multicultural populations. *Journal of Teacher Education, 39:* 2–9.

Anson, R. S. (1987). *Best intentions: The education and killing of Edmund Perry.* New York: Random House.

Apple, M. (1979). *Ideology and curriculum.* London: Routledge and Kegan Paul.

Archbald, D. A. & Newman, F. M. (1988). *Beyond standardized testing.* Reston, VA: National Association of Secondary School Principals.

Arnheim, R. (1985). The double-edged mind: Intuition and the intellect. *Learning and teaching the ways of knowing,* pp. 77–96. Eighty-fourth yearbook of the National Society for the Study of Education. Chicago, IL: University of Chicago Press.

Au, K. (1980). Participation structures in a reading lesson with Hawaiian children: An analysis of a culturally appropriate instructional event. *Anthropology and Education Quarterly, 11* (2): 91–115.

Au, K. & Jordan, C. (1981). Teaching reading to Hawaiian children: Finding a culturally appropriate solution. In H. Trueba, et al. (Eds.). *Culture and the bilingual classroom*. Rowley, MA: Newbury House.

Bailey, G. & Maynor, G. (1985). The Present Tense of be in Southern Black Folk Speech. *American Speech, 60:* 195–213.

Baker, H. (1987). What Charles knew. In L. D. Rubin, Jr. (Ed.), *An apple for my teacher: 12 authors tell about teachers who made the difference*. Chapel Hill: Algonquin Books.

Baldwin, J. (1979). Theory and research concerning the notion of Black self-hatred: A review and reinterpretation. *The Journal of Black Psychology, 5:* 51–77.

Banduar, A. (1986). *Social foundations of thought and action: A social cognitive theory*. Englewood Cliffs, NJ: Prentice-Hall.

Banks, W. C. & Rompf, W. (1973). Evaluative biases and preference behavior in black and white children. *Child Development, 44:* 776–783.

Baratz, J. C. & Shuy, R. W. (Eds.). (1969). *Teaching Black children to read*. Washington, D.C.: Center for Applied Linguistics.

Barsch, R. H. (1971). The processing mode hierarchy as a potential deterrent to cognitive efficiency. In J. Hellmuth (Ed.). *Cognitive studies 2.: Deficits in cognition*. New York: Bruner/Mazel.

Baugh, J. (1988a). Why what works hasn't worked for nontraditional students. *Journal of Negro Education, 57:* 417–431.

Baugh, J. (1988b). Review of E. W. Orr, *Twice as less: Black English and the performance of Black students in mathematics and science. Harvard Educational Review, 58:* 395–404.

Baugh, J. (1987). The situational dimension of linguistic power. *Language Arts, 64:* 84–94.

Baugh J. (1983). *Black street speech: Its history, structure, and survival*. Austin, TX: University of Texas Press.

Baugh, J. (1981). Design and Implementation of a National Neighborhood Literacy Program. In B. Cronnell (Ed.). *The writing needs of linguistically different students*. Los Alamitos, CA: SWRL Educational Research and Development.

Baumarind, D. (1978). Parental disciplinary patterns and social competence in children. *Youth and Society, 9:* 239–276.

Baumarind, D. (1972). An exploratory study of socialization effects on Black children: Some Black-White comparisons. *Child Development, 43:* 261–267.

Baumarind, D. (1971). Current patterns of parental authority. *Developmental Psychology Monographs, 4* (1), Part 2.

Benson, J. & Rentsch, J. (1988). Testing the dimensionality of the Piers-Harris Children's Self-Concept Scale. *Educational and Psychological Measurement, 48* (3): 615–626.

Bereiter, C. & Englemann, S. (1966). *Teaching disadvantaged children in the pre-school.* Englewood Cliffs, NJ: Prentice-Hall.

Bishop, M. (1986). Update. *Sports Illustrated,* 10 February, 43–44.

Blau, Z. (1981). *Black children/White children: Competence, socialization and social structure.* New York: The Free Press.

Blauner, B. (1989). *Black lives, White lives: Three decades of race relations in America.* Berkeley: University of California Press.

Block, J. H., & Anderson, L. W. (1975). *Mastery learning in instruction.* New York: Macmillan Publishing Company.

Borkowski, J. G. & Krause, A. (1983). Racial difference in intelligence: The importance of the executive system. *Intelligence, 9:* 379–395.

Bourdieux, P. & Passeron, J. (1977). *Reproduction in education, society and culture.* Beverly Hills, CA: Sage Publications.

Boykin, A. W. (1986). The triple quandary and the schooling of Afro-American children. In U. Neisser (Ed.). *The school achievement of minority children.* Hillsdale, NJ: Lawrence Erlbaum Associates.

Boykin, A. W. (1983). The academic performance of Afro-American children. In J. Spence (Ed.). *Achievement and achievement motives.* San Francisco: W. Freeman.

Boykin, A. W. (1982). Task variability and the performance of Black and White school children: Vervistic explorations. *Journal of Black Studies, 12:* 469–485.

Boykin, A. W. & Allen, B. (1988). Rhythmic-movement facilitated learning in working-class Afro-American children. *Journal of Genetic Psychology, 149:* 335–347.

Boykin, A. W. & Toms, F. (1985). Black child socialization: A conceptual framework. In H. McAdoo and J. McAdoo (Eds.). *Black children.* Beverly Hills, CA: Sage Publications.

Branch, C. & Newcombe, N. (1988). The development of racial attitudes in black children. In R. Vasta (Ed.). *Annals of Child Development, 5:* 125–154. Greenwich, CT: JAI Press.

Branch, C. & Newcombe, N. (1986). Racial attitude development among young black children as a function of parental attitudes: A longitudinal and cross-sectional study. *Child Development, 57:* 712–721.

Brewer, J. (1986). Durative Marker or Hyperconnection? The Case of -s in the WPA Ex-Slave Narratives. In M. B. Montgomery and G. Bailey (Eds.). *Language Variety in the South*. Birmingham: University of Alabama Press.

Brophy, J. (1981). Teacher praise: A functional analysis. *Review of Educational Research, 51:* 5–32.

Brown, A. L. & Palinscar, A. S. (1986). Interactive teaching to promote independent learning from text. *The Reading Teacher, 39:* 770–777.

Brown, R. & Gilman, A. (1972). The pronouns of power and solidarity. In P. P. Giglioli (Ed.). *Language and social context*, pp. 252–282. Baltimore: Penguin.

Bruner. J. (1960). *The Process of education*. Cambridge: Harvard Press.

Burstein, N. D. & Cabello, B. (1989). Preparing teachers to work with culturally diverse students: A teacher education model. *Journal of Teacher Education, 40* (5): 9–16.

Carnoy, M. (1974). *Education as cultural imperialism*. New York: D. McKay Co.

Casey, K. (1990). Teachers as mother: Curriculum theorizing in the life histories of contemporary women teachers. *Cambridge Journal of Education, 20* (3): 301–320.

Cazden, C. B. (1988). *Classroom discourse: The language of teaching and learning*. Portsmouth, NH: Heinemann.

Cazden, C. B. (1976). How knowledge about language helps the classroom teacher—or does it: A personal account. *Urban Review, 9* (2): 74–90.

Cazden, C. B. & Leggett, E. (1981). Culturally responsive education: Recommendations for achieving Lau remedies. In Trueba, et al. (Eds.). *Culture and the Bilingual Classroom*, pp. 69–86. Rowley, MA: Newbury House.

Chambers, J. W. (1983). *Black English: Educational Equity and the Law*. Ann Arbor: Karoma Press.

Chimezie, A. (1988). Black children's characteristics and the school: A selective adaptation approach. *Western Journal of Black Studies, 12:* 77–85.

Chisman, F. P. (1989). *Jump Start: The Federal Role in Adult Literacy*. Southport, CT: The Southport Institute for Policy Analysis.

Clark, M. (1980). Race concepts and self-esteem in Black children. *Dissertation Abstracts International, 40* (10–A): 5371–5372.

Clark, S. (1962). *Echo in my Soul*. New York: E. P. Dutton.

Coates, D. (1985). Relationships between self-concept measures and social network characteristics for Black adolescents. *Journal of Early Adolescence, 5* (3): 319–338.

Cohen, M. (1991). Growing up segregated. *The Chapel Hill Newspaper,* 24 February, pp. C 1–2.

Cohen, R. A. (1969). Conceptual styles, cultural conflict and nonverbal tests of intelligence. *American Anthropologist, 71:* 828–856.

Conroy, P. (1972). *The Water is wide.* Boston: Houghton-Mifflin.

Cooper, G. C. (1981). Black language and holistic cognitive style. *The Western Journal of Black Studies, 5:* 201–207.

Cross, W. (1987). Personal identity vs. group identity. In Phinrey and Rotheram (Eds.). *Children's ethnic socialization.* Beverly Hills, CA: Sage Publication.

Cummins, J. (1986). Empowering minority students: A framework for intervention. *Harvard Educational Review, 56* (1): 18–36.

Damico, S. B. (1983). Two worlds of school: Differences in the photographs of black and white adolescents. Paper presented at the annual meeting of the American Educational Research Association.

Della Valle, J. (1984). *An experimental investigation of the word recognition scores of seventh-grade students to provide supervisory and administrative guidelines for the organization of effective instructional environments.* Unpublished doctoral dissertation. St. Johns University.

Delpit, L. (1988). Power and pedagogy in educating other people's children. *Harvard Educational Review, 58* (3): 280–298.

Dillard, J. L. (1988). Review of Cleanth Brooks, *The Language of the American South. American Speech, 63:* 376–380.

Dillard, J. L. (1972). *Black English.* New York: Random House.

Dittmar, N. (1976). *A critical survey of sociolinguistics: Theory and application.* New York: St. Martin's Press.

Dornbusch, S., Ritter, P., Liederman, P., Roberts, D., & Fraleigh, M. (1987). The relation of parenting style to adolescent school performance. *Child Development, 58:* 1244–1257.

Dreeben, R. (1968). *On what is learned in school.* Reading, MA: Addison-Wesley Publishing.

Dumont, R. V. (1972). Learning English and how to be silent: Studies in Sioux and Cherokee classrooms. In C. B. Cazden, et al. (Eds.). *Functions of language in the classroom,* pp. 344–369. New York: Teachers College Press.

Eato, L. E. & Lerner, R. M. (1981). Relations of physical and social environment perceptions to adolescent self-esteem. *Journal of Genetic Psychology, 139:* 143–150.

Eicher, J. P. (1987). *Making the message clear.* Santa Cruz, CA. Grinder, DeLazier, & Associates.

Ellison, C. & Boykin, A. W. (1992). Comparing outcomes from differential cooperative and individualistic learning methods. Unpublished manuscript.

Engelmann, S. E., & Sterns, S. (1972). *Distar Reading III.* Chicago: Science Research Associates.

Enggaard, J. (1983). Research and development: Interpreting a child's description of itself and self-esteem. *Skolespsykologi, 20* (2): 156–161.

Entwistle, D., Alexander, K., Pallas, A. and Cadigan, D. (1987). The emergent academic self-image of first graders: Its response to social structure. *Child Development, 58* (5): 1190–1206.

Erickson, F. (1987). Transformation and school success: The politics and culture of educational achievement, *Anthropological and Educational Quarterly, 18:* 335–356.

Farley, F. H. (1981). Basic processes in individual differences: A biologically based theory of individualization for cognitive, affective, and creative outcomes. In F. H. Farley & N. J. Gordon (Eds.). *Psychology and education: The state of the union.* Berkeley, CA: McCutchan Publishing.

Farrell, T. J. (1984). Reply by Thomas J. Farrell, *College Composition and communication, 35:* 469–478.

Farrell, T. J. (1983). I.Q. and standard English. *College Composition and Communication, 34:* 346–350.

Feuerstein, R. (1980). *Instructional enrichment.* Baltimore, MD: University Park Press.

Fields, M. (with K. Fields) (1985). *Lemon swamp: A Carolina memoir.* New York: The Free Press.

Fine, M. (1989a). Silencing and nurturing voice in an improbable context: Urban adolescents in public schools. In H. Giroux & R. Simon (Ed.). *Critical pedagogy, the state and cultural struggle,* pp. 152–173. Albany: State University of New York Press.

Fine, M. (1989b). Perspectives on inequity: Voices from urban schools. *Applied Social Psychology, Annual IV:* 217–246.

Fine, M. (1987). Silencing in public schools. *Language Arts, 64* (2): 57–74.

Fine, M. & Rosenberg, P. (1984). Dropping out: The ideology of school and work. *Education Digest, 49:* 26–29.

Fishman, J. (1972). *Language and nationalism,* Rowley, MA: Newbury House.

Foster, M. (1993). Educating for competence in community and culture: Exploring the views of exemplary African-American teachers, *Urban Education, 27* (4): 370–394.

Foster, M. (1991a). Constancy, change and constraints in the lives of Black women teachers: Some things change, most stay the same. *NWSA Journal, 3* (2): 233–261.

Foster, M. (1991b). The politics of race: Through African teachers' eyes. *Journal of Education, 172* (3): 123–141.

Foster, M. (1991c). African-American teachers and the politics of Race. In K. Weiler (Ed.). *What schools Can Do: Critical Pedagogy and Practice.* Buffalo: State University of New York Press.

Foster, M. (1991d). Just got to find a way: Case studies of the lives and practice of exemplary Black high school teachers. In M. Foster (Ed.), *Readings on Equal Education. Volume 11: Qualitative Investigations into Schools and Schooling,* pp. 273–309. New York: AMS Press.

Foster, M. (1990). Some things change, most stay the same. Examining the pedagogical practice of African American women teachers. Paper presented at the American Anthropological Association Conference. Washington, D.C.

Foster, M. (1989a). It's cookin' now: A performance analysis of the speech events of a Black teacher in an urban community college. *Language in Society, 18* (1): 1–29.

Foster, M. (1989b). Recruiting teachers of color: Problems, programs and possibilities. Monograph of the Far West Holmes Group. Tempe, AZ: Arizona State University.

Foster, M. (1987). *It's cookin' now: An ethnographic study of a successful Black teacher in an urban community college.* Unpublished doctoral dissertation. Harvard University.

Gallo, D. (1969). Student voices: A study of student preferences in a de facto segregated junior high school. Working Paper Number 1. Cambridge, MA: Harvard Graduate School of Education, Pathways Project.

Gardner, H. (1983). *Frames of mind: The theory of multiple intelligences.* New York: Basic Books.

Gay, G. (1975). Cultural differences important in the education of Black children. *Momentum, 2:* 30–33.

Gibson, J. J. (1950). *The perception of the visual world.* Boston: Houghton, Mifflin.

Giroux, H. (1986). Radical pedagogy and the politics of student voice. *Interchange, 17* (1): 48–69.

Giroux, H. (1988). Literacy and the pedagogy of voice and political empowerment. *Educational Theory, 38* (1): 61–75.

Giroux, H. & McLaren, P. (1986). Teacher education and the politics of engagement: The case for democratic schooling. *Harvard Educational Review, 56:* 213–238

Good, T. (1983). Research on classroom teaching. In L. Shulman and G. L. Sykes (Ed.). *Handbook of Teaching and Policy.* New York: Longman.

Good, T., & Brophy, J. (1987). *Looking in classrooms* (4th ed.). New York: Harper & Row.

Goodson, I. (1988). Teachers' lives: Qualitative research in education: Teaching and learning qualitative traditions. Proceedings from the Second Annual Conference of the Qualitative Interest Group, Athens, GA.

Goody, E. (1975). *Toward a theory of questions.* Cambridge University, England: New Hall, mimeo.

Gopaul-McNicol, S. (1988). Racial identification and racial preference of Black preschool children in New York and Trinidad. *Journal of Black Psychology, 14* (2): 65–68.

Gordon, E. W., Miller, F. & Rollock, D. (1990). Coping with communicentric bias in knowledge production in the social sciences. *Educational Researcher, 19:* 14–19.

Greeno, J. (1989). A perspective on thinking. *American Psychologist, 44:* 134–141.

Guttman, H. (1976). *Black family life in slavery and freedom.* New York: Pantheon Books.

Hagen, M. A. & Jones, R. K. (1978). Cultural effects on pictorial perception. How many words is one picture really worth? In R.D. Walk & H. L. Pick, Jr. (Eds.). *Perception and experience.* New York: Plenum Press.

Hale, J. E. (1982). *Black children: Their roots, culture, and learning styles.* Provo, Utah: Brigham Young University Press.

Hakuta, K. (1986). *Mirror of language: The debate on bilingualism.* New York: Basic Books.

Hall, E. (1989). Unstated features of the cultural context of learning. *The Educational Forum, 54:* 21–34.

Hanna, J. L. (1988). *Disruptive school behavior: Class, race, and culture.* New York: Holmes & Meier.

Harris, M., Rosenthal, R. & Snodgrass, S. (1986). The effects of teacher expectations, gender, and behavior on pupil academic performance and self-concept. *Journal of Educational Research, 79* (3): 173–179.

Haynes, N., Comer, J., Hamilton-Lee, M., Boger, J. et al. (1987). An analysis of the relationship between children's self-concept and their teacher's assessments of their behavior: Implications for prediction and intervention. *Journal of School Psychology, 25* (4): 393–397.

Heath, S. B. (1983). Ways with words: Language, life, and work in communities and classrooms. New York: Cambridge University Press.

Heath, S. B. (1982). What no bedtime story means: Narrative skills at home and school. *Language in Society, 11* (1): 49–77.

Henry, A. (1990). Black women, Black pedagogies: An African-Canadian context. Paper presented at the American Educational Research Conference. Boston, MA.

Hernandez, M. (1984). Children's racial attitudes and self-esteem. *Dissertation Abstracts International, 45:* 1914.

Hill, R. (1972). *The strengths of Black families.* New York: Emerson Hall.

Hilliard, A. G. III (1989). Teachers and cultural styles in a pluralistic society. *Today: National Educational Association, 7:* 65–69.

Hollins, E. R. (1982). The Marva Collins story revisited. *The Journal of Teacher Education, 33* (1): 37–40.

Hollins, E. & Spencer, K. (1990). Restructuring schools for cultural inclusion: Changing the schooling process for African American youngsters. *Journal of Education, 172* (2): 89–100.

Irvine, J. J. (1990). *Black children and school failure: Policies, practices and prescriptions.* Westport, CT: Greenwood Press.

Jagers, R. (1988). *Communal orientation and cooperative learning among Afro American college students.* Unpublished doctoral dissertation. Howard University, Washington, D.C.

James W. & Galbraith, M. (1985). Perceptual learning styles: Implications and techniques for the practitioner. *Lifelong Learning, 18:* 20–23.

Jensen, A. R. (1969). How much can we boost IQ and scholastic achievement? Harvard Education Review, 39: 1–123.

Johnson, D. D., Pittelman, S., & Heimlich, J. (1986). Semantic mapping. *The Reading Teacher, 39:* 778–783.

Jones, J. (1985). *Labor of love, labor of sorrow: Black women, work and the family from slavery to the present.* New York: Basic Books.

Joseph, G. & Lewis, J. (1981). *Black mothers and daughters: Their roles and functions in American society. Common differences: conflicts in Black and White feminist perspectives.* Boston, MA: South End Press.

Katz, J. (1985). The sociopolitical nature of counseling. *Counseling Psychologist, 13:* 615–624.

Kelly, J. A. (1984). *Influence of culture, gender and academic experience on cognitive style.* Unpublished Dissertation, Vanderbilt University, Memphis, TN.

Khan, V. (1982). The role of the culture of dominance in structuring the experience of ethnic minorities. In C. Husband (Ed.). *Race in Britain: Continuity and change.* London: Hutchinson.

King, J. (1991). Black student alienation and black teachers' emancipatory pedagogy. In M. Foster (Ed.). *Readings on Equal Education. Volume 11: Qualitative Investigations into Schools and Schooling,* 245–271. New York: AMS Press.

Kluger, R. (1975). *Simple justice.* New York: Vintage.

Kochman, T. (1972). The kinetic element in black idiom. In T. Kochman (Ed.). *Rappin and stylin out: Communication in urban black America.* Urbana, IL: University of Illinois Press.

Kohr, R., Coldiron, J., Skiffingten, E., Masters, J. et al. (1988). The influence of race, class, and gender on self-esteem for 5th, 8th, and 11th grade students in Pennsylvania schools. *Journal of Negro Education, 57* (4): 467–481.

Labov, W. (1969). The logic of nonstandard English. In *Report of the 21st annual round table on linguists and language studies,* Monograph Series on Languages and Linguistics, 23. J. E. Alatis, (Ed.). Washington, D.C.: Georgetown University Press.

Labov, W. (1982). Objectivity and Commitment in linguistic Science. *Language in Society, 11:* 165–201.

Labov, W. (1972). *Language in the inner-city: Studies in the Black English vernacular.* Philadelphia, PA: University of Pennsylvania Press.

Labov, W., & Harris, W. (1986). Defacto segregation of Black and White vernaculars. In D. Sankoff (Ed.). *Diversity and diachrony.* Amsterdam: John Benjamins Publishing Co.

Ladson-Billings, G. (1991a). Like lighting in a bottle: Attempting to capture the pedagogical excellence of successful teachers of black students. *International Journal of Qualitative Studies in Education, 3* (4): 335–344.

Ladson-Billings, G. (1991b). Returning to the Source: Implications for Educating Teachers of Black Students. In M. Foster (Ed.), *Readings on*

Equal Education. Volume 11: Qualitative Investigations into Schools and Schooling, 227–244. New York: AMS Press.

Ladson-Billings, G. (1990). Culturally relevant teaching: Effective Instruction for Black students. *The College Board Review, 155:* 20–25.

Ladson-Billings, G. & Henry, A. (1991). Blurring the borders: Voices of African liberatory pedagogy in the United States and Canada. *Journal of Education, 172* (2): 72–88.

Lanborn. S. & Mounts, N. (1990). Patterns of competence and adjustment among adolescents from authoritative, authoritarian, indulgent and neglectful families. Madison, WI: National Center for Effective Secondary Schools, University of Wisconsin at Madison.

Lerner, G. (1972). *Black women in White America: A documentary history.* New York: Vintage.

Levine, L. (1977). *Black culture and Black consciousness.* New York: Oxford University Press.

Levy, N., Murphy, C. & Carlson, R. (1972). Personality types among Negro students. *Educational and social psychology, 1:* 39–41.

Lightfoot, S. (1978). *Worlds apart: Relationships between families and schools.* New York: Basic Books.

Lightfoot, S. (1973). Politics and reasoning: Through the eyes of teachers and children. *Harvard Educational Review, 43* (2): 197–244.

Lipsitz, J. (1984). *Successful schools for young adolescents.* New Brunswick: Transaction Books.

Lubeck, S. (1988). Nested contexts. In L. Weiss (Ed.). *Class, race and gender in United States education.* Albany: State University of New York Press.

Lubeck, S. (1986). *Sandbox society: Early education in Black-White America—A comparative ethnography.* London: Falmer Press.

Lyons, N. (1983). Two perspectives: On self, relationships and morality. *Harvard Educational Review, 53* (2): 125–145.

Mangan, J. (1978). Cultural conventions of pictorial representation: Iconic literacy and education. *Educational Communication and Technology Journal, 26:* 245–267.

Marsh, H. & Shavelson, R. (1985). Self-concept: Its multifaceted, hierarchical structure. *Educational Psychologist, 20* (3): 107–123.

Massey, G. C., Scott, M. V. & Dornbusch, S. M. (1975). Racism without racists: Institutional racism in urban schools. *The Black Scholar, 7* (3): 10–19.

Mathews, J. (1988). *Escalante: The best teacher in America*. New York: Henry Holt & Co.

McAdoo, H. (1985). Racial attitude and self-concept of young Black children over time. In H. McAdoo & J. McAdoo (Eds.). *Black children: Social, educational and parental environments*, 213–243. Beverly Hills, CA: Sage Publications.

McAdoo, H. (1971). *Racial attitudes and self-concept of black preschool children*. Unpublished doctoral dissertation. University of Michigan, 1970. *Dissertation Abstracts International, 31:* 8–A, 3963.

McDermott, R. P. (1977). Social relations as contexts for learning in school. *Harvard Educational Review, 47:* 198–213.

McDermott, R. P. (1974). *Achieving school failure*. In G. D. Spindler (Ed.). *Education and cultural process*. New York: Holt, Rinehart & Winston.

McLaughlin, M. & Talbert, J. (1990). Constructing a personalized school environment. *Phi Delta Kappan, 72* (3): 230–235.

Metropolitan Life (1988). *Strengthening the relationship between teachers and students*. New York: Metropolitan Life Insurance Company.

Moll, L. C. (1988). Some key issues in teaching Latino students. *Language Arts, 65:* 465–472.

Monroe, S. & Goldman, P. (1988). *Brothers: Black and poor a true story of courage and survival*. New York: Ballantine Books.

Morgan, H. (1990). Assessment of student's behavioral interactions during on-task classroom activities. *Perceptual and Motor Skills, 70:* 563–569.

Morgan, H. (1981). Factors concerning cognitive development and learning differentiation among Black children. In A. O. Harrison, (Ed.). *Conference on Empirical Research in Black Psychology*. Rochester, MI: Oakland University.

Moses, R., Kamii, M., Swap, S., & Howard, J. (1989). The Algebra Project: Organizing in the spirit of Ella. *Harvard Educational Review, 59* (4): 413–443.

Murray, A. (1970). *Black experience and American culture*. New York: Vintage.

Murrell, P. (1991). Cultural politics in teacher education: What's missing in the preparation of minority teachers. In M. Foster, (Ed.). *Readings in Equal Education. Volume 11: Qualitative Investigations into Schools and Schooling*, 205–225. New York: AMS Press.

Myhill, J. (1988). The rise of be as an aspect marker in Black English vernacular. *American Speech, 63:* 304–325.

Myhill, J. (1986). The use of the verbal -s inflection in BEV. In D. Sankoff (Ed.). *Diversity and diachrony.* Amsterdam: John Benjamins Publishing Co.

Nobles, W. W. (1991). African philosophy: Foundations for Black psychology. In R. Jones (Ed.). *Black psychology,* (3rd Ed.). Berkeley, CA: Cobb and Henry.

Noblit, G. (1991). Power and caring. Paper presented at American Educational Research Association. Chicago, IL. April.

Noddings, N. (1984). *Caring.* Berkeley: University of California Press.

Noddings, N. & Shore, P. J. (1984). *Awakening the inner eye: Intuition in education.* New York: Teachers College Press.

Norman, D. A. (1982). *Learning and memory.* San Francisco: Freeman Co.

Ogbu, J. (1987). Variability in minority school performance: A problem in search on an explanation. *Anthropology in Education Quarterly, 18* (4): 312–335.

Ogbu, J. (1978). *Minority education and caste: The American system in cross-cultural perspective.* New York: Academic Press.

Orasanu, J., Lee, C., & Scribner, S. (1979). Free recall: Ethnic and economic group comparisons. *Child Development, 50:* 1100–1109.

Orr, E. W. (1987). *Twice as less: Black English and the performance of Black students in mathematics and science.* New York: W. W. Norton & Co.

Pasteur, A. B. & Toldson, I. L. (1982). *Roots of soul: The psychology of Black expressiveness.* Garden City, NJ: Anchor Press/Doubleday Press.

Payne, C. M. (1984). *Getting what we ask for: The ambiguity of success and failure in urban education.* Westport, CT: Greenwood Press.

Perney, V. H. (1976). Effects of race and sex on field-dependence-independence of children. *Perceptual and Motor Skills, 42:* 975–980.

Philips, S. (1983). *The invisible culture: Communication in the classroom and community on the Warm Springs Indian Reservation.* White Plains, NY: Longman Press.

Philips, S. (1972). Participant structures and communicative competence. In C. B. Cazden, et al. (Eds.). *Functions of language in the classroom.* New York: Teachers College Press.

Piestrup, A. (1973). *Black Dialect Interference and Accomodation of Reading Instruction in First Grade.* Monograph of the Language Behavior Research Laboratory. Berkeley, CA: University of California.

Pitts, W. (1986). Constrastive use of verbal -z in slave narratives. In D. Sankoff (Ed.). *Diversity and diachrony.* Amsterdam: John Benjamins Publishing Co.

Pitts, W. (1981). Beyond hyperconnection: the use of emphatic -z in BEV. *Chicago Linguistic Society, 17:* 303–310.

Provenzo, E. (1988). Black and White teachers: Patterns of similarity and difference over twenty years. Paper presented at the Annual Meeting of the American Educational Research Association. New Orleans, LA.

Reagan, T. (1985). Cultural unity, cultural pluralism and the school: Toward a pedagogical synthesis. *Journal of Research and Development in Education, 18:* 21–24.

Reed, I. (1990). Reading, writing and racism. San Francisco Examiner *Image Magazine.* 19 August, pp. 27–28.

Rist, R. (1973). *The urban school: A factory for failure.* Cambridge: MIT Press.

Rist, R. (1970). Student social class and teacher expectations: The self-fulfilling prophecy in ghetto education. *Harvard Educational Review, 40* (3): 411–451.

Rosenshine, B. V. (1986). Synthesis of research on explicit teaching. *Educational Leadership, 43,* (7): 60–69.

Ruggiero, V. R. (1988). *Teaching thinking across the curriculum.* New York: Harper & Row.

Rychlak, J. F., Hewitt, C. W., & Hewitt, J. (1973). Affective evaluation, word quality, and the verbal learning styles of black versus white junior college females. *Journal of Personality and Social Psychology, 27:* 248–255.

Rychlak, J. F. (1975). Affective assessment, intelligence, social class and racial learning style. *Journal of Personality and Social Psychology, 32:* 989–995.

Salamon, G. (1981). *Communication and education. Social and psychological interactions.* Beverly Hills, CA: Sage Publications.

Sattler, J. (1970). Racial "experimenter effects" in experimentation, testing, interviewing, and psychotherapy. *Psychological Bulletin, 73:* 137–160.

Schmeck, R. R. & Meier, S. T. (1984). Self-reference as a learning strategy and a learning style. *Human Learning, 3:* 917.

Schneider, E. W. (1983). The origin of the verbal -s in Black English. *American Speech, 58:* 99–113.

Scribner, S. & Cole, M. (1981). Unpacking literacy. In. M. Farr-Whiteman (Ed.). *Variation in writing: Functional and linguistic-cultural differences,* pp. 71–88. Volume 1 Writing: The Nature, Development, and Teaching of Written Communication. Hillsdale: Lawrence Erlbaum.

Shade, B. J. (1990a). Cultural ways of knowing. Paper presented at the Summer Institute, Council of Chief State School Officers. Mystic, CT.

Shade, B. J. (1990b). Engaging the battle for African American minds. Paper presented at the National Association of Black School Educators. Dallas, TX.

Shade, B.J. (1990c). African American perceptual style: Implications for future research. Paper presented at the annual meeting of the American Psychological Association. Boston, MA.

Shade, B. J. (1989). *Culture, style and the educative process.* Springfield, IL: Charles C. Thomas.

Shade, B. J. (1983). Afro-American patterns of cognitive (Final report). Madison: University of Wisconsin Center for Education Research.

Shade, B. J. & Edwards, P. (1987). Ecological Correlates of the educative style of Afro-American children. *Journal of Negro Education, 56:* 88–99.

Sherif, C. W. (1973). Social distance as categorization of intergroup interaction. *Journal of Personality and Social Psychology, 25:* 327–334.

Shulman, L. S. (1987). Knowledge and teaching: Foundations of the new reform. *Harvard Educational Review, 57* (1): 1–22.

Silva, C., Moses, R., Rivers, J. & Johnson, P. (1990).The Algebra Project: Making middle school mathemaatics count. *Journal of Negro Education, 59* (3): 375–391.

Silverstein, B. & Krate, R. (1975). *Children of the dark ghetto.* New York: Praeger.

Simmons, W. (1979). *The role of cultural salience in ethnic and social class difference in cognitive performance.* Unpublished Doctoral Dissertation. Cornell University.

Smith, W. I. & Drumming, S. T. (1989). On the strategies blacks employ in deductive reasoning. *Journal of Black Psychology, 16:* 1–22.

Smith, R. R. & Lewis, R. (1985). Race as a self-schema affecting recall in black children. *Journal of Black Psychology, 12:* 15–29.

Smitherman, G. (1987). Opinion: Toward a national public policy on language. *College English, 49,* (1): 29–36.

Smitherman, G. (1981). *Black English and the education of Black children and youth: Proceedings of the National Invitational Symposium on the King Decision.* Detroit, MI: Wayne State University Department of Afro-American Studies.

Spencer, M. (1984). Black children's race awareness, racial attitudes, and self-concept: A reinterpretation. *Annual Progress in Child Psychiatry and Child Development, 616–630.*

Spencer, M. (1982a). Personal and group identity of black children: An alternative synthesis. *Genetic Psychology Monographs, 106:* 59–84.

Spencer, M. (1982b). Preschool children's social cognititon and cultural cognition: A cognitive developmental interpretation of race dissonance findings. *Journal of Psychology, 112:* 275–286.

Spencer D. (1986). *Contemporary women teachers: Balancing school and home.* New York: Longman.

St. John, N. (1971). Thirty-six teachers: Their characteristics and outcomes for black and white pupils. *American Educational Research Journal, 8:* 634–648.

Stack, C. (1974). *All our kin: Strategies for survival in a Black community.* New York: Harper Row.

Steinberg, L. Mounts, N., Lanborn., S. & Dornbusch, S. (1990). Authoritative parenting and adolescent adjustment across varied ecological niches. Madison, WI: National Center on Effective Secondary Schools, University of Wisconsin at Madison.

Sterling, P. (1972). *The real teachers: 30 inner-city school teachers talk honestly about who they are, how they teach and why.* New York: Random House.

Stroman, C. (1986). Television viewing and self-concept among Black children. *Journal of Broadcasting and Electronic Media, 30* (1): 87–93.

Stuckey, S. (1987). *Slave culture: Nationalist theory and the foundations of Black America.* New York: Oxford University Press.

Szwed, J. & Abrahams, R. (1979). *After the myth: studying Afro-American cultural patterns in the plantation literature.* In D. Crowley (Ed.). *African folklore in the New World,* pp. 65–86. Austin, TX: University of Texas.

Talbert, C. (1973). Studying Education in the Ghetto. In T. Weaver (Ed.). *To see Ourselves: Anthropology and modern social issues.* Glenview, IL: Scott, Foresman.

TenHouten, W. D. (1971). *Cognitive styles and the social order.* Final report, Part 2, OEO, Book–5135, University of California, Los Angeles.

Teplin, L. (1976). A comparison of racial/ethnic preferences among Anglo, Black and Latino children. *American Journal of Orthopsychiatry, 46:* 4–19.

Tharp, R. (1989). Psychocultural variables and constants: Effects on teaching and learning in schools. *American Psychologist, 44:* 349–359.

Thompson, R. (1983). *Flash of the spirit: African and Afro-American art and philosophy.* New York: Random House.

Torrance, E. P. (1982). Identifying and capitalizing on the strengths of culturally different children. In C. R. Reynolds and T. B. Gutkin (Eds.). *The handbook of school psychology,* pp. 481–500. New York: John Wiley & Sons.

Treisman, U. (1985). *A study of the mathematics performance of Black students at the University of California at Berkeley.* Unpublished Doctoral Dissertation. University of California Berkeley.

Tuck, K., & Boykin, A. W. (1989). Task performance and receptiveness to variability in Black and white low-income children. In A. Harrison (Ed.). *The eleventh conference on empirical research in Black psychology.* Washington, DC: NIMH Publications.

Turner, L. (1949). *Africanisms in the Gullah dialect.* Chicago: University of Chicago Press.

Vallance, E. (1974). Hiding the hidden curriculum. *Curriculum Theory Network, 4:* 5–21.

Vaughn-Cooke, F. B. (1987). Are Black and White vernaculars diverging? *American Speech, 62:* 12–32.

Villegas, A. M. (1990). Culturally responsive pedagogy for the 1990s and beyond. Unpublished manuscript. Princeton, NJ: Educational Testing Service.

Vygotsky, L. S. (1978). *Mind in society: The development of higher psychological process.* Cambridge: Harvard Univeristy Press.

Vygotsky, L. (1962). *Thought and language.* Cambridge: MIT Press.

Whimbey, A. (1985). Reading, writing, reasoning linked in testing and training. *Journal of Reading, 29:* 118–123.

Wiggins, J. D. (1987). Self-esteem, earned grades, and television viewing habits of students. *School Counselor, 35* (2): 128–133.

Williams, J., Apenahier, L. & Haynes, N. (1987). Dimensionality of the Piers-Harris Children's Self-Concept Scale for minority gifted children. *Schools, 24* (4): 322–325.

Wolfe, L., Cross, L. & Culver, S. (1990 summer). Testing a model of teacher satisfaction for Blacks and Whites. *American Education Research Journal, 27* (2): 323–349.

Wolfram, W. (1987). Are Black and White vernaculars diverging? *American Speech, 62:* 40–48.

Woods, P. (1979). *The divided school.* London: Routledge & Kegan Paul.

Young, V. H. (1974). A Black American socialization pattern. *American Ethnologist, 1:* 405–413.

Contributors

Kathryn H. Au is an Educational Psychologist at the Kamehameha Schools, Honolulu. She currently heads a team responsible for development of a K–6 grade whole literacy curriculum, being used by about 150 public school teachers affiliated with the Kamehameha Elementary Education Program (KEEP) throughout the state of Hawaii. Her major research interest is in the literacy development of students from cultural minority backgrounds. She has published over thirty journal articles and book chapters and is co-author of *Reading Instruction for Today,* a college reading methods textbook.

John Baugh is professor of Education, Linguistics, and Anthropology at Stanford University. His research interest includes working on an integration of economic and linguistic theories for educational application. He is presently completing a National Science Foundation Project on Linguistic Diversity and Access to health care. One of his recent publications is "Changing terms of self-reference among African slave descendants," published in *American Speech,* 1991.

A. Wade Boykin is professor of Psychology at Howard University. He also serves as an educational and psychological consultant. Over the years, he has done extensive work in the areas of research methodology; the interface of culture, motivation and cognition; Black child development; and academic achievement in the American social context. He presently serves as a consultant for the UCLA Center for Research on Evaluation Standards and Student Testing; and the American Institute for Research Project on Educational Reforms for At-Risk Students.

Curtis W. Branch is assistant professor of Educational Psychology at Teachers College Columbia University. He was previously a clinical psychologist with special interests in the areas of cultural diversity and identity formation (transformations) and its impact on psychological functioning. He conducts research in the areas of social cognition and identity development among African American children and adolescents.

Michele Foster is associate professor in the School of Education at the University of California at Davis. She specializes in anthropological research with a particular focus on discourse analysis and classroom interaction. Publications representative of her work include: "Its cooking now: A performance analysis of the speech events of a Black teacher in an urban community college," published in *Language in Society;* and co-author of "Peer-peer learning: Evidence from a student run sharing time" published in A. Jaggar and M. T. Smith-Burke (Eds.).

Eugene E. Garcia is professor of Education and Psychology and Dean of the Division of Social Sciences at the University of California at Santa Cruz. His research interests include Bilingual Education, effective schooling for bilingual education, particularly Mexican American populations. He is Co-Director of the National Center for Research on Cultural Diversity and Second Language Learning (A U. S. Department of Education Center).

Warren Hayman is on the faculty at Johns Hopkins University and is coordinator of the Hopkins/Dunbar Health Professions Program. His primary research interest is in community involvement in educational decision-making. He is presently engaged in developing an interdisciplinary program in mathematics, science, social studies, and English for an urban high school.

Etta R. Hollins is professor of Teacher Education at California State University, Hayward. Her research interests are designing appropriate curriculum for culturally diverse students at the elementary and secondary levels, particularly African American students. She directed two national teleconferences on "The challenge of cultural diversity in teacher preparation and assessment" with over three hundred colleges and universities participating. Her most recent publication is *Applying the Wisdom of Practice in Teaching Diverse Populations,* Longman Publishing Group (in press).

Alice J. Kawakami is Director of Research Services for the Pacific Regional Educational Laboratory, Honolulu. Previously, she was a classroom teacher, curriculum developer, and director of training for the Kamehameha Elementary Education Program (KEEP). One of her current projects involves co-ordinating research in several Pacific island nations on cultural practices with implications for improving schooling.

Joyce E. King is associate professor and Director of Teacher Education at Santa Clara University where she teaches courses in the sociocultural foundations of education and interpersonal/cross-cultural communication. Her research focuses on culture and pedagogy, the sociology of knowledge that functions as ideology, Afrocentric education and participatory research for social change. She co-authored *Black Mothers to Sons: Juxtaposing African American Literature with Social Practice* and edited a theme issue of the *Journal of Education* on African liberation pedagogy.

Gloria Ladson-Billings is assistant professor of Teacher Education at the University of Wisconsin at Madison. Her areas of specialization include multicultural education and social studies curriculum and instruction. Publications representative of her work include: "Culturally relevant teaching: Effective instruction for Black students," "The teacher education challenge in elite university settings: Developing critical perspectives for teaching in democratic and multicultural societies" (with Joyce King).

Irving P. McPhail is provost and vice president for Academic Affairs at Pace University. His research interests include literacy acquisition for African American students. He was founder of the "Real Men" project at LeMoyne Owens College. This project paired African American college students with low income elementary and secondary students to promote a sense of self-determination and academic success.

Carmen I. Mercado is a faculty member in the Department of curriculum and Teaching at Hunter College of CUNY. Her primary interest is collaborative research on learning with teachers, students, and parents in culturally and linguistically diverse classrooms. For the past few years she has shared her world as an educational ethnographer with sixth grade intermediate school students with whom she has made numerous presentations at research forums.

Cornel D. Pewewardy is principal at the newly-established Mounds Park All-Nations Magnet School in the Saint Paul, Minnesota Public Schools. In 1991, he was named the National Indian Educator of the year by the National Indian Education Association. The Minnesota Administrators' Academy named Dr. Pewewardy as a recipient of a Transformational Leadership Award in 1991. In

1992, he was selected as "Indian of the Year" by the American Indian Exposition Board of Directors.

Rebecca G. Eller Powell is currently on the faculty at Kentucky State University. Her research interests include linguistic diversity and its relationship to student achievement; the teaching of literacy to minorities; and issues related to teacher empowerment. Publications representative of her work include: "Dialect effects on Appalachian students' written composition" in C. Ross, Ed., *Contemporary Appalachia: In search of a usable past,* 1987; "Johnny can't talk, either: The perpetuation of the deficit theory in classrooms," *The Reading Teacher,* 1989.

Ana Helvia Quintero is professor of Mathematics at the University of Puerto Rico. She has been involved in research on children's learning difficulties in mathematics and strategies for teachers' involvement in school improvement. She has also participated in various projects directed at improving learning in school. Recently she was named Director of the Center for Research and Innovation in the Education of the General Council on Education of Puerto Rico.

Diana Rivera Viera is currently Dean of the School of Education at the University of Puerto Rico, Main Campus en Rio Piedras. She is also a professor in the Graduate Studies Department. Her research interests are in educational change reading and learning disabilities. She is also involved in university and school collaborative projects.

Barbara J. Shade is professor of Education and Dean of the School of Education at the University of Wisconsin-Parkside. She specializes in the study of the social-psychological characteristics of successful people with an emphasis on African Americans and other racial or ethnic minorities. She is the editor of *Culture, Style, and the Educative Process* which examines the issue of teaching to culturally different information styles.

Helen Smiler is the National Projects Coordinator for Project SEED, a nationwide, nonprofit mathematics education program. She has worked with Project SEED since 1968 in school districts around the nation as a mathematics specialist, trainer, coordinator, director and national administrator. She has demonstrated Project SEED discovery methods at local and national conferences and worked with corporations such as Bell Laboratories, Prudential and Pacific Power and Light regarding their involvement in Project SEED programs in their communities.

Kathleen Spencer is a doctoral candidate at the University of Utah at Salt Lake City. She is employed as a multicultural specialist at the Utah State Department of Education. She is an experienced teacher of bilingual and monolingual children. She has served as a consultant to numerous school districts on the education of ethnic minority youth, issues related to desegregation, bilingual education and the education of children learning to speak English as a second language.

Maria E. Torres-Guzman is associate professor of Bilingual Education and Director of the Program in Bilingual/Bicultural Education at Teachers College, Columbia University. Her research interests include parental and community involvement in education, classroom ethnography, and the relationship between language, culture and instruction. She has co-authored (with Bertha Perez) a book entitled *Learning in two worlds: An integrated Spanish/English biliteracy* approach published by Longman, Inc.

Index

Ability groups, 70
Academic: achievement, 16–17, 28, 37, 39, 101, 173, 215, 233, 240; excellence, 209, 221; Learning Time, 97; motivation, 251; performance, 1, 3, 25–26, 40, 96, 172, 197, 254; skills, 233; standards, 231; success, 21, 37, 192, 201, 237
Accommodation, 30, 181
Acculturate, acculturation, 38, 244
Achievement, ideology, 36; individual, 19
Adjustment, psychosocial, 95
African American: 21, 25–27, 29–35, 37–38, 42, 225, 236, 249, 250; adolescents, 213; children, 18, 27, 33–34, 42, 212–213, 220, 222, 243, 248, 250–251, 254; cultural identity, 32; cultural knowledge, 25–27, 29, 32–33, 42–43; cultural practice, 40; culture, 27–28, 33, 134, 141, 244, 251, 255; English, 191, 200; experience, 248; expressive cultural style, 139; Language, 7, 191–205; learners, 33, 219–220; males, 41; negative beliefs about, 136; teachers, 131; scholars, 134–135, 210; students, 7–8, 27; 115, 129, 132, 135; 243 (See also Black)
African, 32; civilizations, 34; culture, 32; ethos, 249; history, 141; humanism, 34; orality, 34, 42
Afro-American culture, 34, 37
Afrocentric perspective, 210

Afrocultural: attributes, 249–250; expression, 243–257; integrity, 244
Alaska Native youth, 92
Alaskan Athabaskans, 11
Algebra Project, the, 237
Algebraic problems, 200; structure, 168
Alienate, alienation, 49–41, 82; and Appalachian population, 62, 67, 82; and Black students, 134
American Indian(s), 77, 248; education, 78; Elders, 80, 88; Magnet School, 78–81, 91–92; literature, 85; philosophy and thought, 79, 81; sports, games and music, 80; worldview, 79, 91–92 (See also, Indian and Native Americans)
Anglo-European American, 246 (See also White American)
Ann Arbor case, 19–193, 238
Appalachian: culture, 72, 74, 76; homogenizing the population, 67; identity, 71, 75–76 (See also mountain population)
Asian(s), 141; students, 169 (See also Chinese)
Assessment, authentic, 188
Assimilation, assimilationist, 37, 134, 181
Attitudes toward learning, 175
Attributions, teacher, 209, 216, 222

Balance of rights, 14
Bandura, A., 218, 220

281

WITHDRAWN